MILITARY HISTORY

OF THE

IRISH NATION,

&c. &c.

MILITARY HISTORY

OF THE

IRISH NATION,

COMPRISING

A MEMOIR OF THE IRISH BRIGADE

IN THE SERVICE OF FRANCE;

WITH

AN APPENDIX

OF OFFICIAL PAPERS RELATIVE TO THE BRIGADE, FROM THE ARCHIVES AT PARIS.

BY THE LATE
MATTHEW O'CONOR, ESQ.,
BARRISTER-AT-LAW.

The Naval & Military Press Ltd

in association with

The National Army Museum, London

Published jointly by

The Naval & Military Press Ltd
Unit 10 Ridgewood Industrial Park,
Uckfield, East Sussex,
TN22 5QE England

Tel: +44 (0) 1825 749494
Fax: +44 (0) 1825 765701

www.naval-military-press.com
www.military-genealogy.com
www.militarymaproom.com

and

The National Army Museum, London
www.national-army-museum.ac.uk

In reprinting in facsimile from the original, any imperfections are inevitably reproduced and the quality may fall short of modern type and cartographic standards.

CONTENTS.

CHAPTER I.

THE CAMPAIGN OF TYRONE; A. D. 1550 TO A. D. 1607.

PAGE

Irish valour displayed at home as well as abroad.—Hugh O'Neal, Earl of Tyrone.—His abilities.—Revolts against the English authority, and maintains his ground against Sir John Norris and the English army.—Proposals of accommodation made by England, and rejected.—Norris displaced by Lord Burrough.—Tyrrell's exploits.—Death of Lord Burrough.—The English army defeated, and their commander, Sir Henry Bagnall, killed at the Blackwater.—The Earl of Essex.—Lord Mountjoy appointed Governor.—His skill and energy.—Spanish expedition arrives at Kinsale.—Incompetency of its commander, Don Juan D'Aguila.—Defeat at Kinsale.—O'Neal is forced to submit.—Dunboy.—Flight and attainder of O'Neal,   1

CHAPTER II.

CAMPAIGNS IN THE SERVICE OF SPAIN; A. D. 1585 TO A. D. 1609.

The Irish auxiliaries of the Dutch, under Sir Edward Stanley, seduced from their allegiance.—The four nations.—Their successful gallantry at Bois-le-duc.—The Spanish Armada.—Stanley's advice.—Campaign in France.—Dourlen taken by storm.—Amiens surprised by Portocarrero.—Its siege by King Henry IV., and the Duke de Biron.—Death of Portocarrero.—Montenegro succeeds him.—Defence of Amiens.—Montenegro surrenders.—Capture of Rhinberg.—Licentiousness of the soldiers.—Campaign in the Netherlands in 1599.—Lodgment effected in the Island of Bommel.—Fort erected in the Island in the face of the enemy.—Battle at Nieuport, between the Archduke Albert and Prince Maurice, . . 31

CHAPTER III.

CAMPAIGNS IN THE SERVICE OF FRANCE ; A. D. 1652 TO A. D. 1654.

Regiment raised by Lord Bristol.—An Irish regiment offer their services to the Duke of York and enter the French service.—Siege of Ligni.—Campaign of 1653.—Irish engaged on both sides.—Siege of Moinon.—800 Irish nearly all cut off by the French.—Lines of Arras, . . 69

CHAPTER IV.

FURTHER SERVICES IN THE ARMIES OF SPAIN; A. D. 1656 TO A. D. 1660.

Charles II. and his brother obliged to leave France.—The Irish colonels offer their services to the Duke of York.—Circumstances under which Richard Grace of Gracefield, and other Irish colonels, had entered the French service.—Siege of Condé.—Charles and Ormond tamper with Lord Muskerry.—St. Gerlain betrayed by the Irish garrison.—Campaign of 1657.—Siege of Ardres.—Unsuccessful attack on Mardyke.—Spanish distrust of the Irish.—Siege of Dunkirk.—Battle of the Downs.—Colonel Grace and his regiment make good their retreat.—The other Irish regiments taken prisoners.—Dunkirk taken by the English.—Restoration of Charles II., ... 74

CHAPTER V.

FURTHER CAMPAIGNS IN THE SERVICE OF FRANCE; A. D. 1673 TO A. D. 1689.

PAGE

Sir G. Hamilton, in 1673, raises an Irish regiment for the service of France.—Cruelties committed by the troops under Turenne in the Palatinate.—Montecucoli opposed to Turenne.—Death of Turenne.—Retreat of the French. Glory acquired by Hamilton and the Irish on that occasion.—Distinguished services at Altenheim.—Death of Hamilton.—Gradual decay of the Irish regiments.—Defence of Cambray, ... 87

CHAPTER VI.

FIRST FORMATION OF THE IRISH BRIGADE IN THE SERVICE OF FRANCE, A. D. 1690–1.

Original formation of the Irish Brigade.—Exchange of troops favourable to France.—Pay and arrangement of the Irish regiments in the French service.—Operations in Savoy.— St. Ruth commands the Irish auxiliaries.—The passes of the Alps forced by the valour of the Irish.—Savoy overrun.—Services in Catalonia, ... 97

CHAPTER VII.

CAMPAIGN OF 1690–1 IN IRELAND.

Battle of the Boyne.—Errors on James's side.—Incompetency of the French commander.—Mistakes of William.— James's flight ill-advised.—William delays in prosecuting the war.—James's cold reception in France.—William approaches Limerick.—Views of different parties.—The French forces retire to Galway.—Siege of Limerick.— Imperfect state of the fortifications.—Bravery displayed on both sides.—William defeated.—The French a hin-

CONTENTS.

PAGE

drance instead of a help.—Recal of Lausun's corps.—Character of Sarsfield.—Luttrel's intrigues.—The confidence of the Irish forfeited by Tyrconnel.—He goes to France and obtains assistance.—Deputation sent to James at St. Germain.—St. Ruth appointed commander-in-chief.—Marlborough takes Cork and Kinsale.—Arrival of St. Ruth and the French succours.—Opening of the campaign.—Siege of Athlone.—Heroism of the Irish garrison.—Athlone taken.—Battle of Aughrim.—Death of St. Ruth.—Treachery of Baldearg O'Donnell.—Other instances of desertions.—Death and character of Tyrconnel.—Treachery of Luttrel.—Siege of Limerick.—Turned into a blockade.—Surrender of Limerick.—Military provisions of the treaty.—The English enter Limerick.—Attempts to induce the Irish troops to enter the English service.—Departure of the Irish army, . . 105

CHAPTER VIII.

FINAL FORMATION OF THE IRISH BRIGADE IN THE SERVICE OF FRANCE, AND CAMPAIGNS TILL THE PEACE OF RYSWICK; A. D. 1691, TO A. D. 1697.

The Irish troops arrive in France, and are new formed into regiments.—List of the new regiments, and their commanders.—Position of the French Monarch's affairs.—The new-formed corps ordered to the Rhine.—Bridge at Dudenhaven defended by the Irish.—Posture of affairs on the Piedmontese frontier.—The allied forces invade Dauphinè.—Defence of Guillestre and Embrun.—The Allies re-cross the Alps.—Savoy invaded by Catinat.—Battle of Marsiglia.—Death of Sarsfield.—Operations in Germany and Spain.—Campaign of 1694.—Invasion of the Vaudois territory.—Operations on the Rhine.—Death of Lord Mountcashel.—Campaigns of 1696 and 1697, ... 193

CHAPTER IX.

SERVICES DURING WAR OF THE SPANISH SUCCESSION, A. D. 1701, TO A. D. 1738.

Prince Eugene takes the command of the Imperialist forces.—Forces the French lines on the Adige.—Catinat superseded by Villeroy.—Attack on Prince Eugene's position at Chiari.—Affair between Sheldon's horse and the Imperialists, under Count Merci.—Prince Eugene attempts to surprise Cremona.—Valiant and successful defence of Cremona by the Irish.—Villeroy taken prisoner.—The Imperialists repulsed.—Modesty of Mahony.—Vendôme appointed to command the French army.—Distinguishing characteristics of the two generals.—Battle of Luzara.—Battle of Spire.—The Imperialists defeated at Gremen.—The Electorate of Bavaria sides with France.—Determined opposition of the Tyrolen peasantry.—Riva surrenders to Dillon.—Marlborough carries the lines of Schellenburg.—Incapacity of the French commanders.—Battle of Blenheim.—Operations in Piedmont.—Augmentation of the officers in the Irish regiments.—Persecutions in the Cevennes.—Rising of the Camisards.—Eugene attempts to cross the Adda.—Battle of Cassano.—Campaign of 1705 in Germany.—Battle of Ramillies.—Bravery of Lord Clare and Colonel O'Brien.—Fame of Marlborough.—Brave defence of Alicant.—Successes of the English in Flanders.—Prince Eugene relieves Turin. Battle of Castiglione.—Vendome surprises the Imperialists at Calcinato.—Successful defence of Toulon.—The lines of Stolhoven stormed by the French.—Battle of Almanza.—Mahony takes Alcira and Xativa.—Siege of Lerida.—Carthagena surrenders.—Mahony's services in Sicily.—Siege of Tortosa.—Operations in Flanders.—The French defeated at Gavern.—Siege of Lille.—Tournay surrenders.—Battle of Malplaquet.—Operations of

Eugene and Marlborough in 1710.—Philip V. of Spain forms two regiments of Irish deserters.—The Archduke Charles reinforces Stharemberg in Catalonia, who gains several advantages.—Battle of Almanza.—Villa-Viciosa. —Marlborough superseded by the Duke of Ormond in the command of the Allies in Flanders.—Storming of the lines of Denain.—Peace of Utrecht.—Termination of the war.—General remarks, ... 231

APPENDIX.—Memoirs concerning the Irish troops, &c., . . . 310

INTRODUCTION.

THE following pages comprise Mr. O'Conor's labours on the general Military History of his countrymen, so far as he had completed the arrangement of his papers at the time of his death. If the life of this excellent Irishman and assiduous scholar had been spared, his work would doubtless have been presented to his country, in a form much worthier of the subject and the Author. As it is, the liberal indulgence of the reader must be solicited for errors incident to all posthumous publications, and from which it cannot be expected that the present volume should be wholly free.

Dublin, April, 1845.

MILITARY MEMOIRS

OF

THE IRISH NATION.

CHAPTER I.

THE CAMPAIGN OF TYRONE.

A FRENCH writer, whose cursory remark has grown into a sort of historical apothegm, observes that "the Irish who shew themselves the bravest soldiers in France and Spain, have always behaved shamefully at home."

Had the lively M. Voltaire condescended to read the annals of an obscure people, shut out by distance and insularity from European history, he probably would not have indulged in this disparaging contrast: for he would have found Irish valour the same at Clontarf, at the Blackwater, and at Aughrim, as at Luzara, Cassano, and Fontenoy; the same at Dunboy and Limerick, as at Guillestre, Embrun, and Cremona; therefore, although my chief object in these Memoirs is to preserve the remembrance of

B

my gallant countrymen, whose valour, when proscribed at home, shone with such distinguished lustre in foreign service, I have judged it right to couple the memoirs of the Brigade with a short review of the military achievements of the Irish at home and abroad, during the century of active service that preceded its formation.

Prior to the sixteenth century the wars of the Irish were either petty intestine feuds, not worthy of historical notice, or uncombined efforts in resistance to Norse and Anglo-Norman invasion: yet even in these the impartial mind will find subjects of no humiliating comparison with the military recollections of other neighbouring countries.

That the Irish, from the ninth to the eleventh century, were unable to free themselves from Danish and Saxon aggression, was a misfortune equally shared by Britain and France, in both of which countries those piratical powers won territory to a large extent, and permanently established themselves and their institutions; but neither France nor Britain has the glory of having expelled their invaders, after two centuries of oppression, in a great pitched battle, as the Irish, led by their national monarch, Brian of the Tributes, did at Clontarf. In the military annals of these ages, therefore, if the balance of valour were to be struck among the three nations we have named, it would incline, not to M. Voltaire's countrymen, who submitted to the yoke of Rollo; nor to the countrymen of those writers who have so often from England taunted us with his petulant observation; but it would be awarded to us, who, from that very home in which they suppose us incapable of valour, set to both this example of successful warfare which neither of them was able to imitate.

Again, our subjugation by the Anglo-Norman adherents of Dermod Mac Murrogh, imperfect as it was, was not, in any sense of the word, a greater conquest than the English themselves had recently endured at the hands of the invading Duke of Normandy; nor will the character of our Roderick in any wise suffer in the comparison with that of their Harold. Roderick erected towns, built bridges, constructed highways, founded religious houses, and endowed professorships in learning. With causes of dissension and defeat palpable in the circumstances of the times in which he lived, it is harsh to charge such a man with individual want of conduct, because, at the head of only a section of his nation, opposed or deserted by those who ought to have been his natural friends and allies, he failed in resisting an invasion invited by an entire province, and prosecuted by the united valour and policy of England and Rome; yielding to the same force, in an aggravated degree, that had overturned the dynasty of Alfred in the person of Harold, though the latter monarch fought at the head of an united people, and free from that greatest embarrassment that can befal a king contending for the liberties of his country, the treachery of his ecclesiastics.

The Irish, therefore, do not shrink from a fair comparison with other nations, since grown to be great military powers, in the wars of those ages. But I conceive it would be unprofitable to detail the series of inglorious petty contests in which we might be able to match rude valour here with equally ill-employed, though better disciplined, force in the intestine wars of Stephen, or of the Roses in England, or in the provincial conflicts which desolated France during the same periods. I therefore proceed at once to the first demonstration of a really national kind made by the Irish since their subjugation, when, in the reign of Elizabeth, the great house of O'Neal began to measure arms with its opponents in an open war of independance.

Hugh Earl of Tyrone was the leader under whom this strife of a single clan against individual tyranny, ripened into a national struggle, which occupied the whole power of England for many years, and may be regarded as opening the school for that national military genius which afterwards rose to so noble a pitch of fame in all the most warlike services of Europe. The first blow, however, was struck by his uncle, Shane the Proud. If we credit Camden's account of this chieftain, we must imagine a barbarian. The less suspected records of history display us a hero. The Statute-book, in attainting his blood and proscribing his name, pronounces his loftiest panegyric, enacting that "Forasmuch as the name O'Neal, revived by him, in the judgment of the common people of Ireland, conveys in itself a great sovereignty, as they suppose, and that all the people of Ulster should rather live in servitude to that name, than in subjection to the Crown of England, the name of O'Neal, the manners and ceremonies of its creation, and all its dignities, preeminences, tributes, and exactions should cease for ever, and any person assuming the name of O'Neal should be guilty of high treason."

But, however easily Acts of Parliament were carried in those days, extinguishing the ancient dignities and liberties of the country, the name of O'Neal was not to be blotted out of the Irish history without a much more serious struggle than attended the desultory efforts of John the Proud; for on his murder by the Mac Connells, or Mac Donnells of Antrim (formerly subjugated to his arms, but who treacherously turned and assassinated him on his taking refuge in their camp, after a temporary defeat by the English at Derry), a new claimant, not only to the name of O'Neal, but to the loftier title of a national warrior and liberator of his country, though stained by the vices of duplicity and cruelty, arose in the person of Hugh, the son of his illegitimate brother Ferdoragh or Matthew.

Hugh O'Neal, the famous Earl of Tyrone, while he equalled his uncle in strength of body, in perseverance, courage, and constancy; far surpassed him in knowledge of military affairs, in cultivation of mind, and personal accomplishments. In genius, fertility of resources, address, and manners, none of his cotemporaries, whether English or Irish, could compete with him. Even Camden admits that "he had a strong body, able to endure labour, watching, and hunger; that his industry was great, his soul large, and of a capacity for the weightiest businesses."

His vices were those of the times, and of his position in early life among the courtiers of Elizabeth, where he necessarily became familiar with dissimulation and all the arts of intrigue. During the life-time of Shane, jealousy or caution induced him to side with the English. He had a command in their army, had accepted of the title of Earl of Tyrone, had not refused a commission to execute martial law, and had even imbrued his hands in the blood of his nephews. Though a professed Catholic he would attend the Lord Deputy to church, and stay for divine service, whilst the Lords of the Pale stopped short on the threshold. He had even carried his compliance so far as to engage to banish monks, nuns, and friars out of Tyrone. But these were only concealments of deep designs upon the sovereignty of Ireland. Whilst practising these exterior marks of attachment to the government, and of loyalty to the Queen, he was secretly encouraging his countrymen to enter into the Spanish service, and learn the rudiments of war under its great masters, the Duke of Parma, Count Ernest of Mansfield, and the Count De Fuentes. He was, at the same time, in the habit of training men in the corps which he commanded under the Queen's commission, discharging them when expert, raising recruits in their place, and discharging those again when sufficiently trained.

To restore himself to the confidence of his natural friends after so many years of apparent alienation required no ordinary abilities. But in Hugh O'Neal's character tact was a conspicuous quality. He had scarcely thrown off the assumed title and policy of the Anglicised partisan, when he found himself at the head of an enthusiastic people, and aided by all the power of a clergy whom he had so shortly before engaged to persecute. A broil with his brother-in-law, Sir Henry Bagnall, Marshal of the Queen's forces in Ireland, concurring with the revolt of O'Donnell and Maguire, was the immediate occasion of his casting off the mask. Bagnall preferred an impeachment; the Earl repelled the accusation, but withdrew beyond the Blackwater into O'Neal's country. The fort of Portmore had shortly before been erected to command the principal pass into this principality, and an English sheriff had been intruded within its bounds. O'Neal, seeing the time ripe for action, expelled the functionary, and levelled the fort, and the Queen's forces were immediately marched on the scene of the outbreak, under the conduct of Sir John Norris.

The skill and renown of Sir John Norris promised a speedy conquest. To the veteran army of 10,000 men, led by this able general, trained in the wars of the Low Countries, and supplied with all the improved implements of war, O'Neal could oppose only a few thousands of undisciplined and half-armed clansmen, without artillery, commissariat, or ammunition. But he was conscious of his own abilities, of the difficulties of the country and climate, and of the enthusiasm of his followers, and calmly rested on his arms, to fight or negociate, as occasion might demand.

The operations of the English army were retarded and counteracted by disunion. Russell the Deputy envied the glory of Norris, and Norris was jealous of the interference of Russell. The acuteness and energy of Tyrone never suffered a decisive moment to escape. By the disunion of the commanders he calculated upon obtaining a truce, and so suffering the season for action to pass over, while the severity of an Irish winter would guard his territory from invasion. He accordingly offered submission, complained of the tyranny of the Queen's officers, required liberty of conscience, oblivion of the past, and exemption of his territory from the sheriffs and garrisons of the shire lands. The sympathy of Norris, a soldier, was excited by the recital of cruelties exercised upon the unfortunate natives; and his ingenious mind suggested measures of inquiry and redress. Russell, a statesman, more accustomed to the policy of the times, doubted the sincerity of O'Neal, suspected his objects, delay and succour from Spain, and prudently pressed a vigorous prosecution of the war. O'Neal's arts effected a truce, which, however, soon broke off, and the English began their march from Dundalk on Armagh. Then O'Neal, issuing from the woods, hung upon their rere, attacked them in front, assailed them in flank; when pressed, retired to his fastnesses, again returned to the charge, and convinced Sir John Norris that the talents of his opponent were at least a substitute for the deficiencies of his means. As he approached Armagh the *elite* of the Irish army made an unexpected and furious assault; the steadiness of discipline repelled the attack, but the army was forced back on Dundalk, and 600 of these veterans left on the field of battle(*a*).

Norris next proceeded to raise the siege of Monaghan, invested by the insurgents. A rivulet separated the armies, each of which seemed to dread the event of a battle. A sharp encounter ensued, in which Norris had three horses killed under him, and he and his brother were forced by their wounds to retire from the heat of the conflict. Segrave, an English officer, at the head of a body of cavalry, made a furious assault upon O'Neal's quarters. Tyrone encountered him in single combat; their lances being shivered on their cuirasses, the vigorous arm of O'Neal, wielding a ponderous sword, clove down his adversary. Norris sounded a retreat, and Monaghan surrendered to the victorious army(*b*).

These successes, occurring in the autumn of 1595, spread the flame of insurrection throughout the country, gave new vigour to O'Neal, and alarmed

(*a*) Hist. Cath. lib. iv.; Pet. Lombard, p. 393.
(*b*) M'Geog. tom. iii. p. 509.

the fears of Elizabeth for the safety of Ireland. Proposals of accommodation were made and were rejected, and in the intoxication of success O'Neal openly aspired to the throne of his ancestors. His negociation with the King of Spain, and the Governor of the Netherlands, promised him arms and ammunition, and induced an exaggerated estimate of his strength. In these projects he passed the winter. In the summer of 1596 Norris again advanced from Dundalk, was, as usual, harassed in his march(*a*), but at length succeeded in recovering Armagh and Portmore. At this latter position he erected new fortifications, and also built the strong fort of Mount Norris, to secure the communication between the important ports of Newry and Armagh. Upon his retiring to his quarters in Dundalk, Tyrone blockaded his garrisons, intercepted their supplies, and forced them to capitulate, and, as his own troops were unequal to the defence of fortified towns, left them dismantled(*b*).

Lord Burrough, who had acquired a name in the wars of Flanders, was now appointed Lord Deputy. In the pride of power, and the presumption of ignorance, he displaced Norris, and assumed the conduct of the war in Ulster. Norris, removed to the Presidency of Munster, sunk to an untimely grave, his laurels withered, his fame blotted, and his last moments embittered by insult(*c*). His successor's fate

(*a*) Pet. Lombard, p. 397.   (*b*) Ib.
(*c*) Hist. Cath. Hib. v. 3. C. Pet. Lombard, 397. Camd. 543.

would not have provoked his envy. Burrough marched to the Blackwater, having ordered a body of troops from Leinster to join him by another route. Richard Tyrrell, one of O'Neal's lieutenants, a man experienced in the Irish wars, and famous for his guerilla excursions, waylaid the division in a narrow defile in Westmeath, and out of 1000 one man only is said to have escaped. The memory of the achievement is still preserved in the name of Tyrrell's Pass(a).

Burrough having garrisoned Armagh and Portmore, was preparing to fall back upon Leinster, when the victorious Tyrrell's approach recalled him. The united force of the Ulster army encountered at Drumflough, near Benburb. Here O'Neal displayed the courage of a soldier, and the conduct of a general, exhibiting consummate talents in the art of war. Burrough also behaved with a valour worthy of the steadiness and discipline of his veteran army, and exposed himself in the thick of the encounter, until, endeavouring to force his way through the Irish lines, he received a mortal wound. The Earl of Kildare, the second in command, exerting every nerve to restore confidence to the troops, dispirited by the wound of their general, met with a similar fate. Discipline and steadiness alone saved the English army from a decisive and irreparable defeat.

(a) M'Geoghegan, iii p. 517.

They retired in order from a field of battle covered with their dead(*a*).

The Earl of Ormond, Lieutenant-General of the army, was now directed to seek an accommodation with O'Neal. Success, general insurrection, succours from Spain, disinclined the latter from submission. He temporized, demanded terms which he knew were inadmissible, as usual protracted the war, harassed the English, and declined an engagement.

Sir Henry Bagnall next undertook the prosecution of the war. His ardent mind anticipated victory without calculating chances, exploring roads, or ascertaining the strength or position of his antagonist. At the head of 7000 veterans, trained in the wars of Brittany and the Low Countries, he marched from Dundalk to relieve the fortress of Portmore, again besieged by the Irish. O'Neal, ever cautious, raised the siege, and was about retiring into the fastnesses of Tyrone, but was dissuaded by his bard, O'Clery, who assured him that, according to the prophecy of Saint Ultan, the Irish were to gain a great battle at a neighbouring pass on the Blackwater, called the Yellow Ford.

O'Neal, taking advantage of the enthusiasm kindled by this lucky coincidence, marched to the spot, called in Irish Beal an atha Buidhe, which naturally

(*a*) Peter Lombard, p. 398. Camden, p. 545, who claims the victory on the part of the English, is silent as to the wounds of the Deputy and of the Earl of Kildare. He mentions that Sir Thomas Waller, a man renowned for valour in the wars, was wounded.

offered one of the strongest positions in the neighbourhood, being skirted by a bog on one side, and a wood on the other, and approached by a narrow causeway.

He had studied the character of Bagnall. Bravery approaching to temerity, presumptuous confidence in his own talents and skill, implacable hatred towards O'Neal, and sovereign contempt for the Irish, were calculated to precipitate him into an engagement under every disadvantage of position. O'Neal had no cannon, little ammunition, and few musqueteers. He supplied these deficiencies by his admirable disposition. In the pass leading to the plain he placed 500 light-armed infantry; in the plain itself in front of his position, he dug pitfalls and trenches, and covered them with green sods, supported by wattles and branches. Before the engagement he sought to animate his men by a speech instilling revenge and inspiring hope, exciting fanaticism, and rousing patriotism, by every topic which an ardent mind could suggest. "The object of our most ardent prayers, to fight the Protestants upon equal terms, we have at length obtained. Inferior in number you have often routed them; you have now superior masses to oppose to them. My hopes of victory are not placed in the thunder of artillery, but in your valour. Recollect how often you have defeated greater forces, nobler chiefs, and even Bagnall himself, when less prepared and less disciplined than you are now. The Catholic Irish in the ranks of your enemies will shrink from the contest; the consciousness that they are arrayed against their religion and country must unnerve them. You are about to fight for your country, your wives, your children, and possessions. Bagnall, the bitterest of your enemies, not content with the plunder of your properties, seeks to exterminate your race. Here he must meet the just retribution for his cruelty; here we must avenge our wrongs, and the death of our companions killed at Portmore. St. Ultan has promised and prophesied our victory."

Bagnall also, after the manner of the ancients, addressed his troops in the language of valour, but without the soul-stirring topics that excite the passions, and inflame to enthusiasm.

" Relying on your bravery I selected you as my companions in arms; the undisciplined I left in garrisons, the cowardly with Ormond. From your exertions alone I anticipate victory. I have often witnessed your valour. Will these men, unarmed and undisciplined, dare to encounter troops, accoutred, armed, trained as you are, and inured to war? I should be mad if I could suppose they would sustain your shock for a moment. Remember how you drove O'Neal from his camp at Mullachban. On him who this evening brings me the head of O'Neal or O'Donnel I bestow a thousand pounds. March then! and delay not the moment of victory."

A veteran army did not require a speech to animate its courage. Contempt for an enemy unprovided with artillery, and untrained to the ordinary evolutions of war, military music, clarions, trumpets, and fifes, elevated the spirits of the men. A finer array had never appeared in the Irish wars: 600 cuirassiers, covered with armour, glistening in the rays of the sun of a summer's morning, armed with lances, nine feet in length, led the van. The infantry, trained in the wars of Flanders, who had often withstood the shock of the renowned Spanish pikes, marched in gallant array, divided in three columns, followed by parks of artillery, and ammunition waggons. The general at their head, mounted on a fine charger, by his military carriage, seemed to advance to assured victory. But in his contempt for the Irish, and his hatred to O'Neal, he pushed on more with the courage of a soldier, than with the circumspection of a general. With his front column he entered into the defile, unsupported by the second division. The Irish light troops posted there opened a galling fire from behind underwood and trees. Many of the English fell; but Bagnall's intrepidity forced the pass. His infantry debouched into the plain. His artillery being planted against the rampart four feet high, thrown up by O'Neal in front of his position, his heavy horse charged the Irish light-armed cavalry with irresistible fury, but were thrown into confusion by the concealed pitfalls and ditches, into which they were precipitated by their headlong bravery. O'Neal saw, and seized the decisive moment. His whole force, bounding over their rampart, attacked on all sides the body that had entered the plain, and was yet unsupported by the other divisions. Bagnall did all that courage and conduct could effect to inspire confidence, maintain the ranks, and restore order; until, raising the beaver of his helmet to have a fuller view of the field, he was struck by a musket ball, and fell lifeless to the ground. Dismay succeeded to confusion; the Irish burst in and annihilated the leading columns; then assailed the second division, already thrown into confusion by the explosion of a large quantity of gunpowder, and disheartened by the death of the general. O'Reilly, who commanded it, did all that an officer accustomed to the vicissitudes of war could do, to encourage and rally; but the impetuosity of the victors bore down all opposition, and completed the rout; the third division and the cavalry commanded by Montague, an old and experienced officer, abandoning their cannons, ammunition, and wounded, and leaving 2,400 men dead on the field of battle, effected a precipitate retreat to Armagh.

This victory, the most important that had ever been gained by the Irish over the English, furnished the victors with what they were in great need of, cannon, musquets, ammunition, provisions, clothing; and inspired them with the utmost confidence in their general, whose genius supplied their deficiencies in the implements of war, and removed their impression of inferiority in military skill. Consternation, as happens on all such occasions, magnified the defeat. Armagh was abandoned; Portmore surrendered; all the Irish of Connaught joined the standard of O'Neal; his emissaries in Munster represented the state of the English in Ireland as hopeless; and his lieutenant, Owny M'Rory O'Moore, and Tyrrell, his bravest captain, dispatched to that province with 1,000 men, forced the Lord President to abandon the whole country to insurrection, and take shelter in Cork.

To stem this tide of success a great and experienced commander was required; but intrigue and partiality, overlooking the claims of many tried men at court, pitched upon D'Evereux, Earl of Essex, the personal favourite of the queen, whose inexperience required instructions too minute to suffer any display of individual genius. Against the successive defeats of the Pass of Plumes, Ballyfiniter, the Curlews, and the repulse of Harrington by the O'Moores, the new Chief Governor could only set off the reduction of Cahir, a petty fortalice on the Suir, defended for several days against the royal army for James Galdie Butler; and when at length he sought out the great rebel whom he had been commissioned to subdue, it was to accept his terms, and compromise the dignity of his sovereign, by a pusillanimous and disadvantageous truce. Romance amuses us with the tale of a ring, intercepted by jealousy, which was to have saved the unhappy favourite; but historical justice contemplates his fate without emotion, and acquits his executioners of any graver imputation than that of resolute obedience to the stern necessities of the times.

Since the fall of Edward Bruce at Dundalk, no chieftain had arisen round whose standard the Irish could rally with so much confidence and unanimity as now seemed to attend the splendid career of O'Neal. But these bright prospects were soon dissipated, and shades descended on the opening scene of victory and independence. Charles Blount, Baron Mountjoy, was appointed Chief Governor. Unaccustomed to the perils of war, and delighting in literature and retirement, this nobleman's arrival in Ireland excited little alarm; but the vigour of his mind, his capacity, and courage, soon appeared in his measures, and admonished the Earl of Tyrone, that a statesman now directed the public councils who could neither be approached by flattery, nor misled by artifice; that a soldier wielded the sword of state who had skill to plan and resolution to accomplish the suppression of the most enterprizing efforts of Irish disaffection.

Success had swelled the troops of O'Neal; continued warfare had advanced their discipline, victories supplied them with arms, and Spain with ammunition. Mountjoy felt that Tyrone's power was not to be borne down by open violence, but to be undermined by disunion, weakened by desertion, and paralyzed by suspicion and distrust. Rival tanists were accordingly set up as chieftains in the revolted native lordships, and money and troops were supplied to support their pretensions(*a*). This policy soon began to tell. Desertion, ere long, weakened O'Neal, suspicion distracted his councils, but his courage never deserted him. Mountjoy intercepted his communications, enclosed him within his own territory by a chain of strong posts and fortresses, repelled his attacks, and declined to entangle himself in the woods and morasses of Ulster. But whatever could supply food to the inhabitants of Tyrone was wasted with fire and sword. The desolation of famine was relied on for the restoration of peace, and the solitude of the wilderness was regarded as the securest restoration of the dominion of England. Tyrone tried the fortune of war in the plain—he was repulsed with slaughter, and driven back to the woods, with a decline of reputation, and a falling off of adherents(*b*).

Experience of the caprice of fortune, knowledge of the skill and talents of his opponent, and the miseries brought upon the wretched inhabitants, should have induced submission, and the acceptance of terms; but great talents inspired confidence. The hatred of the people to the name and connexion with England, the active exertions of the Catholic clergy, excited by past persecutions, the flattering encouragement of

(*a*) Hist. Cath. Hib. v. 3. c. 5, Neal Garv was set up as the O'Donnell, Maelmorha Dhas as the O'Reilly, and Sir A. O'Neal, the son of Turlogh Lynagh, as the O'Neal.

(*b*) Camden, 583.

the Pope, and the promises of Spain, still upheld the hopes of O'Neal.

The activity of the British Government, apprized of the preparations of Spain, provided large reinforcements for Ireland. Its policy conciliated the Pale by a relaxation of the penal code, and intrusted the English by blood with civil and military authority. In every vicissitude of fortune, under the pressure of persecution, and the yoke of ecclesiastical tyranny, the Catholics of English descent clung to the mother country with unshaken fidelity. The philosophic reader will be inclined to believe that hatred to the wild Irish, the dread of expulsion, and apprehension of the loss of their estates, was the source of this singular and unexampled attachment. At this period the De Burgos, Plunketts, Barnewells, Prestons, all Catholics, supported the cause of England with the most fervent zeal, supplying the State with men and contributions, exposing their persons to the hardships of war, rejecting the allurements of Irish independence, and disdaining alike the representations of the priesthood and the rescripts of the Roman Court.

In the month of September, 1601, the expected succours from Spain reached Kinsale, a place, from its distance, unpropitious to the fortunes of the northern Irish. In our own times a similar expedition, more formidable from numbers, the skill of the commanders, and its military apparatus, invited by the descendants of the conquerors of Ulster, experienced a similar failure in Bantry Bay.

The commander of the Spanish expedition was Don Juan D'Aguila, the least competent of all the generals whom Philip could have chosen for such a service. He had signalized himself by defeats and miscarriages. Commanding the Spanish in Brittany, he had, in 1594, allowed the French and English to capture Morlaix, Quimper, and other towns without an effort to relieve them. At Crodon, an unfinished fort erected by the Spaniards at the mouth of Brest harbour, he exhibited pusillanimity equalled only by the heroism of the garrison who depended on him for relief, and whom he suffered to perish unaided within sight of his lines. The fort was assailed by the French and English under Marshal D'Aumont and Sir John Norris by land, and by the English, with ten ships of war, under the famous Sir Martin Frobisher, by sea. On the 10th of October, 1594, the trenches were opened: the unconquerable firmness and indefatigable perseverance of the garrison (only 400 men), sustained incessant attacks, repaired breaches, made repeated sallies, and often pursued the besiegers into their trenches. Two large breaches at length invited a general assault. The French, headed by the Count de Milac, mounted the one, the English, led by Sir John Norris, the other. The example of their leaders and national emulation impelled them to extraordinary exertions; nevertheless they were repulsed with great slaughter. Notwithstanding the heavy fire from the batteries, the Spaniards repaired the breaches, fenced them with palisades, and in a few days after sustained and repelled a second assault even more furious than the first. The garrison, from one breach, pursued the French to their trenches, and spiked their cannon; on the other a great number of English fell, including several of their best officers. Norris, reproached by Elizabeth for his failure, resolved on a fresh effort. An incessant fire from the ships and batteries, together with the explosion of mines, had crumbled the remaining defences, when D'Aguila approached at the head of the Spanish forces. The French and English, notwithstanding, mounted the breaches opposite their respective quarters, and the conflict re-commenced with greater fury than ever. Frobisher was killed, and Norris carried from the breach severely wounded; De Parcedes, the heroic Governor, also fell in the breach; still the garrison held their ground; 600 of the assailants filled the ditch dead or disabled; the allies were virtually repulsed, and D'Aguila's advance must have secured him a certain and splendid victory; but he stood aloof, an inactive spectator of the fate of his brave countrymen, who, exhausted by fatigue and the pressure of fresh assailants, were cut to pieces without stirring a foot from their breaches, where they fought heroically to the last man. After passively witnessing the massacre of his comrades in arms, D'Aguila the following day retired unmolested, a proof of the inability of the allies to have resisted his advance, had his pusillanimity suffered him to attack at the propitious moment(*a*). It is certain, that if Barlotta, or Vitelli, or Montenegro, or any other of the renowned Spanish generals of the day, had commanded in Brittany at that time, the Spanish arms would have acquired the lustre of a great victory at Crodon, instead of being tarnished by so disgraceful a retreat.

Such was the commander of the Spanish force destined to co-operate with O'Neal in expelling the armies of Elizabeth from Ireland. His selection of a point of debarkation gave early indication of his want of judgment. Instead of making for some port in the west or north-west of the island, where the heads of all the great native families were in arms, and ready to give him an unanimous adhesion, and where his operations must, for a length of time, have been unmolested by the approach of the enemy; he landed at Kinsale, within two days' march of Cork, the depot of the military strength of the province of Munster, among a population whose chieftains were loyal or neutral, and at a distance of the whole length of the island from those friends and allies whom he had been sent to support. Of the great Irish chiefs and gentlemen of the neighbouring district, O'Sullivan Beare, O'Conor Kerry, and the O'Driscolls, alone joined his standard. Mac Carthy More, James Earl of Desmond, and O'Mahony, had been won over by the arts of Carew, the Lord President.

(*a*) Davila's History of the Civil Wars of France, l. xiv.

He was, therefore, constrained on landing to confine himself to the ramparts of Kinsale. Mountjoy, then lying at Athlone, at once determined on blighting the reputation of the invader in the eyes of the natives by compelling him to endure a siege.

Regardless of the severities of a winter campaign, the difficulties of supplies, and the celebrity of the Spanish infantry, alike skilled in the attack and defence of fortified towns, the energetic Chief Governor withdrew his garrisons from Ulster, collected all the disposable force of the kingdom, and early in November sat down before Kinsale. Tyrone's forces were scattered; the greatest part, as usual in the winter, having returned to their homes, to await the return of active service, with the return of endurable weather. By indefatigable exertions, O'Neal collected 6000 men; but this force was inadequate; the distance great, the roads nearly impassable; rivers and mountains, woods and defiles, the hostile territory of the Pale, and a powerful force, under Sir George Carew, protecting the confines of Munster, presented enormous difficulties. But the occasion was pressing, the danger urgent, his engagements with the Spaniards sacred, and the fate of nations and churches at stake; and with energy proportioned to the demands of the crisis, and ability rising with the necessity for its display, O'Neal, without roads, without pontoons, without commissariat, in the depth of winter, and in the face of superior forces, set out on his march for Munster; crossed the rivers swollen by floods, traversed vast tracts of bog, opened a way through almost untrodden forests, and, evading the watchful activity of Carew, on the tenth day displayed the standard of Ulster on the heights approaching Kinsale. But the Queen's army, increased by the return of Carew's division, and by reinforcements from England under the Earl of Thomond, lay between him and the town, 15000 strong. The Irish were exhausted by the fatigues and privations of their march, and in no condition to attack; instead, therefore, of attempting to raise the siege, by assailing Mountjoy in his trenches, O'Neal was constrained to satisfy himself by cutting off his supplies—a policy which, at that season of the year, and in a country only nominally friendly, aided, too, by incipient pestilence in the English camp, and daily increasing desertions, might have been attended with full success, but for an unexpected casualty, which precipitated an engagement at a moment when such an act was least expected in the Irish quarters. A skirmish of outposts with a party of the queen's cavalry, led to a feigned retreat. The feint was mistaken for a flight, and produced a panic. Mountjoy seized the decisive moment, poured his battalions on the Irish camp, and completed the disorder. O'Neal, O'Donnell, and Hugh Tyrrell, in vain endeavoured to rally the fugitives, though they succeeded, by great personal exertions, in partially covering the retreat. With a loss of 1500 men, the camp was abandoned, and the town left to its fate. D'Aguila, who witnessed the engagement inactively from the walls, betook himself to his ships, and carried back the remnant of his army, and the increase of his infamy, to his own country. O'Donnell fled to Spain; O'Sullivan to his castle of Dunboy; O'Neal to the fastnesses of Tyrone. The English entered Kinsale, and the war had a temporary cessation.

But the indefatigable Mountjoy, after a short repose, pursued O'Neal into his remote retreat; re-edified the often razed fort of Portmore, which still preserves the Christian name of this great warrior in its modern appellation of Charlemont—a name glorious also in the peaceful recollections of the nation—and, crossing the Blackwater beyond Dungannon, laid waste the country as far as the confines of Derry. The mountainous and woody district of Glan Conkain, which from the thirteenth century had been a familiar retreat for the descendants of Nial in times of danger, afforded Hugh a last refuge. Here he entrenched himself in an almost inaccessible position, from which not even the talents of Mountjoy could dislodge him, and contemplated, from these savage recesses, the desolation of his territory, the miseries of his people, and the destruction of every vestige of his power and authority. Nothing could be more dreadful than the terrible scene presented to him by the unrelenting energy of Mountjoy.

The sword had failed, and famine, the last of

human calamities, was called in aid. The standing corn was cut down, the grain destroyed, the cattle carried off, the houses burned, and the population left to perish in the fields. Their unburied carcasses, emitting pestilence and death, consummated the destruction of any thing that might escape famine and the sword. Some of the wretched inhabitants prolonged life by feeding on water-cresses and nettles, on the putrid carcasses of their horses, and ultimately on the flesh of their own species. Fynes Morryson, an eye-witness, an Englishman, and a Protestant, cannot be suspected of exaggeration. The picture here drawn is his, though hardly so vivid or so revolting as he has described it. But even this could not subdue the spirit of O'Neal. No longer able to wield the sword, he still exerted the arms of fanaticism, and procured the decision of the colleges of Salamancha and Valladolid, that any Irish Catholic joining the standard of an heretical and excommunicated queen, incurred the everlasting penalties of mortal sin. But the terrors of an invisible world were remote and uncertain; the punishment of secular treason speedy and inevitable. The decision of the doctors proving wholly inefficacious, and news of the death of O'Donnell, who was carried off by fever shortly after his arrival in Spain, having reached his retreat, O'Neal at length, in the spring of 1603, sued for accommodation. Elizabeth had left the scenes of war and worldly policy before these overtures reached her court; and

O'Neal was ignorant that the crown had devolved on another head, until the royal clemency of James had ratified his pardon.

After the submission of O'Neal, O'Sullivan and his companions alone held out against the royal authority. To detail the romantic series of sufferings, dangers, and triumphs, through which these brave men prolonged their defiance of the government, and ultimately effected their escape, would be inconsistent with the plan of this work, in which the greater operations of war only are designed to have a place. Still the defence of Dunboy, although a place of no greater strength than the ordinary houses of the nobility, consisting of a single square keep, with some inconsiderable outworks, was so bravely maintained against a force so formidable for numbers, means, and warlike skill, that it justly claims a place in any record of military virtue respecting these times. Garrisoned by 120 men, under the command of the Irish captain Rickard Mac Geoghegan, Dunboy, standing on the shore of Berehaven, near the mouth of Bantry Bay, occupied Sir George Carew and a force of four thousand men, with a train of artillery, and abundant supplies both by sea and land, fifteen days, before it yielded. The difficulties of the siege, owing to the extreme roughness of the ground, were unusually great; the cannon having to be carried several miles over almost impracticable cliffs and ravines; and when got into position, and a breach at length effected, the resistance of the garrison was so desperate, that the assailants were twice driven to their trenches. When the main hall of the tower was carried, the remnant of the garrison retired to the dungeon beneath, where, for the space of a day, they maintained themselves, firing up through the aperture of the stairs with such vigour, that they at length succeeded in recovering possession of the hall, which was now reduced to a heap of ruins. Here terms were proposed to them, and accepted; but Mac Geoghegan, on the final entrance of the victors, though mortally wounded, would have treacherously blown up the powder magazine; and the capitulants were put to the sword. O'Sullivan and his companions, in all but 1000 men, then retreated northward, crossed the Shannon in corachs covered with the hides of their horses, which they slew for the purpose; and, making their way through Thomond and Connaught, through a series of conflicts, in which their numbers were reduced to thirty-five, found safety at length at O'Rourk's castle of Leitrim.

A comparative tranquillity succeeded, and endured until, in the spring of 1607, on some allegation of an intended rising in the North, O'Neal, O'Donnell, and several others of the principal native nobility of Ulster, deemed it prudent to fly. Their flight was followed by their attainder, and by the well known confiscation and plantation of Ulster. This event, so important in the civil and social history of Ireland, is recorded in the Annals of the

Four Masters, with some touching and appropriate reflections: " This distinguished company embarked (from Loch Swilly, in a ship brought thither by Maguire) on the festival of the Holy Cross, in autumn. It is certain that the sea has not borne, and the wind has not wafted, in modern times, a number of persons in one ship more eminent, illustrious, or noble, in point of genealogy, heroic deeds, feats of arms, and valiant achievements, than they. Would that God had but permitted them to remain in their patrimonial inheritances, until their children should have come to years of manhood. Woe to the heart that meditated, and the mind that conceived, and the council that recommended the project of this expedition, without knowing whether they should, to the end of their lives, be able to return to their native principalities or patrimonies."

CHAPTER II.

CAMPAIGNS IN THE SERVICE OF SPAIN.

WHILE Tyrone was wasting his own and his sovereign's energies in a ruinous religious war in Ireland, the Dutch, animated by an equal but more fortunate enthusiasm on the Protestant side, were striving for civil and religious liberty against Philip of Spain. In this struggle they were aided by the sympathy and arms of Elizabeth, whose favourite, Leicester, commanded the English auxiliaries. Among these troops of the English queen were about 1500 Irish conscripts, raised by Sir John Perrot in 1585, and commanded by Sir Edward Stanley, an English Catholic of high family and distinguished reputation for honour and military ability. The spirit of the times, however, was dangerous to all the nobler qualities of the mind. Fanaticism and rancour had taken the place of religion and manliness. The military character which, in almost all ages and countries, has been peculiarly stamped with honour and fidelity, had caught the prevalent vice of theological partizanship, and desertion to the standard of the deserter's religion was no longer infamous in the eyes of the base bigots and casuists who gave the tone to public feeling. Stanley had served in Ireland for fifteen years against the Catholics of that country, faithful to his colours and his Sovereign; but in Holland his principles no longer remained proof against the solicitations of bigotry. Notwithstanding the remonstrance of the States, Leicester had intrusted the strong town of Deventer to Stanley and his Irish. Common prudence should have guarded against the prevalent spirit of the age; but Leicester's blind confidence or imbecility took no precaution. The Spaniards soon assailed the Catholic commander, through the Jesuits. The Dutch were heretics and rebels; Elizabeth a persecutrix and excommunicate; Philip a Catholic king and lawful sovereign of Deventer. Seduced by such appeals, Stanley fell from his allegiance and his fair fame, and drew the Irish with him. They were easily persuaded: educated in no school of honour, as their recreant commander had been, they grasped with eagerness at the suggestions of national antipathy. They had been dragged by a forced levy from their homes to fight the battles of insurgents, with whom they had no sympathies, against a people with whom they were united by the tradition of a common origin, and the profession of the same creed. Their own wrongs and those of their country rankled in their breasts. They had seen the conflagration of their homes and their harvests, the desolation of their plains, the usurpation of their lands, and the desecration of their altars by English adventurers, who massacred their fathers and brothers, violated their wives and sisters, and indulged in every species of military licentiousness. The exaltation of their religion, and the gratification of a natural revenge, covered the infamy of desertion; and in the shades of a night whose darkness still overshadows the recollection of this campaign, the gates of Deventer were thrown open to the Spaniards. Daylight disclosed the enemy's colours floating on the ramparts. The citizens could make no resistance. Stanley addressed them in a speech intended to extenuate his treachery, and screen his conscience: "He had broken no pledge; to the States he had given none—to Leicester alone he was accountable, and from Leicester he had received letters discharging him from all obligations. He repudiated the charge of perfidy; his conscience, he said, dictated the restitution to Philip of what belonged to him. He had never disgraced his family by any act unbecoming his birth. Necessity would compel the disarming of the citizens, but their effects should be secured from plunder, and their houses from the licentiousness of the military(a)."

Stanley's example of treachery was shortly after followed by another Englishman, Rowland Yorke, who, by practising on the apprehensions of his own troops, with the rumour of a threatened attack by an overpowering force, induced his garrison to evacuate

(a) Bentivoglio, part ii book iv.; Thuanus, ad an.1587; Strada de Bello Belgico.

a fort in the neighbourhood of Deventer, which was, immediately on their withdrawal, occupied by the Spaniards, and by Stanley's Irish. These losses ruined the affairs of the Confederates in those parts, involving the loss of great stores of provisions, ammunition, and artillery. Stanley obtained the government of Deventer: Rowland Yorke, elevated to the same rank in the Spanish, which he had held in the British, service, did not long survive his infamy, being poisoned shortly after(*a*). The Irish were incorporated with the Spaniards, Walloons, and Italians, armed and equipped according to their usage, and shared with them, under the general appellation of the Four Nations, the glory of the succeeding campaigns.

At this time the Duke of Parma was before Sluys, and Count Hohenloe, one of the Dutch generals, to distract his arms from that point, had also sat down before Bois-le-Duc. To raise the siege of this latter place, Hautepeine's division was associated with Stanley's corps of Irish, Walloons, and Spanish. The united force amounted to 3000 foot, and 1000 horse. The besieging army exceeded 5000, half of whom were English, equal in courage, but inferior in discipline, to the Spanish veterans. Hautepeine, relying on the superiority of his troops, advanced confidently from Venlo. The Dutch burned their towns as he approached, and

(*a*) Strada, lib. viii.

he prosecuted his march through a desolated country. Hohenloe then actively prosecuting his attack on the fort of Enghel, adjoining Bois-le-Duc, resolved on giving battle. To this he was induced, as well by his superiority in numbers, as by position, and the presence of the Dutch shipping in the Meuse.

The Meuse forms a crescent to the north of Bois-le-Duc, and with the Dyse, falling into it, covered one of Hohenloe's flanks, while a small fleet of boats, mounted with cannon, protected the other; the front was strengthened by an intrenchment and waggons, so that the post appeared nearly impregnable. Five hundred foot, thrown forward to retard the approach of the Spaniards, were attacked by the Irish, broken, and driven with great loss into the intrenchment. The Walloons, Irish, and Germans, broke through the barrier of waggons: but behind these the English and Dutch presented a compact and firm array within the curve formed by the Meuse : the fire from this body, and the cannon from the ships, taking the assailants in front and flank, did terrible execution, and arrested the advance; but Hautepeine, bringing up his reserve, composed of veteran Spaniards, soon restored the combat, when, in the moment of victory, a shot from the ships arrested his career. The fall of their leader damped not the ardour of the troops of the Four Nations, who, without a general, pressed on, broke the lines of the Dutch, threw reinforcements into Enghel, and, having achieved the object of the attack, fell back, with their faces to the enemy, their respective commanders setting an example of bravery and steadiness, which prevented the English and Dutch from following them beyond the range of the great guns in the river. In this engagement the Irish, though young troops, displayed the steadiness of veterans, and a spirit of gallantry not surpassed, even in that military age(*a*).

Philip, victorious in the Low Countries, had resolved upon the conquest of England, and was now preparing the Armada for that purpose. The difficulties were great, but Spanish presumption calculated on Spanish valour as invincible. The plan of invasion deeply engaged the Spanish councils, and whether England, Scotland, or Ireland, should be first assailed, became a subject of deliberation. The Catholic malcontents in England would join the standard of Catholic Spain. The King of Scotland would avenge the execution of his mother. The native Irish were eager to shake off the yoke of English dominion. In the indecision caused by these conflicting considerations, Stanley was called in. His religion protected him from the contempt which usually pursues treachery. He was received by the Spanish monarch with honour, and ushered into the council chamber where (the King and the Marquis Santa Croce, the Grand Admiral of Spain, only, being present),

(*a*) Bentivoglio.

he spoke as follows: "Ireland is the most vulnerable part of the dominions of Elizabeth. The Irish sea affords numerous safe and commodious harbours. Waterford taken, and fortified, would shelter the Spanish fleets; from thence, the opposite shores of England might easily be invaded, or Ireland itself reduced under the dominion of Spain. Fifteen years have I served in that country; I have had sufficient time to explore it; I have ascertained its strength, resources, and the disposition of its inhabitants. The native Irish abhor the English, their manners, laws, and government. To the ancient faith they are ardently attached, and eager to join the standard of a Catholic invader. Give me but 6000 veterans, 6000 stand of arms, and adequate supplies and ammunition for that number, and I will undertake to reduce the island under the dominion of your Majesty. You will there have ports commodious for your fleets, abundance of provisions wherewith to support them; the island will supply an admirable body of cavalry, and more than 6000 well-disciplined infantry. In vain will England resist invasion from Ireland. Ireland is an outwork, which, when taken, will necessarily induce the fall of England itself, just as fortified towns yield, when the outward defences are carried(*a*)."

Fortunately for both England and Ireland, this politic counsel was not adopted. The Duke of

---

(*a*) Strada, p. 532.

Parma, bent on the reduction of the revolted provinces, and desirous of bringing as great a demonstration of force as possible into the neighbourhood of the insurgents, urged Flushing as the fitting point of rendezvous, and England as the proper object of attack.

The Armada, shattered by storms, and foiled by English seamanship, appeared on the coast of Flanders. Perceiving this disaster, the Duke of Parma, who had collected a flotilla at Dunkirk and Newport, to embark the troops for the intended invasion, paused between his sovereign's orders, and the danger of committing to the perils of the ocean the best disciplined army that Europe had seen since the fall of the Western Empire. Pressed by the commander of the Spanish fleet to embark his men, he ordered 1000 Irish and Spaniards to sea in the most tempestuous weather. A sergeant remonstrated; the inexorable severity of the Duke punished this infraction of military subordination, by inflicting a mortal wound with his own hand. The rest of the soldiers obeyed, embarked, and perished in sight of the army(a). Farnese declined to expose further so much bravery to perils, in which neither discipline nor generalship could avail.

A large body of Irish still remained to share the dangers and glory of a campaign, in which they were to fight side by side with the most renowned soldiers

(a) Strada, p. 583.

of Europe. In such a school, as will be presently
seen, they soon became in no respect inferior to their
comrades. The Spaniards, at this period, had not
degenerated from the virtues of their Celtiberian ancestors. In defending towns, they exhibited the
constancy and courage of the citizens of Numantia
and Saguntum. In the field, their firmness and valour revived the memory of Viriatus and Sertorius.
The Guascon infantry could not be brought to face
them; the French men-at-arms could make no impression on their impenetrable array. They had
annihilated the *elite* of the French armies at the
Garigliano, at Pavia, and St. Quintan. The French
fortresses in Picardy now yielded in rapid succession to their arms. Calais, deemed impregnable,
was taken by assault in the presence of an English
fleet, having 4000 land troops on board. Ardres,
Guisne, Ham, Cambray, strong by nature, and fortified by all the rules of art, yielded to the indefatigable labour of the Spanish soldiers, and the matchless skill of Du Rasni, their Quartermaster-General.
Dourlen, a place of some importance, midway between Arras and Amiens, was carried by storm; the
Spaniards, Italians, Irish, and Walloons, vieing with
each other which should be foremost in the assault of
several breaches in the castle and town. Hernando
Tello de Portocarrero, a soldier of fortune, a Spaniard, was the first to plant the standard of Castile
on the parapet, and to bear down all opposition at
the head of the forlorn hope, for which brave achieve-

ment the Count De Fuentes, an eye-witness of his valour, rewarded him with the government of the captured place. Portocarrero was diminutive in person, but of a large and enterprising mind, eager for glory, and watchful after opportunities. Not satisfied with the bare custody of Dourlen, he often sallied forth with his garrison, consisting of Spaniards, Italians, Walloons, and Irish, and attacked the French in the open field; sometimes lay in ambush, and surprised them; at times carried off their cattle; then set fire to their villages, and thus became the terror of the whole French northern frontier. But his aspiring mind, and enterprising courage, were not to be satisfied by successful incursions and inglorious combats. His ambition aimed at some mighty achievement, that would redound to the honour of his nation, and to his own glory.

Amiens, a first-rate city, strongly fortified, and garrisoned by 15,000 armed citizens, attracted Portocarrero's enterprizing spirit. Despising the discipline of citizen guards, he resolved to surprise their negligence. With this view he employed a native Spaniard, Francesco del Arco, to survey the works, and ascertain the weak points, both of the place and garrison: having done which, he despatched him to Brussels, to apprize the Cardinal Archduke, Governor of the Netherlands, of the supine security of the

(a) Davila, book xv.; Strada, book viii.; Thuanus, ad. an. 1599.

citizens, and of the great chance of surprising them. Arco soon returned with the approval of the cardinal, and orders to the neighbouring garrisons to furnish Portocarrero with 2400 of the bravest of the infantry, and 600 horse of the same description. The *elite* of the army were chosen from the different nations: 600 Spaniards, 600 Italians, as many Walloons, and an equal number of Irish—the last wholly infantry.

On the evening of the 10th of March, 1597, these troops assembled within a league of Dourlen. Their destiny was a profound secret. Having ordered them to advance towards Amiens, Portocarrero called the captains together, and apprized them of his design in an animated speech, setting forth the facilities of the enterprize, the glory that would redound to the Spanish arms, and the advantages that would result to their king and country. For himself he would rather act than command, and whether he should live or die, he could not live or die more gloriously. The design being announced, officers and soldiers were astounded by the boldness of the attempt; they could scarce credit the reported negligence of the citizens; could scarce hope to overpower 15,000 men; but Portocarrero's enthusiasm and eloquence soon dissipated doubt, inspired confidence, and all cried out, they would achieve whatever he commanded.

At sunrise ten resolute Spaniards, dressed as peasants, approached one of the gates, followed by a waggon seemingly loaded with beams; three of the foremost carried bags of nuts and apples; one of whom falling down at the gate, the citizen guard fell to collecting the scattered fruit. During the scramble the waggon was introduced into the gateway, while the disguised Spaniards instantly overpowered the guard. The sentinel at the top of the gate cut the ropes of the portcullis, but the waggon prevented its descent, and the Spanish officers, armed cap-a-pie, marched into the town. Two hundred Walloons and Irish, concealed outside the pallisadoes, under Captain Bostock, rushed after, bore down all opposition, got possession of the principal points, and, in a word, enforced the surrender of this important city, with its citizen guard of 15,000 men.

This surprise alarmed all France, and excited murmurs against the Marshal Biron and the king, as negligent of, or incapable of sustaining, the military glory of the nation. The king, to stem the tide of unpopularity, resolved on a mighty effort for recovery of this important city. He collected forces from all quarters, and being joined by 4000 English, about the middle of May he laid siege to Amiens, giving the command of the besieging force to the Marshal de Biron, one of the most enterprizing and active captains of that age.

The Irish, having had a most distinguished share in the defence of this town, I am induced to give a more detailed account of the siege, being one of the most memorable of the sixteenth century, and a subject of the greatest pride and glory in Spanish military recollections.

Amiens, the capital of Picardy, a city nearly two leagues in circumference, divided by the Somme, was strongly fortified with a thick wall, having towers, ravelines, and outworks, which required a great garrison to man the different points, and keep down a numerous and warlike population, indignant at their surprise and subjugation.

Biron first blockaded: he drew a line of circumvallation from the upper to the lower part of the right bank of the river, and strengthened it by seven forts, mounted with artillery; another, at some distance on the exterior, with an equal number of forts, protected the French from an attack on the side of Flanders. Thousands of peasants, collected from Picardy and Artois, worked incessantly at these lines; but Portocarrero, neither awed by the disaffection of the townsmen, nor checked by the activity of the French cavalry, omitted no opportunity of interrupting the besiegers. Incessant sallies, successful in many instances, frequently drove the pioneers from the trenches, and often in a few hours reduced the work of days to rubbish. On the 24th of May Portocarrero and Montenegro led two sallies from different gates of the city; a furious encounter ensued; the Spaniards bore down all opposition, until the French cavalry under Montigni took them in flank; then Biron made a desperate effort to cut off their retreat in a narrow pass between the river and his trenches. Captain Bostock, at the head of the Irish, opened a tremendous fire upon the French from some bushes he had occupied, so as to give time to the runaways to rally. The encounter was again renewed; Montenegro's division attacked the cavalry in flank and rere, whilst engaged in front with the Irish, and if the Marshal Biron had not brought up the whole of the French cavalry, Montigni's squadrons would have been cut off to a man.

On the 7th of June the king arrived in the camp. Concealing his chagrin under an air of cheerfulness, he commended the diligence and industry of the troops, but privately urged the Marshal to renewed exertion, especially by sapping and mining, as more effectual against a garrison so resolute and active. Henry fixed his head-quarters at an abbey within cannon range of the ramparts, where he gallantly remained in defiance of the shot of the town, but humanely removed the soldiery into huts outside the lines, to protect them from the incessant fire of the besieged.

The besieged laboured under scarcity of provisions, and diseases that carried off many of the soldiers as well as of the inhabitants; but the spirit of the garrison bore up against all privations: they sallied every day; the fire of their great guns was incessant, and on one occasion the king was nearly buried in the crumbling ruins of his quarters.

Certain friars in the town, and some of the Walloons, conspired to open one of the gates to the

French. Portocarrero's vigilance discovered the plot; the Walloons were executed; respect for the ecclesiastical order saved the friars from the infamy of a public execution. These dangers did not lessen the number, though they weakened the force of the sallies, for the governor, obliged to contend against intestine treachery as well as external force, had to keep constant patroles in the streets, and a great guard in the square, as well as a sufficient number of men on the ramparts.

On the 20th of June, Biron attempted a surprise, by getting some men to descend into the ditch, and fire several bags of powder, the united explosion of which, it was hoped, would open a breach. Some only of the bags exploded. The Spaniards poured a terrible fire into the ditch, drove off the assailants, and got possession of a great deal of powder, of which they were much in need.

Biron was now making rapid progress with his approaches from the Hermitage, when Montenegro sallied with 400 horse, followed by 200 Irish and Italian foot, and commenced a fight so vigorous, that the workmen and Biron's troop of horse were totally routed, and ultimately rescued from utter destruction by the Count D'Auvergne, with a strong body of cavalry; but the Irish and Italians came on so briskly as this critical moment, that the French were routed with a loss of 200 killed. Not above ten of the besieged fell in this brilliant sally.

Every day, for an entire month, such sallies retarded the approaches, until disease, want of supplies, and the increasing numbers of the French, defeated the efforts to destroy the works, and Biron was at length enabled to batter in breach from the Hermitage. Portocarrero, perceiving that a desperate effort alone could defeat the approaches of the besiegers, directed 300 Irish, headed by two of their captains, 200 Spanish, 200 Italians and Walloons, 80 men at arms, and 350 horse, to sally precisely at noon, on the 17th of June. They fell with their customary fury upon the trenches, dispersed the foremost guards, attacked, and totally routed, the regiment of Picardy, and drove it into the redoubt of the Hermitage, with the loss of most of its officers. The regiment of Champagne, in front of the redoubt, endeavoured to stop the runaways; but so ardent was the emulous onset of the Four Nations, that the French broke and fled in all directions. Biron, Bonsi, a Florentine, and some resolute guards, defended for a few moments the narrow passages of the redoubt with the utmost resolution; but the fury of the assailants bore them down, routed a reinforcement under the Prince of Joinville, and filled the camp with dismay. Portocarrero's men at arms now came up, to sustain the Spanish and Irish infantry. Biron, covered with sweat and blood, having all the hair of the right side of his head scorched off, continued to animate his men in the battery, calling loudly for reinforcements. At this moment the king came up. Henry, whose courage was always kindled by the appearance of danger, alit from his horse, snatched a pike, plunged into the midst of the conflict, and was followed by D'Auvergne, St. Paul, and the bravest of the French nobility; and thereupon a conflict ensued in defence of the cannon, that resembled a mighty battle. Two hours it raged, the king, at the head of his troops, encouraging them by his voice and gestures, was exposed to the utmost danger, and repeatedly rescued by the enthusiasm of the French nobility. Intense heat, and heavy armour, embarrassed the efforts of the Spanish men at arms, and the French at length drove the assailants from the trenches; but being, in their turn, attacked by the Spanish cavalry, on their debouching on the plain, were suddenly cut through and surrounded. The king, Biron, and Joinville, were at length extricated from their desperate, almost hopeless situation, by the Duke of Maine, at the head of 600 fresh cavalry, who drove the exhausted Spaniards back to their works. On this memorable occasion, so glorious in the Spanish annals, the French had 900 men killed, and probably some thousands wounded, among the latter Henry Davila, the admirable writer of the Civil Wars of France, from whom we have drawn these particulars(*a*).

The numbers killed in these desperate sallies, scarcity of provisions, and malignant fevers, slackened the sorties, and enabled the French to make

(*a*) Davila, book xv.

their approaches with less difficulty. The counterscarp was now in danger of being carried; but the Irish and Italians constructed a pallisade in the covered way, which protected it till the 1st of August, when the besiegers, after the most obstinate resistance, succeeded in carrying it. The Spaniards, at the time of this disaster, were exhausted by a recent assault upon the trenches, in which the loss of the French was great, many of them being slain in their lines, and forty being blown up by the springing of a mine. The following days were employed by the French in endeavouring to destroy the casemates by fougades, fireworks, and other means. The assaults and defence were carried on by day and by night without intermission, but so great was the industry and perseverance of the besieged, that only a few spans were gained upon them for an entire week. The constancy of the Spaniards in this memorable siege has no parallel, but in the valour of their ancestors at the sieges of Saguntum and Numantia, and of their descendants in the defence of Saragossa and Gerona, in our own times. The French endeavoured, by sapping, to destroy the works; by countermining, the garrison defeated these efforts: their valour under ground was as fatal to the French miners, as their compact array, and impetuous assaults, were destructive in the trenches.

Biron's ardour had now carried a gallery close to the walls; a ravelin protected the gate of Dourlens and the bridge over the fosse; by the incessant fire of the French batteries, it was reduced to ruins; and on the 24th of August the French and English severally assaulted it: national emulation impelled them to extraordinary efforts. The resolution of the Spaniards maintained the post for several hours, until exhausted nature yielded to overpowering numbers; but so wearied were the assailants, that they could not cover themselves, and were at the first light on the morning of the 25th attacked with such fury by the garrison, that they were driven out of the ravelin with immense loss; but returning on the evening of the same day with fresh numbers, and under cover of the batteries, and of a cavalier mounted with artillery, they retook it; and the regiment of Cambray made a lodgment, whereby the rampart was irretrievably lost.

The governor had performed all that bravery and the laws of war required to justify a surrender, if not to make it imperative, to save his garrison, and obtain honourable terms; but Portocarrero was not a man to yield to ordinary pressure: death had no terrors to subdue him; dangers and difficulties infused into him additional vigour; and on this occasion, confiding in the constancy and heroism of his garrison, he resolved to hazard the last extremities of war, sooner than surrender a conquest made by his enterprising spirit, and so long maintained by his indefatigable exertions.

He immediately set about making a little halfmoon on the edge of the rampart, which was constructed by carrying earth in baskets, a labour almost incredible in the exhausted state of the garrison. Neither privations, nor a scorching sun, nor the tremendous fire of the French batteries, could impede or retard this work, which had been completed before a practicable breach was made in the wall. At the same time Montenegro, the lieutenant-governor, was employed in digging a deep trench inside the rampart, to serve as a fresh line of defence, after the breach should be carried.

The French batteries thundered on the great tower over the gate, and having made a practicable breach, it was stormed with great gallantry by the besiegers, but was ultimately maintained by the obstinate resolution of a few men in guard of it. The French, at the same time, sprung a mine under it; a portion came down with a great crash, that filled up the entrance into the tower on the side of the city, so that it was deprived of all relief from the body of the place, and must have yielded to a second assault, if the governor had not laboured incessantly to have the rubish removed, which was effected in the course of the night, and 80 Irish and 80 Italians were introduced to relieve the heroic defenders who had maintained it with so much glory.

During four successive days the Irish and Italians maintained this post against the united efforts of the French and English. By sapping, at length, the miners effected what the fire of the artillery and the gallantry of the assailant troops had altogether failed in; and on the 30th of August the French standards were planted on the tower, the wall, and the rampart; but the assailants were checked in their career by the half-moon erected by the governor, and two other half-moons, constructed at the same time by Pachiotto, a celebrated Italian engineer.

By this time the Spanish army of the Netherlands was in motion to raise the siege, and the French king pressed on the works with increasing ardour. On the 4th of September he caused a general assault to be given on the half-moons, which was sustained by the Spaniards with their usual resolution. Under the eye of their king, the French behaved with the intrepidity characteristic of their nation; mounds of dead bodies filled the ditches, and the works must have been carried, if Spanish resolution had not surpassed French loyalty, and if the emulation of the Four Nations—Spaniards, Italians, Irish, and Walloons—had not presented an array which the Gascon and English infantry were unable to break.

But this victory was dearly bought. Portocarrero was struck dead by a musket ball:—alike lamented by the Spaniards, whom he had often led to victory, and the French, whom he had often defeated. A great man, this, cut off in his early bloom, before he ripened to great achievements, and consigned by the inevitable fate of war to an early grave. His countrymen long bewailed his loss. He had sustained the honour of the Spanish arms by matchless intrepidity, invincible perseverance, adventurous enterprize, and cool and calculating science. In the cathedral church of Amiens a monument was erected to his memory, with an inscription recording the great qualities of his mind, and the attachment of his troops, and enumerating his triumphs over the enemies of his king and country.

He was succeeded in the command by the Marquis of Montenegro, of the noble house of Carraffa, so fruitful of great men, and upon which he reflected as much lustre as he derived from it—an officer not inferior to the deceased governor in industry, perseverance, vigilance, constancy, or courage; who did honour to the Spanish arms in an age when every soldier of that nation was animated with a spirit of heroism not surpassed in the annals of ancient or modern warfare.

St. Luc, the French engineer in chief, with the king's favourite regiment, that of Navarre, and Biron at the head of the English, now cut two trenches across the ramparts, in order to protect their flanks, when storming the Spanish half-moons. Montenegro and Frederico Pachiotto were continually present in the works; and because the infantry was in a manner consumed by hardships, the men at arms and cuirassiers worked with spades and shovels, doing the duty of infantry, and fighting with pikes and muskets. On the night of the 8th of September, St. Luc was struck by a ball which terminated his career, to the exceeding grief of the king, on account of his loyalty, and great skill in engineering. His attachment to Henry and his country had induced him to exchange the agreeable pursuits of science and literature for the camp, where the purity of his mind, the elegance of his genius, and extent of his learning, and his graceful figure, and noble aspect conciliated the affections of all who knew him. In the field his courage was prominent; in council his wisdom was conspicuous. His fate and that of Lord Falkland, at different periods, and in different countries, were alike deplored. Their fortunes were nearly similar. Both were confidential advisers of their respective sovereigns; both lovers of the Muses; both urged by ardent loyalty from the retreats of science to the bustle of war; both adorned by the noblest qualities of mind and the most elegant and graceful form of body; both victims in early life to a chivalrous spirit, paramount to every consideration of interest and every inclination to ease and retirement.

On the 12th of August the half-moons were stormed at sun-rise. French and English vied with each other which would be foremost in planting the Fleur de Lis or the Cross of St. George on the Spanish works. The firmness of the Four Nations opposed to them was equal to the valour of the assailants. Hunger, thirst, and the heat of a scorching sun added to the horrors of the combat. Biron led the French troops repeatedly to the assault, and continual reserves supported them as often as beaten back by the Spaniards.

Montenegro, with a pike in his hand on the rampart of the half-moon, in the foremost ranks, animated his men with unflinching resolution to perish or to remain masters of the works. Ten hours the conflict raged: Biron calculated that weariness and hunger would finally effect what the thunder of his artillery and the fervour of his numerous host were unable to accomplish; but Spanish constancy finally triumphed over hunger as well as French impetuosity and British steadiness. Diminished and exhausted as the garrison now were, they yet on the following days repelled several assaults, and continued to overawe the citizens, eager for insurrection, but cowed by the astonishing resolution and vigour of the Spanish infantry.

The Archduke, assured by Montenegro of his utter inability to hold out much longer, and sensible of the importance of preserving Amiens, as a first-rate fortress, opening a road into the heart of France, and covering the Netherlands, had by this time collected an army of 20,000 infantry and 4000 cavalry, and now marched into Picardy, resolved to try the chances of war, if he could not otherwise raise the siege. The united French and English armies exceeded 40,000 men; but the Spanish, though consisting of various nations and languages (4000 native Spaniards, 6000 Germans, 4000 Italians, 7000 Walloons, Burgundians, and Irish), were united in spirit as one nation, and in discipline far superior to their opponents. This magnificent army, descending from the heights of Dourlens to the plain of Amiens, presented an imposing spectacle to the besiegers and the besieged. Its order was the finest, its equipment the most magnificent, its discipline the most perfect of any equal body of men in the world. Henry, his infantry remaining entrenched, made several charges at the head of his cavalry, but could not sustain the terrible fire of the Spanish foot as they moved over the plain near Picquiny in battle array, till they came within half cannon shot of the French circumvallation. All was disorder and confusion in the French quarters. Sutlers, waggoners, artillery, and infantry were abandoning the lines, and seeking to cross the Somme above Amiens. Mendoza, Barlotta, and other renowned colonels of Spanish infantry, counselled an immediate assault. Count Ernest of Mansfield, eighty years old, hesitated; his courage had not failed, but his energies were chilled, and the decisive moment was lost. The king and his nobility restored order, and a splendid conflict of cavalry ensued. A plain, free from all obstructions, extended from the entrenchments to the front of the Spanish army, an admirable theatre for the evolutions of cavalry. The whole of the French horse, 8000 strong, charged with the gallantry peculiar to their nation; the Spaniards, though not half in number, declined not the conflict.

The field exhibited a magnificent tournament; the evolutions and charges, directed by science, and conducted with valour, excited the admiration of the infantry on both sides. The French carbiniers and cuirassiers had invariably the advantage over the Spanish cavalry, of the same description; but the men-at-arms of Flanders and Burgundy bore down all before them, until superiority of numbers and the opening of the French squadrons to break the violence of their lances, forced them behind the battalia of their army.

During these operations the Walloons attempted to pass the Somme, and throw succours into Amiens, as Farnese had done in relieving Paris and Rouen; but the vigilance and activity of the Duke of Mayenne defeated these efforts; and on the morning of the 17th the Archduke's army commenced its retreat towards Dourlens. The king pressed them with his cavalry, but could make no impression. The Duke of Parma was then dead, but his great soul, that had formed this army, seemed still to exist in the order and skill of the retreat, and the imperturbable resolution of the Spaniards. The rere guard retired in the form of a crescent, the centre composed of pikemen, the wings of musketeers; when the French assailed this crescent, they were exposed to the fire of the wings, and met a phalanx of pikes in the centre: when the wings alone were assailed, the Spanish lancers came on furiously to the charge, whilst the musketeers poured in destructive vollies into the enemy's squadrons. The losses thus sustained forced the king to keep at a respectful distance, until the Archduke's army approached a stream between

Dourlens and Amiens. Henry anticipated confusion and disorder on the passage; and pushed on with all his cavalry, resolved not to miss so favourable an opportunity; but the Spanish rere-guard instantly faced about, stood firm, observed the same order, poured in the same destructive fire, and stirred not till the rest of the army had passed over, and then observing the same order, passed through the water knee-deep. This marvellous retreat, in face of such superior numbers, excited the wonder of Henry, who gave utterance to his admiration, saying, " that no other troops could do so much, and that with that infantry and his own cavalry he would set all the world at defiance."

Henry, on his return to the lines, offered Montenegro honourable terms, because he desired not the destruction of so many gallant soldiers. The Governor had had permission from the Archduke to surrender; his own officers pressed it; contagious mortality in the town, scarcity of ammunition, want of men to guard the works and keep down the citizens, rendered it imperative. Montenegro, to gain time, required a safe conduct for an officer to the Archduke, to know his pleasure. On the 24th of September the terms were agreed upon, as honourable to Spanish pride as the defence was glorious to Spanish valour. The first article, that " the monument of Portocarrero should not be disturbed, nor its inscription defaced," indicated the veneration of the garrison for the military virtues of their deceased

Governor, and the respect of the king for departed greatness, even in an enemy. The other articles were equally honourable: that the troops should march out in battalia, with all the honours of war, and should be furnished with carriages for their baggage to Dourlens; and that there should be a truce for six days, at the end of which, if not relieved, the city should be surrendered.

On the 18th of September the garrison, reduced to 1800 foot and 400 horse, marched out, headed by the Marquis of Montenegro, in splendid military apparel, mounted on a noble charger, with a truncheon in his hand. Being come to the place where the king and the army in battalia expected him, laying aside his truncheon, he alighted, kissed the king's knee, and said, he delivered the city of Amiens to a soldier king, since it had not pleased the king his master to cause it to be relieved by a soldier commander, alluding to the Archduke's misconduct in not taking advantage of the disorder in the trenches, and afterwards in not forcing a passage across the Somme, and entering by the left bank of the river(a).

With the siege of Amiens the war between Phi-

(a) Davila, Strada, Thuanus, Bentivoglio. The stranger who visits that most beautiful monument of Gothic architecture, the Cathedral of Amiens, after admiring the colossal grandeur of the edifice, the splendid altar, the lofty and beautiful arched ceiling, pillars, and stained glass windows, of this the finest church in France, will seek in vain for the monument erected by Spanish honour to the matchless valour of Hernando Tollo de Portocarrero.

lip and Henry terminated. The peace of Vervens restored to the French king Calais and all the fortified towns in Picardy, relieved Philip from the pressure of the French war, and enabled him to direct all his forces to the suppression of the insurrection in the Netherlands.

In 1598 the Irish were at the capture of Orsoy, and the siege of Rhinberg. The Walloons, Italians, and Spaniards, under their respective campmasters, the Irish under Stanley vied with each other which should be foremost in every encounter. They attacked an island, crowned by a fort, an outpost covering Rhinberg; the Walloons and Spaniards on one side, the Italians and Irish on the other. The troops who defended it, awed by the impetuosity of the assailants, abandoned the fort, and fled into the town. The besiegers now converted the fort into a battery, and played on the ramparts and castle with such effect, that the powder magazine blew up. The explosion operated like an earthquake; for miles round houses and whole villages fell to the ground, and a great portion of the garrison, including the Governor and his family, were buried in the ruins. The survivors surrendered. All the great towns in the neighbourhood, Buriem, Rees, Emeric, and Wesel, opened their gates to the Spanish army. They thus effected the conquest of the Duchy of Cleves, and part of the Electorate of Cologne, but being ununfortunately commanded by a general deficient in ability, Mendoza, Admiral of Arragon, they disgraced their arms by pillage, plunder, and cruelty. It cannot be doubted that the Irish indulged the licentiousness of plunder, but it is to be hoped that they did not participate in the cruelties practised by the native Spaniards, who committed every outrage of military licentiousness, tortured the wretched inhabitants to extort confessions of hidden treasures, and often, in the rage of disappointment, massacred indiscriminately, and set fire to houses and whole villages(*a*).

In 1599 the Irish served under the Cardinal Andrew of Austria, Governor of the Netherlands. The town of Bommel, on the Wahal, made a most vigorous defence. The Spanish, Irish, and Walloon brigades, under the command of Zapena, Stanley, and Barlotta, were ordered to pass the Wahal into the island of Bommel, preparatory to the siege. The vigilance and activity of Prince Maurice foiled the efforts to pass the river, but were ultimately defeated by the rapid movements of the three brigades, who, unopposed and unnoticed, brought their pontoons to the western extremity of the island, launched them at the confluence of the Wahal and Meuse, crossed the united streams, and ascending the left bank of the Meuse, crossed that river, and made a lodgment in the island of Bommel, and secured the passage into it by forts erected on both banks. The difficulties of this achievement will be best understood by viewing the

(*a*) Bentivoglio. Watson's Philip III.

situation of the island. It is formed at the junction of the Meuse and Wahal at its eastern extremity, having the Wahal river on the north, the Meuse on the south side of the island. After securing the passage across the Meuse, the three brigades besieged and took Creveceur, and returned to the island to besiege the town of Bommel. Never was town attacked or defended with more constancy. The native Spaniards attacked it on one side, the Walloons, Burgundians, and Irish on the other. The sallies made in large bodies were incessant and determined. Prince Maurice had collected 18000 foot and 3000 horse in the neighbourhood, an army far superior in numbers, but in courage and discipline far inferior to the besiegers. He prudently declined an engagement, the stream of the Wahal, on which he had a flotilla, enabling him to throw succours into the town. The Spaniards nobly defended their quarters, which were attacked by 3000 foot and 400 horse, and raked by the artillery of 30 boats moored in the Wahal. The Germans, Burgundians, and Irish were at the same time assaulted by 4000 infantry and 400 cavalry. The fight was resolute on both sides, the one striving to get into the works, and the others as resolutely defending; the business was as hotly disputed by the horse, and the artillery played on both sides with incessant and murderous discharges. The conflict swelled to the magnitude of a mighty battle, and after three hours the troops of the States were repulsed, and retreated into their own works. On the next night the Walloons and Italians were surprised. Avalor, the campmaster, was badly wounded, and the success of the assailants was great, but ultimately the discipline and valour of the besiegers prevailed. In three days after, La Nui, son of the celebrated Huguenot of that name, who inherited the shining qualities of his father, sallied out at the head of 5000 English and French Protestants, and fell furiously on the quarters of the Walloons, who were thrown into great disorder, but rallying, and being supported by the Italians, they beat back the assailants.

Despairing of taking Bommel, the Cardinal resolved on building a fort on the island, at its eastern extremity, where the Meuse and Wahal unite and branch off. Such a fort would give him the command of both rivers; but the difficulty of executing such a work, in the presence of an army superior in numbers, seemed insuperable. The Spanish general, Mendoza, had not the fortune of Cæsar to second, nor his genius to push on, so hazardous an undertaking. The genius, the skill, and experience of the campmasters of the different nations, and the valour of the soldiers, supplied every deficiency, and achieved one of the most difficult military operations of modern warfare. In the erection of this fort, the tactics of Cæsar, and the laborious duties of the Roman legionaries, were revived; for the difficulty of erecting it was much greater than that of throwing up a fortified camp within six hundred paces of an enemy, drawn up in order of battle.

The art of war had been changed, and artillery had given Prince Maurice an advantage which Petreius had not: both, with superior forces, declined an engagement. Petreius could not disturb his enemy without coming to close quarters. Maurice, from the opposite high bank of the Wahal, annoyed the workmen by discharges of artillery, which Velasco returned, but without much effect, from the left bank, which was lower. Three thousand soldiers, and 2000 pioneers, laboured incessantly at the trenches, which extended from the Wahal to the Meuse, and at the rampart which extended along the Wahal. The intrepidity, labour, and perseverance of the workmen, in the course of a few days, erected a rampart sufficient to cover them from the enemy's fire. Two royal bastions were raised towards the Wahal, two towards the Meuse, and a fifth towards the land; these were furnished with curtains, and the rivers served as ditches on two sides, and filled the excavated ditches on the land side with their waters. When finally completed, it was called Fort St. Andrew, and was considered impregnable. The Irish shared with the other nations the honour of erecting this fort; never troops displayed more determined intrepidity, and even when surprised, and thrown into confusion, recovered their ranks, and rallied with astonishing facility, the effect of the military discipline established by the great Duke of Parma.

The Irish continued to serve in the Netherlands until the peace of 1609, between the States and the

Archduke Albert. They were not infected by the spirit of mutiny and desertion that prevailed amongst the Spaniards, Italians, and Walloons, who lived at free quarters upon the inhabitants, levied contributions, expelled their officers and appointed others in their place, and betrayed the forts of St. Andrew and Creveceur to the Dutch. The native Spaniards and Italians returned to their colours; most of the Walloons took part with Prince Maurice, who availed himself of these disorders to advance into Flanders and besiege the town of Nueport. Prince Albert, having collected a small army of veteran troops, composed of these repentant mutineers, of Irish, and of other corps, marched from Bruges to raise the siege. Prince Maurice detached a large body of English and Scotch to retard the march of the Spaniards, and gain time to make his arrangements for an impending battle. These troops were attacked by the mutineers, were broken, and 500 of the Scotch were killed. Prince Maurice was in a most perilous position: to continue the siege or retreat to Ostend was impossible, without the risk of an engagement; to attempt to embark such a number of men in the presence of the enemy would be utter ruin. He resolved to meet the coming storm; drew up his army on the sand-hills, and ordered off his fleet to Ostend, to leave his troops no alternative but victory or death. The Archduke, inferior in numbers, hesitated; Zapena advised delay; the enemy had no means of retreat; but Barlotta counselled an immediate attack, lest they should escape on board the fleet. The boldness of Barlotta suited the Spanish army better than the prudence of Zapena: and it marched to the attack. Prince Maurice drew up his army, composed of English, Swiss, Germans, French, and Dutch, on the Downs; the English, under Sir Francis Vere, forming the van. The Spanish army, composed of Germans, Italians, Irish, and Walloons, elated by numerous victories, and confident in their discipline, advanced to the charge, regardless of the strong position of the enemy, and of the incessant and well-directed fire of the batteries on the sand hills. The British troops yielded to the impetuosity of the mutineers, who were animated to wipe away the disgrace of their late disorders, by more than usual efforts. Sir Francis Vere, dismounted and wounded, and Sir Horatio, his brother, with fresh troops, could not sustain their impetuous charge, and were broken and routed. But Prince Maurice brought up two battalions, gave time to the English to rally, and restored the battle. The resolution of the mutineers was unequal to the superiority of numbers. Another battalion of Swiss and Walloon deserters forced Albert to bring up the Irish to sustain the yielding ranks. A terrible encounter ensued, such as exceeded all that had occurred during the wars of the Low Countries. Troops from all the countries of Europe were engaged, Irish against English, Wal-

(a) Tuanus, 1. 126, 904 ; Watson's Philip III.

loons against Walloons; Italians, Spaniards, and Germans, against Dutch, Swiss, and French. National antipathies, religious animosities, and mutual emulation inspired the utmost efforts of which each were capable. The sun, wind, and sand hills favoured the Dutch. Valour and discipline sustained their opponents. When pushed and forced to yield they formed without the slightest confusion, and, under the deadly fire of the Dutch batteries on the sand hills, returned to the charge, filling up the chasms made by the artillery. The English troops, exposed to the furious onset of the Irish and the mutineers, suffered most. National feuds and religious hatred fired this quarter of the battle, and the field was covered with slain. Here Bostock, who led on the Irish, who had distinguished himself at Amiens, and was one of the renowned leaders of the Spanish infantry, lost his life; eight English captains fell, and all the rest but two were wounded. Sir Francis and Horatio Vere, supported by the Swiss and Walloons, maintained their ground against the efforts of the Irish and Walloons, who although behaving with admirable order and constancy, were unable to break the dense ranks and determined valour of the Swiss.

At length the Dutch and Frisians broke in the centre, and fled to the shore. Prince Maurice then, with reproaches and exhortations, brought up his reserves, under the command of his brother Frederic. " They had no alternative but victory or death. The hostile squadrons pressed them in front, the ocean, in the rear, was ready to swallow them up. They had to fight for life, liberty, and fortune. All around was adverse; their valour was their only resource; could they then abandon, in this last extremity, that which they had experienced as their chief refuge in all former difficulties, the instrument of many glorious victories?" Dauntless, in the midst of a shower of balls, Maurice led on his battalions with the courage of a soldier and the coolness of a general. The English remaining firm, gave him time to restore the ranks in his centre. Albert displayed not less heroism, and with the hereditary valour of his family, performed the duties of a common soldier in the foremost ranks, and at the same time displayed the presence of mind and skill of a veteran commander. Perceiving the sun and wind aiding the enemy, he made a desperate effort on their flanks to evade the sand and smoke that were blown into the faces of his troops; but the superiority of the Dutch cavalry defeated his evolutions. At length, wounded by a pike, his attendants forced him from the field, and that circumstance, together with the blowing up of a Spanish powder magazine, relaxed the fire of the Spaniards, whose intrepid valour yielded for the first time, and in a slow and menacing retreat, evinced the same resolute front and contempt of their enemy as it displayed four hours before in marching to the attack.

Prince Maurice remained on the field of battle, not da.·ing to pursue a foe still anxious for a renewal of the fight. The English and Scotch, who had lost 600 men the day before, and 1000 men on the day of the battle, he with difficulty restrained from massacreing their prisoners. The chief loss of the confederates fell upon the British subjects, caused by the national hatred, not less than by the impetuous valour of the mutineers, seeking to wipe away the stain of insubordination and mutiny by an extraordinary effort of valour.

The Irish regiments served during the subsequent campaigns in the Netherlands till the peace of 1609, with their accustomed valour. They shared in the glory of the capture of Ostend and Grave, and in the raising of the siege of Rhinberg. In this celebrated school their officers learned the art of war, but from 1609 to 1653, when Cromwell transported 40,000 Irish to France and Spain, I have not been able to trace them in any foreign service.

CHAPTER III.

CAMPAIGNS IN THE SERVICE OF FRANCE.

THE sympathy with France, cultivated by the house of Stuart, led to the formation of several regiments of Irish in that service during the exile of Charles II. Of these a regiment of horse, commanded by the Earl of Bristol, served with distinguished reputation during the campaign of 1652, under the Marshal Turenne and De la Fertè. Towards the close of the same year an Irish regiment in the service of the Duke of Lorraine entered the same service under the following circumstances. The French had laid siege to Bois-le-duc, garrisoned by these Irish. The lower town being easily accessible, the French easily constructed their batteries under shelter of the houses in the suburbs, and having soon opened a practicable breach, mounted to the assault. Here a deadly conflict ensued: Lieutenant-general Baron De Toll was killed leading the forlorn hope: the regiment of Picardy, with its characteristic bravery, at length entered ; but the garrison defended their barricades, the streets and houses, until driven to the upper town and citadel by superior numbers. The assailants derived vast encouragement from the presence of Cardinal Mazarin, from whose favour all promotion and advancement were at that time derived, and under whose eye officers and soldiers were animated to the utmost exertions. Still the obstinacy of the garrison held out, and at length the great Condè approached to relieve the place. Marshal D'Aumont remained to superintend the siege. The Cardinal Turenne and La Fertè marched to give battle to the Spaniards, whose supineness and want of videttes in the village of Voubcourt, would have exposed them to an irreparable defeat; but La Fertè, jealous of the glory of Turenne, discountenanced an immediate attack, and procrastinated the march. Condè perceiving the approach of the French, to rouse the Spaniards, set fire to their quarters, forced them to march out in order of battle, and effected a masterly retreat. The Cardinal and La Fertè returned to the siege; a breach in the upper town was immediately assaulted, but the storming party were valiantly beaten off. A fresh breach, however, was soon after effected; and the town and citadel being no longer tenable, the garrison surrendered prisoners of war(a).

The Irish, always loyal, considered that, though mercenaries in the service of foreign powers, they owed a paramount duty to their own king; and the regiment in garrison at Bois le Duc, as soon as the surrender of the place had discharged them from the standard of Lorraine, made a tender of their services

(a) Thuanus.

to the Duke of York, which was accepted by the Cardinal. Their numbers had been much reduced during the siege, their colonel being dead, and their lieutenant-colonel having escaped, so that not being qualified to act as a separate body, they were incorporated into the duke's own regiment(a), which was then engaged at the siege of the Castle of Ligni. The Marshal De la Fertè directed the operations. It was then the depth of winter, and the water of the fossè being frozen, and a wide breach effected, the Irish regiment of York, those of Douglas and La Fertè, under the orders of the Count D'Estrees, pushed over the ice, and gained the summit of the rampart; but being unable to burst through a pallisadoe raised inside, owing to the failure of a mine, had to retrace their steps. In retreating, the ice broke, and four captains, several inferior officers, and 100 privates of the regiment of York, lost their lives(b).

Irish were now opposed to Irish in the campaign of 1653, in the French and Spanish armies. Moinon, on the Meuse, this year withstood an obstinate siege. The York regiment, with those of Picardy and Turenne, mounted the trenches alternately. A sergeant of York's performed a very gallant action in carrying drink and candles from the trenches into a mine exposed to the fire of the garrison, and escaped unhurt. The Spanish and Irish garrison defended the

(a) Thuanus.   (b) Ibid.

place with unusual bravery. Twice they beat the besiegers out of the fossè, and by sallies and mines destroyed the works, while by means of bombs, fireworks, and hand-grenades, they killed the workmen in the mines, and retarded the approaches. In all these sanguinary conflicts the Duke of York and his regiment took a very distinguished part. The skill of the engineers, and the perseverance of the troops, ultimately forced the garrison to a capitulation, after seventeen days of open trenches.

In this siege, the vigilance, activity, and skill of the French were beyond all praise. The Marshals Turenne and La Fertè every day and night examined the trenches: an officer was therein killed in the act of saluting Turenne. The engineers, captains of miners, and officers were always at their posts, and performed all the duties attached to their station with the utmost exactitude(a). The rest of this campaign was consumed in sieges of very little note.

Before the opening of the campaign of 1654, 800 Irish, quartered at Eterre and Gorque, were surprised by the Count De Broglio. These villages were divided by the Lis, and had been guarded by the Spaniards and Irish during the winter. The Spaniards had suddenly withdrawn, leaving the Irish unsupported, exposed to the attacks of the enemy, and unable to act unitedly in any emergency,

(a) Clarke's Memoirs of the Duke of York.

being divided by the river. The ever-wakeful eyes of the French perceived the difficult position of these troops, and with their wonted activity assailed, routed, and nearly destroyed the whole corps. Murphy, the colonel, fought with intrepidity, and effected his escape(*a*).

At the lines of Arras, gained by Turenne over the Spaniards under Condè, the regiments of York and Dillon shared with the French the honour of that great victory.

(*a*) Quincy, Louis le Grand, vol. i. p. 183.

CHAPTER IV.

FURTHER SERVICES IN THE ARMIES OF SPAIN.

THE alliance between the English commonwealth and the Court of France, effected through the policy of Mazarin, having compelled the Duke of York to retire to Flanders, while the exiled monarch, his brother, sought protection from the Spanish Court at Cologne, the Irish colonels, in the armies of Turenne and La Fertè, were placed in a position of conflicting duties, very painful to men of honour, sensible of their duty to their legitimate Sovereign on the one hand, and to their adopted flag on the other. In this predicament they addressed a letter to the Duke of York, offering their services, and that they would obey his orders as far as would be consistent with their honour. The Duke advised them to keep their regiments together, and that he would accept of their loyal and generous offer as circumstances might suggest.

Richard Grace of Gracefield, in the Queen's County, commanded one of these regiments. He had distinguished himself in the Irish wars, and brought his regiment, 1200 strong, to Spain, where he had obtained an advantageous capitulation for them from the Spanish government. But the disorders in the Spanish finances, or the misconduct of the Spanish authorities, violated the terms, and Grace lost half his men before he reached his quarters in Catalonia. Having fought in the Spanish service with great reputation he had been sent with the remnant of his regiment to a castle on the French frontier. Here he had resolved to join the king, his master, in Flanders, and accordingly wrote to the Marshal Dé Hochincourt, the French general in Catalonia, that he would march out of the fort on a certain day, on condition that his regiment should be put on the same footing with the other regiments in the French service. His terms were accepted, and great offers made to him to deliver up the place to the French. His feelings of honour rejected these offers; he apprized the Spaniards of his intention of joining the French, and desired them to send 200 men to take possession of the fort, whom he allowed to enter at one gate as he marched out at the other. Such had been the introduction of Grace's regiment into the French service.

Justin M'Carthy, Lord Muskerry, afterwards Lord Mountcashel, commanded another regiment; he was nephew to the Duke of Ormond, a very gallant officer, and most sensibly alive to the feelings of honour. Sir John Darcy, another of these colonels, could not reconcile to his principles desertion from the service in which he had engaged, and neither Charles the Second's commands nor personal influence could induce him to bring over his regiment to the Spaniards.

Charles having now concluded a treaty with the Spaniards, which rendered it necessary for the Duke of York to quit the service of France, wherein he had made many friends, particularly the Marshal Turenne, advised the duke to obtain privately his brother's consent that he should remain in France, whilst his Majesty should ostensibly affect displeasure, and that this connivance should be kept a profound secret. This duplicity was wholly unworthy of the great Turenne, and was too subtle to elude the suspicion and jealousy of the Spaniards. Charles feeling it degrading to his dignity, as well as to his honour, at length laid absolute commands on the duke to come to Bruges, where he resided, in the house of General Preston, then Lord Tara, who had been born and was married in Flanders, and had there inherited a considerable estate in right of his mother. Condé, a small but a strong fortress on the Meuse, between Cambray and Valenciennes, was at the time besieged by the Spaniards. The garrison consisted principally of an Irish regiment commanded by Muskerry. Skill, vigilance, bravery, and incessant sallies, maintained the place against Don John of Austria, the Spanish commander, who, fatigued by the obstinacy of the besieged, applied to Charles to exert his influence with the garrison to surrender. The king had the meanness, through the agency of Ormond, to tamper with the garrison.

Condé was reduced to the last extremity, and forced to surrender when the marquis arrived at the camp. His intrigues were now confined to inducing Muskerry to bring over his regiment to the Spaniards. Muskerry was a stranger to the perfidy of courts. " It was not," he said, " consistent with his honour that either he or his men should quit their colours, until, according to his articles, he should march into France; he would then leave his regiment in their quarters, demand his pass, which, by contract, he was entitled to whenever his own king should demand his services, and his regiment should be permitted to march with him." He desired his uncle to satisfy himself, that he would return within six weeks, and his regiment would in a few days be after him(*a*).

Upon his return to France Mazarin did all he could to divert Muskerry from his purpose. He remonstrated that the service of his own king was but a colorable pretext for joining the Spaniards; that if he remained, every indulgence should be granted to, and care taken of his regiment. Strict principles of honour and morality may be inconsistent with the conduct of Muskerry, who insisted on and obtained a pass for himself alone, and afterwards all the officers and soldiers, by sixes and sevens, quitted their quarters, and went over to the

(*a*) Quincy, Louis le Grand.
(*b*) Clarendon's History of the Rebellion, vol. iii. p. 350.

Spaniards to the number of 800 choice veteran troops, who were immediately incorporated with the Spanish army.

St. Gerlain, another strong fortress, was at the same time betrayed by the Irish garrison to the new friends of the king. Schomberg, the governor, a brave officer, infested the whole country to the gates of Brussels by his incursions. An attempt by the Spaniards on the place had failed. Sir George Lane, secretary to the Marquis of Ormond, tampered with the garrison. They agreed, if it should advance the king's interest, to let in the Spaniards. Don John, the Marquis of Caracena, the King, and the Duke of York were apprized of the intended treachery and encouraged it. Don John, assembling his army in the depth of winter, sat down before the fortress. Schomberg, vigilant and indefatigable, was near defeating the whole project. He arrested several of the Irish officers, and would have defeated the whole project, had not the soldiers in the outworks betrayed them and let in the Spaniards, which forced Schomberg to surrender. In the annals of the Irish in foreign service, this and the affair at Deventer are the only acts of treachery that stain the character of the nation, but the Stuarts and the Marquis of Ormond share with them the infamy, and were the chief instigators to these foul transactions(*a*).

By these means the Spanish army was reinforced

(*a*) Clarendon's Rebellion, vol. iii. p. 352.

by four Irish regiments, accustomed to all the hardships of war in their own country, and disciplined in France under the eye of the great Turenne. They were engaged in all the marches, counter-marches, evolutions, sieges, and battles of the years 1656 and 1657.

The Duke of Lorraine and the Prince of Condè had separate corps, foreigners and French, in the Spanish camp. The hostility of both to the Cardinal Mazarin was an ample guarantee for their fidelity; but the desertion of the Irish at Condè, and their treachery at St. Gerlain, alarmed the Spaniards, and an oath of fidelity on their part was insisted on by the Spanish government. The Duke of York and Lord Muskerry felt indignant, but were obliged to submit to this humiliation. The Spaniards considered that religion would operate as a safeguard, where honour, the paramount law of military men, had lost its control. The commands of Charles may plead some extenuation, but can never justify the abandonment of the French colours by these Irish regiments.

During the subsequent campaigns of 1657 and 1658 they do not appear to have displayed their wonted valour, owing probably to the stigma of desertion, which paralyzes the bravest; or, perhaps, to the slow, ill-judged, and irresolute conduct of the Spanish generals. Courage is often the mechanical impulse of example in leaders. Don John and the Marquis of Caracena were naturally brave, but their indolence was extreme. They slept long, and would not suffer their slumbers to be disturbed by reports of the enemy's movements; suffered surprises and opportunities of attack to escape; and neither capacity nor courage can counterbalance the disadvantages of inactivity and want of vigilance(a).

On the 23rd of August, 1657, Don John undertook the siege of Ardres, midway between Calais and St. Omer. Three several attacks were fixed for the Irish, Condeans, and Spaniards. Lord Muskerry, at the head of one of the battalions of York, pushed on with great bravery, and effected a lodgment on the ditch of the raveline, which covered the point of one of the bastions. The Dukes of York and Gloucester followed the men into the ditch, got a sergeant to sound the depth of the water, and ascertaining it to be shallow, gave orders to the men to pass it, and make a lodgment close to the wall, in order to spring a mine. But success having attended the attack of the Prince Marshal Turenne in taking St. Venant, he now approached, and it became necessary to raise the siege. To bring off the men and miners was a matter of great difficulty, as they had no trench or covered communications behind, and must, on falling back, be exposed to the fire from the ramparts. To favour their retreat, Muskerry kept up a hot and well-directed fire on the garrison stationed on the parapet, whereby the miners and

(a) Clarke's Memoirs, vol. i. p. 313.

soldiers who had made the lodgment, running with full speed, escaped almost unhurt.

About this time the French took Mardyke, and delivered it to the English, pursuant to their treaty with Cromwell, who directed new fortifications there, as well as repairing the old. Before the works were finished, Don John, who had determined to destroy them, marched out of Dunkirk in the dead of night, using lights to conduct the troops. The Duke of Gloucester's regiment formed part of the infantry. They put out their lights when they came within cannon shot, but Ormond, the king, and Don John, stayed in the rere with the cavalry, out of reach of the cannon. The garrison and some English frigates in the harbour having caught the alarm, opened a brisk fire, but in the confusion and darkness of a nocturnal attack, chance, and not aim, directed the shot, which passed over the infantry, killed a horse under the Marquis of Ormond, and several of the cavalry. Gloucester's regiment, all Irish, did whatever could be effected by valour and discipline. Finding the ditch too deep in one place, they attempted to fill it up in another, and kept up a heavy fire, until the approach of day warned them that their efforts were vain, and compelled a retreat to Dunkirk. One captain and a few soldiers of Gloucester's were killed, and a few more wounded in the affair.

This regiment was quartered in Mont Cassel during the winter, and the Duke of York's at St. Omer, as being contiguous to Dunkirk, with a view of throwing them into that place if it were attacked. Mont Cassel was open: the French attacked it. The place was defenceless, and 400 Irish were obliged to surrender(a).

Spaniards have been at all times open to the influence of jealousy, and are by nature distrustful. The French, a chivalrous race, free from every taint of dishonour, never suspect vices in others by which they are themselves uninfected. Upon several occasions the outposts of both armies met without the appearance of hostility, and the Duke of York being often the object of their anxious inquiries, they sometimes dismounted to pay him the respect due to his rank, and to testify their sympathy for his fall from his high station. This chivalrous courtesy was calculated to create jealousy, and a proposition made by the Earl of Bristol to the Prince of Condè, to join the Irish with the Condeans, in order to extort conditions from the Archduke, increased the suspicion of the Spaniards, so that the oath taken by the Irish appeared no longer a guarantee for their fidelity. The Duke of York's regiment at St. Omer, and the king's at Dermude, were shut out from the defence of Dunkirk, by either the distrust of the Spanish councils, or the activity of the French generals. The Marquis De Lodi, whose innate courage impelled him into the military profession, though his unaffected piety and ardent devotion might better

(a) Life of James II., vol. i. p. 336.

have aspired to the repose and solitude of a cloister, defended Dunkirk with a garrison of 2000 foot and 800 horse, and by his valour, vigilance, and bravery made up for the deficiency of his troops, double their number being scarce sufficient to man the works. The English blockaded the place by sea; 6000 English, under Lockart, who had been substituted for Reynolds as commander, on account of some respect shewn by the latter for the Duke of York, were encamped at Mardyke, whilst Turenne formed lines all round to intercept relief. The Spaniards under Don John, the Marquis of Caracena, Condè, and the Duke of York, approached the lines. Turenne, confiding in his own great talents, and in the superiority of his troops, and sensible that lines are liable to great vicissitudes, marched out to give battle. Don John, instead of being assailant, was forced on the defensive unexpectedly. His cannon and gunpowder had not arrived, half of his cavalry were out foraging; his infantry, composed of 2500 native Spaniards, 2000 Irish, and 2000 Walloons, were inferior in numbers to the enemy, and defeat seemed inevitable. Condè advised a retreat; Don John and Caracena persisted in the experiment of a battle. Their position on the sand hills was strong; their right reached the sea, their left the canal of Furnes; their centre occupied the line of sandy elevation.

The native Spaniards, supported by 100 Irish, were first attacked by Lockart's regiment, with the steadiness of veterans and the valour of Britons. They halted at the foot of the sand hills, like Cæsar's men at Pharsalia, to take breath, keeping up a deadly fire; they then began the ascent with a great shout, and notwithstanding the steepness of the hill, and the yielding of the sand, they reached the summit, after losing their colonel, and several officers, and men. The resistance of the Spaniards was not less brave. Eleven captains of one regiment (Boniface's), and Slaughter and Farrell, two Irish captains, were killed before they were forced off. Pursued down the sand hills, the English were attacked in flank by some squadrons under the Duke of York, but their firm battalions were impenetrable, and the Spanish right wing sustained an irreparable defeat; but still it fought, and the Duke states in his Memoirs, that having rallied a few of his own English, he called to a Spanish major to follow the example, and that it being the custom of the Spaniards not to run when others stand, they faced about with the most determined resolution, and penetrated into the English battalion, not one soldier of which asked for quarter, or threw down his arms, the matter being debated hand to hand, and with the butt ends of their muskets. The left wing of the Spaniards fared no better than the right. Colonel Grace, in the centre, seeing the disorder on the right and left, marched off his Irish regiment in three divisions, and reached the canal of Furnes, by which he made his retreat, without the loss of a single man. The king's regiment, composed of English, and the Earl of Bristol's, composed of Irish, were in line next to the native Spaniards. James, in his Memoirs, states that the English stood firm, although they saw all around them broken and routed; but some of the Irish, notwithstanding the efforts of their officers, on this occasion disgraced their colours, and ran away. Of Muskerry's regiment the leader was almost the only man who escaped. The king's battalion still stood firm. A French colonel, with the hereditary gallantry of his generous nation, offered them quarter, which they had at first declined, but finding their whole army routed, they surrendered, upon the terms of not being stripped, or delivered up to the English Cromwellians. The whole of the Duke's and Bristol's Irish regiments were made prisoners; Lord Muskerry, and about twenty men, escaped, but the prisoners, in a few days, by bribery and artifice, contrived to return to their colours(a).

Dunkirk had no resource after the irretrievable defeat of the Downs. The dispirited garrison would have surrendered, but its leader made another desperate effort: careless of his own fate, insensible to danger, he headed a sally, received a mortal wound, and the English became masters of the town and citadel.

Cromwell's glory ended with this conquest: his ambition and plans were soon after buried in his

(a) Clarke's Memoirs of James II., vol. i. p. 338.

grave. Charles was restored to the throne of his ancestors. The Irish, who had followed his fallen fortunes, returned to their own country; but their services, though acknowledged in the most fervent language, were requited with the basest ingratitude. In his first speech to his Parliament, Charles coldly remarked that Ireland only did not deserve to be excluded from his clemency; though in his Declaration for the settlement of Ireland, he had alluded to the Irish troops who accompanied him in his exile. "We remember," states the Declaration, " and shall always remember, with the greatest affection, the loyalty borne to us by a considerable portion of the Irish nation, during our residence beyond sea: our Irish troops having always received our orders with the greatest joy, and conforming to them, not hesitating to join the service we pointed out to them as most serviceable to us, however injurious to their own interests; which conduct, on their part, is entitled to our protection, justice, and favour."

CHAPTER V.

FURTHER CAMPAIGNS IN THE SERVICE OF FRANCE.

IN 1673 Charles II. sent directions to Essex, Lord Lieutenant of Ireland, to give Sir G. Hamilton liberty to recruit a regiment of foot for the service of France. Some French ships were sent for them to Dingle, a remote corner of Kerry, but came to Kinsale, where their appearance created suspicion, and caused the connivance of the Government to be made public, which for a time defeated the project. The men were ultimately raised, and served under Turenne on the Rhine, during the campaigns of 1673, 1674, and 1675. The details of the actions in which they distinguished themselves have not been transmitted; but they had a part in the plunder and destruction of the dominions of the Elector Palatine, which tarnished the glory of the great Turenne. Two cities, twenty-five towns, and innumerable villages, in flames, excited the execration of the civilized nations of the world against the monarch who commanded, and the general who perpetrated these enormities.

In the virtues and the vices of soldiers the Irish may well rank with the troops of any other nation: on the present occasion they indulged their propensity for plunder, derived not less from the habits of a rude life, than from military education. Houses were first plundered, then set fire to; the women violated, the old and the young turned adrift without food or raiment. These unheard of cruelties were retorted upon the soldiery by a furious peasantry driven to despair. The body of a soldier, who had been assassinated, was exhibited on the highways in a horrible, mutilated, and disgusting condition. The Irish recognized some of their comrades in this plight, and gave vent to their rage, by lighted straw in one hand, and the sword in the other, consuming and exterminating all around them. The Elector beheld from the ramparts of his capital the waste and desolation of his country. He wrote a letter to the marshal, reproaching him with his cold-blooded barbarity, and challenged him to single combat. Turenne sheltered himself behind the commands of his master, had some of the Irish punished, and in some measure put a stop to these horrible excesses(*a*).

We gladly turn from these atrocities to the record of the subsequent campaigns, in which the discipline and valour of the Irish troops were conspicuous. The details of the part they had in the battle of Enghein are not known, but Quincy mentions that Count Hamilton, who commanded them, performed great acts of valour.

Turenne had with a small army gained the bat-

(*a*) Quincy, vol. i. p. 396.

tles of Mulhausen, Turkheim, and Senzheim, and had carried terror and devastation to all the countries bordering on the right bank of the Rhine. The Austrians had one general only equal to him in science. This was the celebrated Montecucoli: he had gained the victory of St. Gothard against the Turks; he had out-generalled Condè and Turenne in the campaign of 1673, and under feints of giving or accepting battle, had avoided it, and formed a junction with the Prince of Orange. The safety of the empire required that he should command the army opposed to Turenne. During the summer of 1675, in a very narrow stripe of land between the Black Forest and the Rhine, a few miles above and below Strasburg, these great men practised all the evolutions of war, one covering the empire, and the other Alsace, from hostile invasion. Turenne fixed his camp near Strasburg, on the left bank, to defend the passage of the river. Montecucoli marched down to Phillipsburg, to draw out Turenne to protect the passage lower down. Turenne, penetrating his design, passed to the right bank, and occupied the important post of Welstel, two leagues from Strasburg, just as Prince Herman of Baden, with 6000 horse, was approaching to take possession of it by order of Montecucoli, who was well aware of its importance. He then marched his whole army to Offenburg, the river Kenig, every where fordable, dividing the two armies; but both generals declined battle on equal ground, each seeking some advantage of position, and four months were consumed in marches and counter-marches, within a narrow space of ten miles, enclosed on two sides by a mighty stream and lofty mountains, intersected by streams and rivulets, and containing great inequalities and undulations : the equal skill of these great men alternately offering and refusing battle, according as superiority of position or difficulties of ground rendered the event certain on one side, or hazardous on the other. All Europe had their eyes fixed on these evolutions. It was the great game of war, played with more skill than had ever been observed in the annals of military history. In these marches and counter-marches not the slightest confusion occurred, a thing unexampled in armies so near to each other, always in battle array, and each hour expecting the signal of a mortal encounter. At Sallsbach the two armies were separated by a rivulet, the French left and centre being in line ready for an engagement, and the right moving to its ground. Turenne now fancied he had obtained a fair opportunity for attack. Montecucoli perceived his design, and threw 600 men, with some pieces of cannon, into the church and churchyard, in his front. His baggage was in full retreat through a defile,—a precaution of prudence,—but his position was strong on the declivity of a hill. The stream protected his front; and he seemed not to wish to decline the menaced engagement. Turenne, though determined, yet cautious, was weighing the inequalities of the ground, the least difficult fordes on the rivulet, and had just given directions where to place his batteries, when a cannon ball from the churchyard struck him to the ground, and terminated his earthly career. The right wing of the French halted, its colours fluttered, advanced some paces, and then fell back, while the centre and left remained paralyzed and motionless. The command of the French army devolved on De Lorges, the lieutenant-general of the day, but Vaubrun claimed it by seniority, and each aspiring to the command in chief, added irresolution to dismay. The eagle eye of Montecucoli penetrated into these convulsive motions. The soul of the French army had perished, but the soldiers of that army were fired with rage to avenge the death of their beloved general: desperation might supply the want of generals; and the over-cautious Italian would not descend from his strong position to cross a rivulet in face of his enemy, in a position equally strong. The fire of the great Condè would not have hesitated a moment. But the caution acquired by the imperial general in the Italian school—that of the princes of the house of Savoy, the Farnese's, and the Spinolas—would not commit itself to hazard; and instead of an immediate attack, Montecucoli sent his cavalry by a circuitous rout, to intercept the retreat of the French by their bridge over the Rhine to Altenheim. Inclosed by the Rhine and the Black Forest Mountains, pressed in front by the imperial infantry, and threatened on the rear by Caprara's cavalry, no alternative remained but a precipitate retreat to Altenheim.

A dreadful storm and a dark night concealed from the Imperialists the retrograde movement of the French. A nocturnal retreat in an enemy's country, diffidence in their generals, disunited councils, and contradictory orders, produced the utmost disorder. Cavalry, artillery, infantry, and baggage, in one mass of confusion, sought a passage over the stream of the Kenig. Fortunately the bridge of Achera, over a narrow stream, and of Welstel, over the Kenig, were not occupied by the enemy, and the baggage and cavalry, and a great portion of the infantry, passed unmolested. But the rear-guard, Bloufler's dragoons and Hamilton's foot, were here attacked by 4000 foot and 2000 dragoons. The Irish presented an impenetrable phalanx: the reiterated charges of cavalry only rendered their ranks more compact. After repeated efforts the cavalry, though under the eyes of Montecucoli, were successively repulsed, and Hamilton covered himself with glory in covering this memorable retreat(*a*).

Contrary to all the rules of war, the rear-guard was left without cavalry, and without information of the advance and near approach of the enemy. Montecucoli, pressing on with his infantry, after passing the Kenig, kept his army out of sight, in or-

(*a*) Quincy, vol. i. p. 427.

der to lull the French into security, and hoping for an opportunity of surprising them at the passage of Schullern, or of the Rhine at Altenheim. At the Schullern the Irish brigade were relieved from the rear guard by the brigade of Champagne, which was afterwards surprised and cut to pieces by the Imperialists on the right bank of the stream. Sixteen captains and all the subaltern officers of this corp lay dead on the field, and, unfortunately for the French, their commander, Vaubrun, was killed in heading a charge of calvalry.

Montecucoli was now advanced in years, slow and cautious, and not possessing that activity whose eagle wing darts upon opportunities, and never suffers them to escape. Instead of plunging into the stream after the French, he sent his cavalry higher up to pass the Schultern, and take them in the rere, so as to intercept their retreat to the bridge of Altenheim. Hamilton's Irish and the French infantry had thus time to form on the left bank, and by a tremendous fire, baffled every effort of the German infantry to pass the stream: attacked behind by the cavalry, their rear ranks faced about, and poured into them a destructive fire, until the French cavalry, recrossing the Rhine at full gallop, overpowered the Imperialists by the rapidity and weight of their charges, and extricated their infantry from its perilous position. The battle raged till the shades of night separated both armies. The French retained possession of the left bank, and effected their retreat across the Rhine by the bridge at Altenheim. This is the glorious day of Altenheim, so celebrated in the annals of France, in which half their army, without generals, sustained the efforts of the whole of the Imperialists during an entire day, remained masters of the field of battle, and effected their retreat across the Rhine.

Jealous as they are of sharing their fame, the French have admitted the Irish to all the honours of that memorable victory, and the rank of major-general conferred on Count Hamilton, marked the high sense entertained by the French of their obligations to his bravery on that great occasion. Hamilton served under the Duke of Luxemburg in Alsace in 1776.

Charles V., Duke of Lorraine, a general whose valour and capacity, the inheritance of his noble house, was equal to any command, however arduous, now commanded the Imperial army. He had defeated the Marshal Crequi, and shewed himself equal to Luxemburg in the skill and rapidity of his movements, in the selection of his ground, and his quickness and discernment in seizing opportunities. Hamilton had the honour of sustaining a distinguished part, and gloriously lost his life in this campaign. This event occurred in a conflict near Saverne, where, after an undecisive affair at Kochresberg, the opposite armies met in force. The French cavalry, thrown into disorder, fled. Hamilton posted his regiment very advantageously, and checked the enemy's career by a tremendous fire, until Luxemburg came up with a fresh body of cavalry, and forced the Germans off the field. This was the last of Hamilton's fields: he lost his life in the moment of victory: but the regiment continued in the service until the waste of war and the want of recruits from Ireland obliterated it from the military records of France.

The same causes operated to reduce the four Irish regiments that remained in the service of Spain, to one. This regiment upheld its military fame, forming a portion of the garrison of Cambray in 1677. After the town surrendered, the garrison retired to the citadel, and made the most obstinate defence that had been achieved at this period in Flanders. The French stormed a half moon, carried it by a wide and practicable breach, and made a lodgment. In open day, and in presence of the whole of the French army, commanded by the king and Luxemburg, this Irish regiment, with another of native veteran Spaniards, sallied from the town, retook this important post, and maintained it two entire days, under the incessant fire of the batteries and assaults of the besiegers. The citadel surrendered soon after.

This is the last affair in which I find the Irish engaged in foreign service, prior to the formation of the Irish Brigade in 1689, and I trust this brief account, which has long been a desideratum in Irish history, will not be unacceptable to the Irish reader, who may feel an interest in the achievements of his countrymen.

CHAPTER VI.

FIRST FORMATION OF THE IRISH BRIGADE IN THE
SERVICE OF FRANCE.

HITHERTO we have seen the Irish in foreign service advancing to military renown by paths too frequently diverging from the direct line of a soldier's duty. In these scandals they did no more than participate in the evils attendant on mercenary service at all times, and among all nations; still, the desertion of their colours, at whatever instigation, is a subject so painful to contemplate, that it is with inexpressible relief the author finds himself at length arrived at a period in the military history of his countrymen, when, taking service in the most honourable manner with their ancient allies, they began that series of brilliant exploits, performed with unimpeachable fidelity through numerous campaigns, which has rendered the name of Ireland illustrious in the military annals of Europe, in connexion with that of the Irish Brigade in the service of France.

The first formation of this celebrated corps was by way of exchange, and an exchange in which France had much the advantage. One of the great errors of the reign of Louis XIV., after the abdication of James II., was the neglect of Ireland. Had a veteran French army been landed there, aided by the existing Government and by the troops of the country, it would have been an overmatch for the French refugees, Dutch and Danes, composing William's forces, which had often before been defeated by the French alone.

But the French ministers were not united among themselves, nor unanimous in support of James. They concurred in contempt of the Irish, of their strength and resources; nor would they venture any portion of their army in that wild country without an equivalent. When, therefore, they at length conceded their tardy aid to the British monarch, they required in exchange for their own mercenaries and raw recruits, three of the choicest of James's Irish regiments. Had they sent, in Jourville's fleet then victorious on the ocean, such regiments as those of Picardy, Piedmont, Auvergne, and Normandy, they would have inspired the Irish with confidence, and instructed them in the movements and manœuvres for which they were themselves so conspicuous. But the troops sent were unnoticed in the French military annals: Fimoreon regiment, about 1000; Zurlauben's mercenaries of all nations, Swiss, Italians, and Germans, 2000; Merode's, 800; La Forest's, 900; La Marche's, 900; Courvassier's, 900—in all 6000; men who fled at the Boyne with the Irish, and abandoned them at Limerick. Far different was the conduct of those given in exchange. On the 7th of April, 1690, Chateau Renaud's fleet took on board at Kinsale 5000 Irish, and landed them at Brest on the 23rd of the same month(*a*). This corps formed the first nucleus of the famous Irish Brigade.

The three regiments drafted out of Ireland were old and disciplined : Mountcashel's, commanded by the Viscount of that name; Clare's, by Daniel O'Brien, eldest son of Lord Clare; and Dillon's, by Arthur Dillon, second son of the Lord Viscount of that name. Each regiment consisted of two battalions of eight companies, each company composed of 100, making in the whole, including officers and cadets, upwards of 5000 men. The colonel's companies of these regiments were not limited to 100, but had attached to them supernumeraries, drawn from the other companies. The colonel's company in Mountcashel's had also twenty cadets, and in Dillon's sixteen, receiving five-pence, or ten sols, per day. Each company had one captain, two lieutenants, one sub-lieutenant, and an ensign, making, for the three regiments, altogether 240 officers. The soldiers were allowed one sol per day more than the French, the officers in the same proportion, and the colonels a sol for every livre expended in the appointments of the officers and the subsistence of the regiments. Lord Mountcashel, as lieutenant-general commanding this brigade, independent of his allowance as colonel of his own regiment, was allowed an additional sol for each livre

(*a*) Quincy, vol. ii. p. 316. Dalrymple states the number to be 2500, but I conceive Quincy to be more correct. He gives the names of the regiments, and the number of the companies, and men.

in the appointments and subsistence of the other regiments.

Soon after its arrival in France, Mountcashel's brigade was ordered to Savoy, where the French *corps d'armée* was too feeble for active operations. After a march of 500 miles, under a burning sun, to which the men were unaccustomed, it joined the French army near the capital of Savoy, towards the latter end of July. Lieutenant-General the Marquis of St. Ruth, afterwards famous in the Irish wars, upon its arrival, commenced active operations, and approached Chamberry. The governor, the Count de Bernix, not having sufficient troops to man the works, abandoned both the town and citadel; which were entered and taken possession of by two battalions of Irish soldiers. Annecy was likewise abandoned, but Rumilly, better fortified, made some resistance, and was carried by assault. 3000 of the militia of the country, and 500 fusileers, defended the passage of the Ruè, but soon took flight. The Iserentaise, the Chablais, the country about Geneva, and Fusilly, submitted in succession; Montmelian, Moutiers, and the higher Alps, only remained to Victor Amadeus.

The Piedmontese troops, commanded by the Count de Bernix and M. de Salles, evacuated the duchy, retreating by the valley of Maurienne, and afterwards crossing the mountains that separate it from the valley of the Isere. That river, rising at the foot of Mount-Iseran, and collecting the cascades and rivulets that flow from the inexhaustible glaciers of the Graian Alps, turns to the north at the foot of the Little St. Bernard, and forces its foaming course through a chain of mountains, winding round projecting rocks, that present admirable positions for the defence of this great pass into Italy. The mountains forming its boundaries rear their snowy tops to the skies, and in many places descend almost perpendicularly to the river, narrowing its channel to a few hundred feet, and deepening it so as to be unfordable. No trees or shrubs facilitate the ascent; impending rocks, whose adhesion is often dissolved by the summer sun, threaten destruction, and fragments and loose stones, as slippery as the glaciers, endanger, at every step, the bold adventurer who dares to climb these precipitous steeps; gloom, barrenness, desolation, the thunder of avalanches, the roaring of cataracts, the very colour of the waters, as dark as Cocytus, and the solitude of these dreary abodes, unnerve the arm and appal the heart. Wildness and grandeur characterize this defile through an extent of forty miles. The Piedmontese generals calculated upon these difficulties, and resolved to defend this passage leading into Italy both by the Little St. Bernard and Mount Cenis. Their knowledge of the country, of its defiles and passes, enabled them to elude the pursuit of St. Ruth. But a general of his capacity, talents, and resources, was not to be deterred by difficulties. He calculated upon the valour of the Irish, and their agility as mountaineers. He therefore ordered the two battalions in the town and citadel of Chamberry to join him, and entered the upper valley of the Isere, determined to drive the Piedmontese beyond the High Alps that separate Savoy from Piedmont(a).

The village of Cintran, on the right bank above Moutiers, retains the name and revives the memory of the *homines intensi et inculti* who opposed, in this very defile, the march of Cæsar to the conquest of Gaul. At Moutiers the valley becomes enlarged, less savage, and has an appearance of industry and civilization, but still bounded by barrenness and desolation. Escaping from this spot of momentary tranquillity, the river again rushes into a defile, precipitating its waters over ledges of rocks into deep chasms, through which it foams on in a lengthened and furious rapid, and after another expansion above Aigue Blanche, rushes through the rocks of La Batie, which it nearly surrounds, and forms a natural, and almost impassable moat, rendering the position of that fortress as impregnable as any that military science could devise. Lower down it enters the Iserentaise,—the Davantasia of the ancients. Here it maintains its original impetuosity, and runs rapidly through a defile equally savage, narrow, and tortuous, where a handful of resolute men, by precipitating loosened rocks and avalanches, might arrest the career of armies, however numerous, though guided by the genius of a Hannibal or a Napoleon. In Cæsar's time the unarmed and undisciplined barbarians opposed him in vain from the high grounds, not daring to encounter in the valley

(a) De Quincy, vol. ii. p. 292.

underneath the disciplined valour of the legions. These same passes, guarded by great bravery, by military science, and all the improved implements of war, were forced by the valour of the Irish, and generalship of St. Ruth.

St. Ruth found M. de Salles in the lower valley, in a position nearly impregnable, on a rock washed by the Isere in front, and protected on its flanks and rere by steep mountains and impracticable defiles, guarded by an abattis; but no obstacles could check the activity and impetuosity of the Irish. Lord Mountcashel, at the head of his regiment, gained the defiles, burst through the abattis, carried the entrenchments, and forced the Piedmontese to fly to the summit of the mountains. Monsieur de Salles was taken prisoner, the next in command killed, and several others in the pursuit were killed or taken. Lord Mountcashel was on this occasion badly wounded.

St. Ruth, following up his successes, ascended towards the sources of the river in the High Alps, between the Little St. Bernard and Mount Cenis. Here the Count de Bernix chose a position still stronger than that which had been occupied by the Count de Salles, in a defile protected by the Isere on the right, and by inaccessible mountains on the left. Deep and broad fossès, filled with water, covered this position, and none but such troops as the Irish, accustomed to climb mountains and scale precipices, could have carried it. Colonel Lee, by incredible efforts, and through paths practicable only to the wild goats or chamois, gained the summit of a mountain in the rere of the position. The Piedmontese, panic-struck, fled to the passes of the Alps, and halted not till they reached the valley of Aosta in Italy. The bread and wine found in their camp were given to the Irish, who were allowed to scour all the surrounding hills, to carry off the cattle, and riot in the plunder of the country(*a*)—a pernicious reward of valour, although well calculated to stimulate rude soldiery to future achievements. Morienne sent its keys to the French camp, and all Savoy, except Montmelian, submitted to the dominion of Louis XIV. The Archbishop, clergy, and magistrates of Moutiers, apprehensive, probably, that their town might be plundered by the Irish, sent a deputation to St. Ruth, congratulating him on his successes ; *Te Deum* was sung there by his orders, and the town was spared. During the campaign of 1691 St. Ruth's corps was embodied in the French armies of Piedmont and Catalonia, and shared with them the honour of the capture of Montmelian, the strongest fortress in the south of Europe, and of Urgel in Catalonia, defended by a large garrison, the *élite* of the Spanish army. Clare's mounted the trenches at Mountmelian, as did Mountcashel's and Dillon's at Urgel(*b*). Such were the achievements of the first draft of the expatriated Irish, who were afterwards to be so famous as the Irish Brigade under the flag of France.

(*a*) Quincy, vol. ii. p. 304.
(*b*) Quincy, vol. ii. pp. 437, 444.

CHAPTER VII.

CAMPAIGNS OF 1690-1 IN IRELAND.

As the Brigade, on its complete formation, included the remaining portion of the Irish army of 1690-1, the campaign of that year forms a very essential part of its history. The existing accounts of this campaign were written when the truth was corrupted by party spirit; when success exaggerated, when defeat extenuated. I propose to give a fairer view, free alike from the prejudices of the victors and the passions of the vanquished.

The defeat of the Boyne was neither irreparable nor absolutely disastrous. The loss on both sides was nearly equal in officers; and in men not more than 1500 fell on the part of the Irish. Schomberg, Caillemote, Walker, and many of the officers of Schomberg's and the Dutch guards, were killed, and were more than an equivalent for the loss sustained by the Irish in the deaths of Lord Carlingford and Lord Dungan, and of those officers of Parker's and Tyrconnell's regiments, who fell in that engagement. The Marshal Duke of Berwick, an actor in this engagement, has, in his own handwriting, left the best account of it. Both parties committed errors. On the 30th of July, 1690, the armies were in front on the opposite sides of the Boyne; yet both neglected the bridge of Slane—the Irish to break it down, the English to possess themselves of it, the same being unguarded and only two miles from their encampment. The Irish neglected to throw up entrenchments opposite the fords in the Boyne, and to level the ditches and hedges that afterwards obstructed the charges of their cavalry. The very selection of the banks of the Boyne for a field of battle was a mistake. They ought to have retired behind the Shannon, and embarrassed their opponents by a desultory war. William could not have long maintained his ground; the French were masters of the sea; they had defeated the English fleet at Dungenness; they could have thrown into Ireland troops and supplies to any extent. Invasion succeeds by celerity; defence is sustained by delay. The Irish troops were raw and undisciplined, and had no experienced officer to command them. Lausun, who directed all the movements, was a Gascon by birth and disposition. Devoid of military talents, he had pushed himself into favour at Versailles by tact and address, till, though no more than a minion of Louis XIV., he had such credit at court, that he was able to treat the ministers and mistresses with the utmost hauteur. Aspiring to marry the king's sister he fell into disgrace, and was imprisoned for years in the citadel of Pignerôle; but having afterwards regained the king's favour, was sent to command in Ireland, where he shewed neither resolution nor capacity. At the Boyne, with

20,000 men he ventured an engagement with 45,000, though he had no advantage but that of a river in front, passable for both infantry and cavalry; this too, after discouraging his troops by sending off his baggage and a great part of his artillery to Dublin on the morning of the engagement, as if he intended to retreat. He then allowed the right wing of the enemy, after passing at Slane, to deploy, and take the Irish in flank, although the Duke of Berwick called on him to resist that movement, and he promised to do so, but remained passive and inactive(a), looking out for a favourable opening for attack, until the opportunity was gone by. The English artillery was very numerous; the Irish had but ten or fifteen field pieces. Under all these disadvantages the Irish cavalry behaved with the utmost bravery. Sir Neal O'Neal's dragoons resisted, for an hour, the passage at Slane, exposed to the fire of a numerous artillery and charges of cavalry greatly their superiors in number. Tyrconnell's and Parker's regiments charged several times with the utmost bravery, and drove the Dutch Guards and Schomberg's regiment back into the river with the loss of a great part of their officers.

The mistakes on William's part were no less flagrant. Lausun had allowed him to outflank the Irish left wing; but William neither pressed the Irish left, nor seized the pass of Duleek; but allowed the Irish cavalry and French infantry to cover the

(a) Memoirs of the Duke of Berwick, vol. ii. p. 83.

retreat without any effort to break them. After the Irish infantry had passed Duleek, indeed, the English made demonstrations of attack, which they repeated at the Naul; but both were feeble and ineffectual(a).

James beheld from the hill of Donore, his left wing outflanked, his centre broken, his right inactive. The spirit of his youth was frozen; the elasticity which gives nerve to enterprize was relaxed; old age and the impression made by unwarlike advisers had chilled those feelings, which, in his earlier years, impelled him to encounter the dangers of the field. The hero, who in Flanders excited the admiration of Turenne, sunk into the coward on the banks of the Boyne, and declined leading the charges of his own horse, when he might have restored the battle, and prevented an inglorious retreat. Panic-struck, and guided by counsels suggested by selfishness and fear, he abandoned an army that was beaten, not broken; that yielded to superiority of numbers and generalship, but had still resources and determination to prolong the contest indefinitely. Wexford, Waterford, Cork, Limerick, Youghal, and the line of the Shannon, all of which were in the hands of the Irish, presented obstacles to William's success, that should have inspired James with confidence in maintaining the contest; but Lausun, sensible of his own incapacity in camps, but conscious of his admirable talents for courts, was

(a) Memoirs of the Duke of Berwick, vol. ii. p. 72.

eager to quit a country where he could reap no harvests of glory, and where he had no field to exercise those arts, and practise those intrigues, which had raised him to the pinnacle of favour at Versailles. He, therefore, advised James to seek safety in flight, to return to France, and thus escape being made prisoner by William. He would give his right hand to have accompanied him, but his duty commanded him to guide the retreat of the French troops, or perish with them (*a*). This ill-judged counsel was seconded by Talbot, Earl of Tyrconnell. Talbot was brave in danger, pusillanimous in disaster. In the route of the Boyne he viewed the cause of James as hopeless, that of William as triumphant. He had estates and dignities to preserve, and only in an accommodation could he see security for them. If James remained, the contest would be prolonged beyond the hope of an accommodation. He, therefore, sent his chaplain to him to press his flight to France, and to work on his fears of falling into the hands of William. James reached Dublin on that same day; and, conscious that his flight would be construed into cowardice, he sought to shelter his fame, not only under the cover of the suggestions of his officers, but likewise under that of the advice of his privy council. Sir Richard Nagle, Riverston, Judge Daly, and those whom he could convene, counselled flight. The disaster of the Boyne

---

(*a*) Memoirs of Berwick, pp. 72, 73.

was considered irreparable, and the flight of James necessary for an accommodation. No terms could be made, if he inspired the troops by his presence; and the estates and dignities of these courtiers would be forfeited, in the result of a struggle which would terminate in the conquest of the country. Lest a spark of courage should revive in James, the colonels of four of the French regiments reached Dublin in full speed to hasten his departure.— They represented the enemy at hand, and the royal fugitive's capture inevitable, if he hastened not his departure. Thus his own fears, worked on by summer friends, false counsellors, and interested foreigners, pretending zeal, and yet anxious to quit his service, precipitated James's flight at a time when the French victories of Fleurus and Beechy Head endangered the position of William's army in Ireland, and when the command of the sea by the French threatened to cut off all supplies from England. And so it was that James, Lausun, and Tyrconnel, gave out that all was lost; that the Irish were cowards, and would not fight—lies circulated by the first to conceal the infamy of running away; by the second as a pretext for retiring to France; and by the third as a cover for an accommodation and making terms. By their representations the war in Ireland was made unpopular in France, and the Irish merchants in the French seaports could not walk the streets without being in-

(*a*) Clarke, vol. ii. p. 401.

sulted(*a*), until the heroic defence of Limerick altered the opinion of the French people, and convinced them that the Irish was as brave as any other of the nations of Europe.

After the retreat from the Boyne, the Irish army was left to shift for itself, without the guidance either of king or general officers ; but the fidelity and enthusiasm of the inferior officers and common soldiers prevented disorder and desertion, and conducted the retreat to Limerick in admirable order(*b*). The French, who sustained no loss at the Boyne, accompanied the Irish, and were quartered in the town and suburbs.

William lost the fruits of his victory at the Boyne by not pressing the Irish on their retreat. Drogheda, a nominal fortress, without ramparts, bastions, or outworks, with only seven iron cannon, a garrison of 1200 men, and a cowardly governor, arrested his career but a single day. Three more days elapsed before his entry into Dublin, a distance of twenty-two miles only. He thus gave his enemies leisure to retreat, and opportunity to reorganize. Even then it was not too late to press and pursue with his whole force. The fortifications of Limerick had mouldered to decay: he gave the Irish time to repair and add to them. He divided his forces, sending Douglass with 10,000 men to besiege Athlone, while he with the

---

(*a*) Narrative of Contests in Ireland, by Colonel Charles Kelly of Aughrim.
(*b*) Ib.

remainder marched southward along the coast. Before Athlone Douglass sustained a signal defeat. William himself did no more than take Wexford, which was betrayed, and Clonmel, which was ungarrisoned—petty conquests, interposing delay when expedition was essential.

James, on his arrival at St. Germain, was visited by Louis; but it was a visit of condolence, without offers of further aid. His fallen fortunes may have excited pity; his flight and misconduct must have challenged contempt; yet he still clung to royalty. Hope pointed to Scotch attachment and to English discontent. He expected that Scotch loyalty would achieve what Irish valour had failed to effect; and that the discontents of the English aristocracy, excited by William's partiality to foreigners, would bring about a counter-revolution. He proposed to the French ministers to go on board a French fleet, and head a French force in an invasion of England or Scotland. He sought a further interview with Louis, but the French monarch declined all further intercourse(*a*). The ministers refused supplies, men, and money, and the French nation manifested disgust. That gallant people always prized valour as the first of virtues. James was left to repent, in the silence and solitude of St. Germain, his having abandoned a people who fought for him, and who still held out for him, and were determined to conquer in his cause, or perish in the last entrenchments of their country.

(*a*) Clarke's Life of James II., vol. ii. pp. 412, 432.

On William's approach to Limerick, a council of war, attended by the French and Irish general officers, deliberated whether the town should be defended or not. Lausun declared the place untenable ; that his master could take it with roasted apples(*a*). The other French generals coincided with him: they were disgusted with a country where incessant rains and eternal fogs damped the spirits ; where want of supplies and bad quarters induced diseases ; where hope never smiled, and pleasure never cheered. In Ireland they had no harvests of glory to reap, no advancement to expect, but had to endure the iron hardships of the field, without acquiring fame or glory, the best recompense of military achievements. The manners, habits, and customs of the people, could not reconcile them to the gloom and desolation of the climate, or the hardships of inglorious warfare. Difference of language prevented communion between them; and the French, in the misery and nakedness of the natives, could view them only as semi-barbarians, without arms, or means to carry on war with a martial and disciplined enemy. The boastings of the Irish, who had claimed the post of honour at the Boyne, and fled on the first discharge, excited their disgust. In the council, therefore, these foreigners were for abandoning all further opposition to William, and returning to the enjoyments of that gay and sprightly land,

---

(*a*) Memoirs of Berwick, vol. ii.

where the toils of war were relieved by mirth and ease, Venus and the Graces dispelling the fatigues and cares of war, in the amusements, fetes, and entertainments, that enlivened the winter quarters of the French military.

On the subject in discussion the Irish themselves were divided; opposite interests, and different prospects, induced conflicting councils. The natives, stripped of their estates in Ulster under the first James, and others under Cromwell, not restored by the Act of Settlement, and hopeless in the event of an accommodation, had no fair prospect but from a continuance of the war, and a separation from England, which they calculated might be effected by French aid and Irish valour. The O'Neals, Maguires, M'Ginnesses, M'Mahons, O'Ferralls, O'Reilys, O'Garas, the Irish bishops, and the discontented officers, Sarsfield, the Luttrells, and the Purcells, formed the strength of this party, and were supported by the common soldiers, enthusiasts in the cause of their country and religion. Lord Tyrconnell headed the peace party, supported by the Hamiltons, Talbots, Nugents, Dillons, Burkes, Rices, Butlers, Plowdens, Sheldons, all of English descent, who preferred William, as king of Great Britain and Ireland, to James, as king of Ireland only, and in despair of reinstating the latter on his ancestral throne, sought to preserve their possessions by accommodation. The embarrassments of William, they hoped, would dictate concessions; private communications from his generals offered terms most advantageous. Nor does it appear that James was adverse to a settlement. He hated the native Irish, because he had, at the Restoration and by the Act of Settlement, plundered them of 150,000 acres, which he appropriated to himself as his private patrimony. He had reaped the harvest of their valour in his exile ; he repaid them by decrying their courage at the battle of Dunkirk. He saw them shedding their blood at the battle of the Boyne in his cause ; he maligned them to the French nation as cowards. He had called into action the energies of Ireland with the sole view of regaining the throne of Great Britain ; and when he fancied his chances of success in that direction hopeless, he abandoned his ill-requited adherents to the scourge of conquest, and the horrors of military devastation.

Lausun, regardless of all entreaties to remain with the Irish army in Limerick, retired with all the French to Galway. Tyrconnell followed his example. To force the Irish to surrender, they removed as much of the ammunition and stores as time would allow. The ardent and enthusiastic spirit of the Irish bore up against every discouragement; against the desertion of the French veterans, the want of supplies, and the taunting declaration of the French general, that his master would take the town with roasted apples. The defence of the place to the last extremity was resolved upon ; officers, soldiers, citizens, women, and children, laboured from sunrise to sunset at the fortifications. Boiseleau, a captain of the French guards, who had some knowledge, which none of the Irish had, of the defence of fortified towns, was appointed governor. Sarsfield commanded the horse: his ardent and enterprising activity intercepted the convoys to William's camp, and at Kellunamona blew up the English artillery destined for the siege.

James, after his departure, wrote to Tyrconnel, ordering such of the officers as wished to follow his fortunes to sail on board the French fleet, absolving the rest from their allegiance, and allowing them to compound with the enemy. The publication of this letter was intended to dispirit the Irish, in order to preserve the reputations of the generals; for if the defence of Limerick should prove ultimately successful, Lausun and Tyrconnel felt they would be disgraced for ever. The stain of cowardice and desertion would never be obliterated. Sarsfield's zeal and popularity counteracted the base design. In the heat of the siege he posted off to Galway, made a strong party of the officers in garrison, protested against the accommodation, represented the letter as the result of misinformation, and shamed both Tyrconnel and Lausun into demonstrations of courage: both set off for Limerick upon the report of the outworks being carried(a).

Tyrconnel had raised his own minions and crea-

(a) Charles O'Kelly's Narrative.

tures to power and places, and thus sowed the seeds of dissension, which ripened nearly to ruin during the siege. Connected with the Hamiltons of Strabane, by his marriage with Frances, the widow of Sir George Hamilton, and sister to Sarah, Duchess of Marlborough, he raised Richard Hamilton to the rank of lieutenant-general, with the enormous pay, at that period, of £499 10s., out of an exhausted treasury; Anthony Hamilton, the elegant writer of the Memoirs of Grammont, an associate of Talbot at the court of Charles II. in pleasures, intrigues, and the gaming table, he raised to the rank of a major-general; and his brother John to that of a brigadier. The Purcells and the Luttrels envied their elevation, and, during the siege, reproached Hamilton with private practices with King William before his victory at the Boyne, and charged all of them with malversations in the commissariat department.

William, having received a fresh supply of artillery, commenced the siege. On the 18th of August he opened the trenches; the old walls crumbled under the fire of thirty pieces of heavy ordnance. The garrison consisted of 30,000 foot, one-half only armed. The cavalry, 3500 strong, under the Duke of Berwick, guarded the right bank of the Shannon, and prevented the English from investing, or even sending detachments on that side, although the river was fordable in many places. It was no wonder that Lausun declared, that his master would deem it an easy conquest. It had no outworks, no glacis, pallisadoes, fosses, half-moons, or horn works, or any of those exterior defences that retard the approach of an enemy. An old wall, flanked with some towers, without a ditch or parapet, constituted its defence. The garrison had made a kind of covered way all round, and a sort of pallisadoed horn work opposite the great gate. The batteries erected to the left of this horn work, in the course of eight days, made a breach 100 feet in breadth. William, to spare effusion of blood, before he ordered an assault, summoned the place to surrender. The summons was received with a haughty defiance, intimating a resolution to perish in the breach, rather than yield. On the 27th of August 10,000 men were ordered for a general assault. The trenches being but fourteen feet from the pallisade, and there being no ditch, the English were at the summit of the breach before the alarm was given. A battery, which Boiseleau had erected inside, arrested the career of the assailants for some time, but confident in their strength, and led on by the officers, they descended into the city. By this time the garrison advanced on all sides, and attacked with such bravery in the streets, that they forced the enemy back to the breach, where they attempted a lodgment. Here a terrible conflict ensued. The women of Limerick mingled with the soldiers; in the midst of the carnage encouraged them with their shouts; assailed the besiegers with stones; and exhibited the valour of their Celtic ancestors in their wars with the Romans. Brigadier Talbot sallying out of the horn work, took the assailants in the rere, bore them down, and entered the breach amidst the shouts of triumph of the besieged(a).

Never was town better attacked or defended; during the siege nothing was unattempted that the art of war, the science of great generals, and the valour of veteran soldiers, could put in execution to carry it; the Irish omitted nothing that constancy and courage could effect to defend it: continued assaults on the one side, and continued sallies on the other, consumed a great number of both armies. The general assault terminated in the utter discomfiture of William, and the triumphs at the commencement, were overbalanced by the failures at the close of the campaign of 1690.

Whilst Mountcashel's brigade was achieving conquests for France in Savoy and Catalonia, the French troops remained in Galway, inactive spectators of the struggles of the Irish in the outworks, and upon the breach of the last stronghold of their country. Lausun and Tyrconnel were mortified at the heroic defence, in which the skill and discipline of veterans were foiled by the valour of raw recruits. On the approach of the enemy towards Limerick, the French general had marched with all his troops straight to Galway, taking with him a great quantity of ammunition; so that, instead of assisting the Irish during the siege, he had weakened them in the department

(a) Memoirs of Berwick, vol. ii. pp. 76, 78.

most important to their defence(*a*). During the siege he was pressed to send back some of the stores and ammunition, and fear of impeachment induced a restoration of part.

The defence of Limerick effected a mighty change in the French councils. The Irish were no longer a cowardly, but a brave people, equal to the veterans opposed to them; they wanted not the aid of French soldiers, but supplies of all kinds were ordered for them—money, arms, ammunition, food, clothing; and on account of the disunion between them and Lausun's corps, the latter were recalled(*b*).

Brigadier Sarsfield obtained, and in some degree deserved, the honour of having defeated William's attempt upon Limerick. His character is a very important one in Irish history; it has been sketched by the Duke of Berwick, an attentive observer of human character, who married his widow, and was intimately acquainted with this most popular character, by whom the passions of the Irish were directed without control, during the last years of the war. Sarsfield was of a noble family, was possessed of £2000 a year—a large fortune at that period—and of all the accomplishments of a perfect gentleman; was well-natured, affable, of a tall and manly figure. He had been an ensign in France in the regiment of Monmouth, and lieutenant of the

---

(*a*) Memoirs of Berwick, vol. ii. p. 411.
(*b*) Ibid. p. 420.

Guards in England. When James came to Ireland he got a regiment of cavalry, and was made a brigadier. The destruction of William's convoy inflated him in an inordinate degree, and raised him to the highest pitch of popularity. Arminius was never more popular among the Germans, than Sarsfield among the Irish—to this day his name is venerated—*canitur adhuc*. No man was ever more attached to his country, or more devoted to his king and religion. Like most men who have acquired popularity, he had sycophants about him to minister to his follies and to inflame his vanities. Of these the most conspicuous was Henry Luttrel, the ancestor of the Carhampton family, who never ceased to extol him as a great general, and this not from any attachment to him, but to serve his own purposes. Luttrel was brave, possessed of great talents, and one of the best officers in the Irish army, but recklessly bent on pushing himself forward by the popularity of Sarsfield, and by raising him to the chief command. He had served in France with distinction, but was so eager of personal advancement, that he would shrink as little from infamy as from danger to promote his fortunes. He was the younger brother of Simon, an officer of great integrity, who followed the fortunes of James, forfeited his estates, and was killed in Piedmont in the year 1696 or 1697. Long before his death, William made a grant of his estates to Henry— a reward for his treachery, which redounded equally to the disgrace of the king who gave, and of the traitor who received(*a*).

Sarsfield, Luttrel, and the native Irish did every thing they could to undermine the power of Tyrconnel, to decry his minions, and hold them up to public scorn(*b*). By these means, and his own misconduct, Tyrconnel deservedly lost the confidence of the Irish. He had advised the flight of James; had fled to Galway on the approach of William to Limerick; had withdrawn the troops who guarded the fords of the Shannon to Galway; had concurred in the retreat of the French, and in the removal of the stores. He had supplied beans and oats to the troops during the siege of Limerick, whilst there was abundance of wheat in the commissariat. He had also, no doubt, increased his unpopularity by descanting on the military inability of the Irish, and on the consequences of their reduction by the English. The war party regarded him, therefore, with justice, as a coward, and as such he was represented to the French ministers. Finding the decay of his popularity and dreading the loss of power, he resolved, in a personal interview with Louis and James, to meet the charges of his opponents, who reproached him with falsehood, and misrepresentation of the state of affairs, in order to prevent French aid. His insinuating address might deceive Louis and

(*a*) Memoirs of Berwick, vol. ii. p. 104.
(*b*) Ibid. p. 87.

his ministers. James's favour would support him against the statements of the malcontents of the army: the true state of affairs in Ireland might be concealed, made known, or perverted, so as to suit the humours and wishes of courtiers, or the exigencies of his own affairs. His misrepresentations after the battle of the Boyne might be excused or justified by the retreat of the French; and the removal of the stores might be thrown off his own shoulders, on those of Lausun. With such notions and prospects, Tyrconnel prepared to follow his exiled master.

As a pretext for quitting his government, he gave out the king's orders to go to France to give a statement of the true posture of affairs. He appointed the Duke of Berwick commander-in-chief, with a council of officers to direct him(a), and nominated, during his absence, twelve of his own creatures to administer the civil government. He then sailed on board the French fleet, which carried back to Brest the French corps, and their commander Lausun. This delinquent hoped to palliate his desertion and flight, by alleging the orders of the viceroy, and representing the country as hideous, the people as savages, the soldiers as cowards, nothing donbting that the viceroy, for his own sake, must concur in these misrepresentations. But Tyrconnel knew that the gallantry of the Irish at Limerick, in Piedmont,

(a) Charles O'Kelly's Narrative.

and Catalonia would belie these statements, and that if such representations alone were relied on, he and Lausun might incur in France the odium of misconduct and cowardice—the Bastile might be the punishment of both. He therefore put all his ingenuity on the stretch to dupe Lausun into a belief that mutual safety depended on mutual justification. Lausun fell into the snare, feeling that recrimination would be the ruin of both, and agreed to represent Tyrconnel as having done every thing that zeal, perseverance, and energy could effect; and Tyrconnel, on his part, was to represent the cause of James as hopeless, and the retreat of the French troops as unavoidable. On their arrival at Brest, Tyrconnel affected indisposition and inability to travel post to Paris; but impressed on Lausun the necessity of anticipating the statements of the malcontents, by prompt explanations. Lausun, proceeding direct to the capital, lavished eulogiums on Tyrconnel. Ireland he represented as a lost country, and that it could not be recovered; the nation was inclined to an accommodation. They who defended Limerick were but few, and animated by Tyrconnel, who was the soul of the cause. Tyrconnel having thus prepared the stage for his own appearance, soon after arrived, and though he had parted at Brest with professions of lasting friendship for Lausun, did not hesitate to lay the blame of all the miscarriages of the king's affairs in Ireland, on the misconduct and desertion of that officer and his troops, representing that if the French could be prevailed on to stay in Ireland, something might still be effected ; and that supplies of money and troops were only wanting to reinstate the affairs of James. Lausun was thunderstruck at being made the dupe of a man not half so well versed as himself in the art of deception : he would have been sent to the Bastile but for the interposition of the queen. Tyrconnel's representations were sustained by the statements of Lausun himself, by the gallant defence of Limerick, and the bravery of Mountcashel's brigade in Piedmont, Savoy, and Catalonia(a).

Lord Tyrconnel, returning to his government after this characteristic stroke of policy, landed at Galway on the 6th of January, bringing with him some clothing, ammunition, and £11,000 in money. He found the soldiers and officers in the extreme of misery and nakedness. During his absence, insubordination, treachery, and discord had altogether disorganized the army. Lord Riverston, the Secretary at War, and Colonel M'Donnell, the Governor of Galway, had been detected in secret practices with the enemy, and were removed from their offices by the Duke of Berwick. Others, calculating upon the chances of defeat, and apprehensive of forfeitures, meditated submission to William. Baldearg O'Donnel, at the head of 8000 of the rabble, had set up an independent command, disclaimed the king's authority, and made demon-

(a) O'Kelly's Narrative; Clarke, vol. ii. p. 435.

strations of maintaining the cause of the native Irish as distinct from James's, and restoring them to the dominion of their native country. Unparalleled misery produced mutiny and desertion in several of the Irish quarters. The soldiers were nearly famished, having no food but horse flesh, sufficient to sustain bare existence; they had neither fuel, clothes, nor pay. The garrison of Thurles laid down their arms, driven to desperation by hunger(a). To punish men who received no pay, and were left without supplies, was impossible. To bring them back to their duty, could be effected by mild courses only, and by appeals to their loyalty and patriotism.

Upon his departure for France, Tyrconnel had appointed the Duke of Berwick commander-in-chief, with a council of officers to direct his youth and inexperience. Policy should have nominated Sarsfield of the council—personal dislike and hatred excluded him. He had also established a new form of civil government, appointing twelve senators, his own partizans, to manage all civil affairs. In these appointments violent factions originated, and burst forth in furious opposition to the new arrangements. The ecclesiastics joined the discontented officers and native Irish. A great council at Limerick, consisting of bishops, nobles, and officers, deputed Sarsfield, Simon Luttrel, and Brigadier Dorrington to represent to the Duke of Berwick that his power was il-

(a) Clarke, vol. ii. p. 437.

legal, but that they would confer on him the civil and military authority, if he would admit a select council of officers to direct his military operations, and two able persons from each of the provinces to direct him in relation to civil affairs. They also stated, that Tyrconnel would not sufficiently represent their wants to the French court, and begged of him to make the necessary representations himself. The Duke expressed his astonishment that they should hold such illegal assemblies—declared that he would accept no authority from the army or nation—that he had unquestionable authority to act as lieutenant-general, under a former commission from the king—and severely reprimanded the dissatisfied officers, whom he ordered to their quarters. Their answer was, that the king had absolved them from their allegiance, and that if he would not accept of the command proffered to him, they were by nature entitled to provide for their own safety. This firmness shook the duke's resolution. He said he would give them a definitive answer on the day following; when having convened the nobles, bishops, general officers, and colonels, he made an harangue similar to that of the preceding day, reprobating such illegal assemblies, and prohibiting them for the future. However, to shew his anxious wishes for the good of the nation, he professed his readiness to send delegates of their own party to France to represent their wants, and to give a true statement of their condition, and proposed the Bishop of Cork, the two Luttrels, and Colonel Purcell. All approved of this arrangement, and in a few days he despatched the delegates, accompanied by Brigadier Maxwell, his own agent, with secret instructions to apprize the king of his reasons for sending them, and not to allow Henry Luttrel or Colonel Purcell to return, they being the firebrands of the army,—in fact, that he had chosen them on purpose to put them out of the way. On the passage, suspecting Maxwell carried private instructions, Henry Luttrel and Colonel Purcell proposed to throw him overboard, but the Bishop of Cork interposed the sanctity, and Simon Luttrel the mildness and honesty of his character, and their united expostulations rescued him from a watery grave(*a*).

Delayed by contrary winds, these agents arrived at St. Maloe, whilst Tyrconnel was at Brest on his return to Ireland. He had intelligence of all the proceedings against him, and advised James to retain Purcell and Henry Luttrel. They proceeded to St. Germain, and represented to James that the reappointment of Tyrconnel as commander-in-chief was pregnant with ruin. His age, infirmities, inactivity, and corpulency, disqualified from active operations, and his ignorance and incapacity rendered him unfit for directing military movements. A general of science and activity must be found to oppose the experience and tactics of the enemy. A

(*a*) Memoirs of Berwick, vol. i. p. 91 ; O'Kelly's Narrative.

commander possessing the confidence of the troops was also necessary Talbot had forfeited their esteem by his desertion at Limerick; Sarsfield had gained it by his activity and exploits. The haughty carriage of the former had alienated—the popular manners of the latter had conciliated. The vacillation of Talbot had discouraged; the resolution of Sarsfield to hold out to the last, had animated. Lord Mountcashel had acquired renown in Piedmont and Savoy. The Irish only wanted a general and supplies. The agents must also have complained of Talbot's general administration—of his inclination for an accommodation with William—and, doubtless, insinuated his insincerity in the cause; and as they dreaded being imprisoned, they represented that the Irish would retort on the Duke of Berwick any ill treatment they might receive. This menace protected them, and James had the meanness to supplicate them not to disparage Talbot in their interview with the French ministers. At this interview they stated the resolution of the nation to hold out to the last. They asked for a general, arms, and ammunition; urged that it was Louis's interest to keep William engaged in Ireland; that such a diversion would ensure his conquests in Flanders, and might regain the throne for James. They extolled the bravery and loyalty of the Irish troops, and gave flattering accounts of their numbers and discipline. These statements induced promises of support. The difficulties of appointing a general were obviated by a patent of an earldom to gratify the vanity of Sarsfield. Mountcashel was attached to the army of Piedmont, and could not be spared. The command was therefore conferred on St. Ruth: his rank, reputation, and achievements silencing the murmurs of the disaffected, and extinguishing all competition. The Luttrels then returned to Ireland, Simon to fight, and Henry to betray(*a*).

Berwick's military operations, during the absence of Talbot, were directed by the Hamiltons, were conducted without skill, and had dispirited the Irish. With his whole cavalry, seven battalions of infantry, and four pieces of cannon he had passed the Shannon at Banagher, besieged the castle of Birr, upon which he could make no impression, from want of cannoneers, and upon the approach of Douglass's army had recrossed the Shannon with precipitation(*b*).

In the month of September the Earl of Marlborough, with 8000 men, laid siege to Cork, which had no tenable fortifications. Berwick advanced with 8000 men to Kilmallock to raise the siege, but a great portion of the enemy's troops from various quarters having joined Marlborough, he found the relief of the place impracticable He then directed Roger M'Eligot, the governor, to burn the town, and withdraw his garrison into Kerry. In violation of these orders, M'Eligot maintained the place for five days, when, escape having become impossible, he

(*a*) Memoirs of Berwick, vol. ii. p. 80 ; O'Kelly's Narrative.
(*b*) Clarke's James II. p. 424.

surrendered himself and his troops prisoners of war. They were treated with great inhumanity, most of them having died through misery in prison, where they remained unburied till they amounted to thirty or forty at a time, so that the infection caused thereby greatly hastened the destruction of the survivors(*a*).

The governor of Kinsale made a more spirited and more fortunate defence : his garrison, not much more than 1000 men, held out ten days, and obtained most honourable conditions. Though a practicable breach had been made, and the enemy were ready to mount, the garrison were allowed to retire to Limerick with arms and baggage.

Never was country in a more wretched condition than the province of Connaught during the winter of 1790 and 1791. Being almost the only part of Ireland in possession of James, the cattle of Ulster had been driven in there, where many of them miserably perished, having no fodder, while great numbers were slaughtered by the troops, who, having no pay, lived at discretion(*b*). Berwick's youth disregarded disorder, and rioted in pleasures. Civil commissioners disclaimed all authority over the soldiery, and Sarsfield maintained his popularity with the troops by countenancing their excesses. The store-keepers and subalterns seized upon cattle, butter, leather, wood, linen, and every other com-

(*a*) Clarke's Memoirs, vol. ii.; Berwick's Memoirs, vol. ii. p. 85.
(*b*) O'Kelly's Narrative; Clarke's Memoirs, vol. ii. p. 433.

modity, regardless of the orders and protests of bishops and nobles, so that little or no provisions found their way to the king's stores.

Discord and privations had nearly dissolved the army. Some efforts were made by Tyrconnel to reorganize it. Sarsfield, the great promoter of disunion, appeased by his patent of an earldom, lent his influence to quell mutinies and restore discipline. Two pairs of brogues and a pair of breeches and stockings were supplied to each foot soldier. Provisions were sent to the different quarters on men's backs; want of carriages, and impassable roads, rendering any other mode of conveyance impracticable.

Although the great firebrands of the army were still in France, the necessities of the men and officers were alone but too well calculated to produce discontent and disaffection. The disproportion of the pay was excessive. The men received only one penny a day; while each colonel had at the rate of 100 crowns, each brigadier of 200, and each major-general of 400—extravagant sums, considering that the whole of the money given by James to Tyrconnel was but £20,000(a). The supplies brought by him to Galway were also soon exhausted. The months of March, April, and May passed, no fur-

(a) Lord Tyrconnel came to Galway with two frigates and five small vessels, escorted across the Channel by the Marquis of Numond's fleet. The Marquis of Quincy states, that he brought with him all kinds of stores, provisions, and clothes for the troops. But this small squadron could not have brought much.

ther succours arrived from France, and universal despondency prevailed, except in Galway, where all thoughts of the approaching campaign were buried in a succession of revelries, balls, and banquets. Tyrconnel was received there with every demonstration of joy, ringing of bells, firing of cannon, and bonfires; was feasted by the citizens, and huzzaed by the soldiers. The thoughtless and excitable populace fancied victory in valour without discipline, and hugged themselves on regal promises, liable to the changes of caprice, irresolution, and ministerial disunion. The ladies of Galway too, famed for their beauty, accomplishments, and address, even in the holy time of Lent, when their love of pleasure had been usually under the control of penance and prayer, did not relax their festivities; for so many young officers of rank, family, and fortune, had never before been quartered in their town; while the young men, under their influence, seemed to have renounced the service of the god of war, and to have devoted themselves exclusively to Venus and Bacchus(*a*). Neither drills nor reviews prepared the soldiers for the approaching contest; no provision was made for the campaign; no magazines or commissariat got together to relieve the existing distresses, or provide sustenance for future operations. But, in their quarters, the poor Irish common soldiers displayed a degree of patience and endu-

(*a*) O'Kelly's Narrative. Quincy, vol. ii. p. 437.

rance unexampled in the annals of history. They vegetated on half a pound of bread for each soldier per day, and sustained all the hardships of a cold, wet, and dreary winter without clothes or fuel(*a*).

On the 8th of June the English army opened the campaign; and on the same day forty French transports, escorted by twelve ships of war, commanded by Count Numond, reached Limerick, having on board Lieutenant-general St. Ruth, sent as commander-in-chief, 106 officers, 150 cadets, 300 English and Scotch, 24 surgeons, 180 masons, 2 bombardiers, 18 cannoneers, 3 engineers, 20 carpenters, 800 horses, 19 pieces of cannon, 12,000 horse shoes, 6000 bridles and saddles, 16,000 muskets, uniforms, stockings, and shoes for 16,000 men, some lead and balls, and a large supply of biscuit(*b*). These timely succours elevated the Irish with an immoderate joy. But any rational calculation must have estimated these supplies as utterly inadequate. The Irish had no corps of artillery, no field pieces, no engineers; so that, notwithstanding these contributions, they were still, in the most effective materials of warfare, wholly deficient. *Te Deum*, however, was sung in the churches of Limerick, and all ranks

(*a*) Quincy, vol. ii. p. 451.
(*b*) Quincy, vol. ii. p. 456. The indubitable authority of the historian of Louis XIV. fixes the day of the departure of Numond's fleet from Brest, and the day of its arrival in the Shannon, which falsifies all the imputations of blunders, made by the English historians against St. Ruth.

and orders exerted themselves to put the army in a condition to take the field. But want of money rendered the preparations dilatory and inefficient. 170 caissons, 400 cars, and carriages for 10 field-pieces, were at last got in readiness; and as much money was put together as was sufficient to pay one penny per day to each soldier for three weeks. But the troops, in the anticipated deliverance of their country, were reconciled to every species of hardship and privation, and in their attachment to their king and cause, found food, raiment, vigour, every thing that sustains the hardships of war.

On the same day the English sat down before the wretched, untenable fort of Ballymore, between Mullingar and Athlone. To maintain this post, Miles Burke had been appointed governor, with a garrison of 800 men, the *élite* of the Irish, being picked men from all the regiments. On the east and north-east Ballymore was protected by a small lake, and had on that side neither outworks, ditch, nor rampart. To garrison such a place, especially with choice troops, was very ill-advised. In the space of twenty-four hours six batteries crumbled all the works to the south, and the appearance of a flotilla on the lake induced a surrender(*a*). The capture

(*a*) Clarke, vol. ii. p. 452. Burke, the governor, is charged with cowardice or treachery in the Memoirs of James. It would appear rather that vanity induced the defence, and incapacity the surrender.

of the fort was of no consideration; but the loss of the men was irreparable.

This paltry place had been constructed by Sarsfield during the winter, to favour incursions into the English quarters; but had never been intended to stand a regular siege, or to retard the march of an army; yet De Ginkle, ever slow and irresolute, remained an entire week encamped here. Had he followed up his success with rapidity, Athlone would have made as little resistance. It had but a small garrison, and scarcely any artillery or ammunition. These phlegmatic proceedings of the Dutchman allowed time to St. Ruth to dispatch to the menaced point a considerable force, who encamped on the Connaught side of the river, and prepared to dispute with De Ginkle the passage of the Shannon.

On the 18th of June the English approached Athlone. On the 19th they were met by Fitzgerald, a gallant officer, who disputed the ground to the foot of the ramparts. Ditches and hedges were defended and carried with equal bravery; but superior numbers forced the Irish into the English town. This part of Athlone, lying on the eastern side of the river, was comparatively untenable. Had the garrison retired into the Irish town on the opposite bank, and made good their position there, by breaking down the bridge, the defence would have proved much more formidable. Whom to censure for this oversight is difficult to determine, whether Sarsfield or Tyrconnel. St. Ruth, at all events, is blameless, not having yet arrived, being then actively engaged in collecting and organizing the army(*a*).

On the day following De Ginkle's arrival, his heavy artillery made a practicable breach. 4000 men were ordered to the assault; 400 men in garrison repelled them, until one-half of their number lay dead or dying, when, after a conflict of several hours, the remainder fell back, and formed a rampart at the foot of the bridge, where they sustained the whole force of the victorious host, until two arches of the bridge were broken down, by which time this immortal band of heroes lay nearly all a mound of lifeless trunks on the spot where they had arrested the career of the victors(*b*). In this war, pregnant with acts of heroism and sacrifice to country, this is an achievement which might claim the pencil of Tacitus, or the descriptive powers of Thucydides, to give it immortality. But the Irish have had no historians, and, notwithstanding numerous such instances of heroism during the campaign, the

(*a*) Clarke's Memoirs, vol. ii. p. 453.
(*b*) Clarke, vol. ii. p. 453. "On the 20th the enemy appointed 4000 detached men to make an assault; there were not above 300 or 400 men in the town, on the Leinster side; however, they defended the breach for some time, till at last 200 of their men were killed or wounded, and the rest so exhausted with eight-and-forty hours' continued action (whereas the enemy were relieved by their whole army), that they were forced to retire to the bridge, where they sustained all the power of the rebels, till they had broken down two arches of it, and thereby stopped, at least, all communication with the other town."

malignity of their conquerors has succeeded in stamping the national character with cowardice in their domestic wars(*a*).

St. Ruth did not reach Athlone, until the siege of the Irish town had commenced. Dissensions are said to have arisen between him and Sarsfield. Possibly upon his arrival at the camp, he may have reproached Sarsfield with the unnecessary and hopeless defence of Ballymore, and of the English town of Athlone, where so many of the best soldiers of the army had been sacrificed in posts which were notoriously untenable. That discord prevailed, most prejudicial to the service, is certain, but whether excited by these reproaches, or by the jealousies too frequently attendant on camps, is a speculation now enveloped in obscurity.

Impartial posterity must do justice to St. Ruth. He considered the Irish an injured and oppressed people, martyrs to their religion, and victims to loyalty; and he devoted to their cause all the energies of his mind and body(*b*). He had not been in Ireland more than ten days, and his activity during that period in collecting the scattered troops, in organizing and providing them with necessaries, had scarcely admitted an intermission for the needful rest which exhausted nature required. He had heard on the 20th, while at Ballinasloe, of the capture of the English town of Athlone, and he instantly set out with 1500 horse and foot, leaving the rest of the

(*a*) Clarke, vol. ii. pp. 454, 455, 456.
b) O'Kelly's Narrative.

troops to follow him. Arriving at Athlone, he pitched his camp at a short distance outside the town, and appointed D'Usson governor, instead of Fitzgerald, as being more versed in the science of defending fortified places. Lord Tyrconnel, and the rest of the army, soon after arrived. Discord blazed anew, Sarsfield and others protested against the presence of Tyrconnel. St. Ruth, a foreigner, could not control their disorders, but whether at his instance, or from mortification, Lord Tyrconnel withdrew.

The English had raised several batteries, mounted with mortars and twenty-four pounders, which had levelled the walls, the castle, and most of the houses in the Irish town. These played from the 21st until the 28th, and left the garrison scarce any shelter. The Irish had only a few field pieces, five and seven pounders, to oppose to the battering artillery of the English, yet fought with extreme bravery and enthusiasm. Daniel M'Neal, an English officer, in a letter to Sir Arthur Rawdon, on the 28th of June, from the camp before Athlone, writes thus: " We have battered the castle all down on this side, and have so cannonaded the enemy's part of Athlone, as, I believe, never town was. All day yesterday and this day, we have played from five batteries, one of eight, one of six, one of five, one of four, and one of three, besides the mortar batteries. We have laid very level a great part of the works to the water side. We have dismounted all the enemy's cannon, so that we can now stand almost at the water side to look over...... The enemy work like horses, in carrying fascines to fill up the breaches, and pass to and fro with more courage than expected..... You may judge how fast we play them with cannon, when our whole artillery is employed. We have lost last night several officers and soldiers in gaining the bridge, which we have now, all to two arches"(*a*). Designing to throw planks over these arches which were broken, the besiegers, on the 28th, pushed a gallery along the bridge, while their batteries kept up a tremendous fire on the opposite works, so that the capture of the place appeared inevitable. The English batteries and trenches were raised so high, that, to use the strong phrase of an Irish officer, a cat could scarce appear without being knocked in the head by great and small shot. In this perilous state a scene occurred, that equals in bravery and contempt of death, the devotion of the Spartans at Thermopylæ, or of our own Richards on the rock of Alicant. The sacrifice of the Spartans was a result of the institutions of Lycurgus, which instilled courage as the first of virtues, and military glory as the first of rewards: that of General Richards was the triumph of military discipline, which enjoins obedience as the first claim of honour on a soldier; but the sacrifice of the Irish on the bridge of Athlone, was a pure act of devotion to their country, on the

(*a*) Rawdon Papers.

impulse of native courage and chivalrous daring. A sergeant and ten men volunteered to throw the planks into the river. The English batteries swept the narrow bridge; a shower of musket balls and hand-grenades covered the approaches with inevitable destruction; the ten volunteers, clothed in complete armour, rushed upon the arches, setting every thing at defiance; but the storm of shot checked their career almost as soon as it was undertaken, and their lifeless bodies lay mutilated on the bridge. A shout of triumph from the English was met on the opposite bank by a still and awful silence, indicating dismay approaching to despair. On a sudden, ten more volunteers, clad also in armour, advance to the arches, undismayed and unchecked by a similar storm;—they destroy the planks, —they tumble them into the stream,—and, until the whole work of destruction is completed, remain firm and undaunted, though falling in quick succession under the showers of balls and grenades;—and now all the planks are removed, and two survivors return, covered with honour, to the shelter of the ruins(*a*). The triumphal shouts of the Irish echoed along their lines, and extended to their camp, two miles distant. Veterans, such as composed De Ginkle's army, were disheartened, but not deterred by this failure. They pushed on a new gallery; but the Irish grenadiers, under a terrible fire from the batteries and from the works, set it on fire, and in half an hour not a trace

(*a*) Clarke, vol. ii. p. 54.

of it remained. This signal success induced security, always dangerous, but especially in presence of an active and enterprising enemy, equally accustomed to successes and reverses. St. Ruth now relieved the garrison with three regiments of infantry and cavalry, and caused the breaches to be filled up with fascines. But the trenches thrown up opposite the fords could not be completed, so numerous was the artillery, so incessant and terrible was the fire, both by day and night, from the opposite bank; and the soldiers had no cover or shelter. Maxwell, a Scotchman, had the guard of these entrenchments to the west of the town, opposite a ford which, if properly defended, would have prevented any passage of the river in that quarter.

St. Ruth finding the works and castle all in ruins, advised D'Usson, on the 29th, to level the rampart on the north side of the town next his camp, that in case of a general assault he might march in a whole battalion abreast to repel the enemy. D'Usson objected, that it was their business to preserve, not to ruin, fortifications; the sounder judgment of the general yielded to that of the governor; the unparalleled bravery of the garrison reconciling him to the opinion of D'Usson. He could not bring himself to think that De Ginkle would venture to cross the broad and rapid stream of the Shannon in the face of an army on the opposite side of the river.

Maxwell, who guarded the ford below the town, had suffered his men to fall asleep, and one of them deserting, apprized the army of the state of the garrison. De Ginkle had resolved upon another desperate effort, and was much encouraged by this information. Three parties were accordingly ordered to attempt a passage; one at the bridge, by throwing planks over it; another through a ford hard by; and another over pontoons, opposite to Maxwell's entrenchments. The bravery of the foreign generals and troops in executing these difficult pieces of service equalled any that modern warfare could exhibit; they plunged into the water breast-high, threw their planks over the bridge, surprised Maxwell's entrenchments, and surmounted every obstacle. The Irish raw recruits made but a feeble resistance, abandoned the works, and fled to the camp; several of their bravest officers were killed, or made prisoners, in attempting to rally them. Colonel A. M'Guire, brave as he was noble, and old Grace, famous for his former defence, were killed; and Oliver O'Gara, the chieftain of Coolavin, was taken prisoner. St. Ruth detached two brigades, under General John Hamilton, to reinforce the garrison, but the enemy were in possession of the ramparts, and drove them back to their camp(*a*).

D'Usson, the French governor, was at breakfast, a mile from the town, when this misfortune occurred. In endeavouring to get back, he was borne down by the runaways, and so rapid were the movements of the enemy, that further detachments from St. Ruth's

(*a*) Memoirs of Berwick, vol. ii. p. 98.

camp arrived too late, and the disaster became irreparable(*a*). Athlone was lost by surprise: so were Bergenopzoom and Schewednitz, two of the strongest fortresses in Europe; but though blame has been attached to St. Ruth, the following extract of a letter from an officer present, Felix O'Neil, to Helena, Countess of Antrim, found on him dead, after the battle of Aughrim, and preserved in the Rawdon Papers, will shew these imputations to be groundless.

"MADAM,—Everybody knows that Athlone could not be thought tenable, either from its situation or works; and that this considered, and the strength of their artillery, no place was ever defended better than it was, till the very day it was lost, by as perfect a surprise as ever was. Whose fault that was, I will not take on me to decide; certain it is, that our men sent thrice for ammunition, and could not have it, and when powder was had, ball was wanting; and that when Major General Maxwell, who was for that day called to, by Cormack O'Neil's men, for ammunition, he asked them often, whether they designed to kill larks (lavracks he called them) ; to which I will add, that the place was so ruined, and the passages so filled up with lumber and stones, that there was not room for two men abreast to pass any way. Besides, they raised their batteries and trenches so very high, that a cat could scarce appear without being knocked on the head."

(*a*) Rawdon Papers.

The Irish officers, on the capture of Athlone, railed at the French as authors of the disaster; the French, no doubt, recriminated the folly of defending a place approachable by so many fords, and requiring the defence of lines so extensive. St. Ruth, on the occurrence of the disaster, retired behind the Suck, and encamped near Ballinasloe, having the river, which is here both wide and deep, in his front. But being a man of great knowledge in his profession, he calculated that the enemy, far superior in numbers as in discipline, would find fords, and compel him to abandon that position. And this he meant shortly to do under any circumstances, his main object being to avoid an engagement, to fall back on the Shannon, and approach Limerick. The diversion in Ireland was ruining the Allies on the Continent; almost the whole of Piedmont and Savoy had fallen into the hands of the French; Luxembourg had taken the town and citadel of Mons, and was carrying all before him in the Netherlands; the combined Dutch and English fleets fled before those of France, and the continuance of the war in Ireland would have weakened the allied armies to the extent of fifty thousand men. The Irish, too, naturally brave, would have acquired discipline and steadiness by a prolongation of the war. St. Ruth, a competent judge of his master's interests, and a profound tactician, saw all this perfectly, but was forced into an engagement by the clamour of the Irish, and the anxiety of some French officers for a speedy termination of the war, to enable them to quit a barbarous country, and to return to the ease, enjoyments, and luxuries of the French capital.

In yielding to their wishes St. Ruth took all the precautions necessary to achieve victory, and, in case of failure, to secure retreat. He was deficient in artillery, having but nine pieces, but his cavalry, about 3000, was equal to any in Europe, and his infantry, though inferior to the horse, had, during ten days, shewn invincible courage within the ruined precincts of Athlone. Position and disposition, with such an army, might afford reasonable chances of success against the veterans of Europe, and, in case of defeat, a secure retreat to the Shannon and Limerick might be relied on. St. Ruth was, therefore, well justified in awaiting the enemy at Aughrim, where, in obedience to the necessities of his position, he resolved to give De Ginkle battle.

The hill of Kilcommodon, about five miles from Ballinasloe, is accessible, from the Leinster side, by two narrow passes only; one, the road from Ballinasloe to Banagher, passing under the old castle of Aughrim, at the northern extremity; the other, a by-road, running nearly parallel past the house and demesne of Uracree, over the declivity at the south. The whole of the intermediate space, fronting the hill on the eastern side, is occupied by a strip of bog, having a rivulet in the midst, the morass being about half a mile in width.

Between the foot of the hill and the edge of the

bog, a considerable space intervened, intersected with hedges and ditches, affording great shelter to any force occupying the hill. Nevertheless, St. Ruth's position was not without several drawbacks. Tyrconnel, anticipating disaster and disunion, had retired from the camp to Limerick. The Connaught levies, to the amount of 6000 men, on the eve of the expected battle, had fled to their bogs and mountains: still there remained 11,000 infantry and 5000 cavalry, men of resolute hearts and disciplined valour, to fight for their estates, liberties, and religion, in the last entrenchments of their country; and St. Ruth resolved to try the issue of a battle. Retreat would have left Galway, and the whole of Connaught, in the hands of the enemy. Clare, Limerick, and Kerry only would remain to the Royal army. A battle lost could scarce be more injurious, and even defeat could hardly be expected to terminate in disaster, as the bogs skirted the line by which he should retire as far as Banagher. His admirable cavalry would check the pursuit of the enemy, and the broad and deep stream of the Shannon, no where fordable, would cover his retrogade movement on the left bank of the river.

When he had made up his mind to try the chances of war, he omitted nothing that could insure victory. He lined the ditches and hedges in front with infantry, having levelled as much of them

(a) Clarke, vol. ii. p. 457. Quincy, vol. ii. p. 462.

as, in case of emergency, would enable his cavalry to charge the enemy whilst storming these natural entrenchments. He directed the infantry, when forced to abandon their position, to retreat from hedge to hedge, and keep up an incessant fire on the front and flanks of the assailants, the ditches being disposed in a curve, which enabled them to take this advantage. Of his seven field pieces, two were placed to rake the pass leading to the Castle of Aughrim, two to command the pass of Uracree, and the remainder on the hill of Kilcommodon, to rake the enemy's centre; and the cavalry were placed in ravines on the right and left, behind the infantry, so as to be ready at a moment's notice to charge.

Story puts a ridiculous speech into the mouth of the French General, before the commencement of the action. St. Ruth is made to boast of his achievements in the persecution of the Protestants in France, in the exaltation of the Catholic Church, and in her defence against the assaults of hell and heresy(*a*). The noble mind of that gallant officer could never have stooped to such contemptible gasconading. He was bred in camps, a stranger to the spirit and language of theological rancour; ignorant besides of both the English and Irish languages, and could not have delivered any personal address to his troops. He may, perhaps, in written orders, read at

(*a*) Story's Continuation, p. 124.

the heads of the regiments, have reminded them that the safety of their country and religion depended on their valour, and that they should on that day conquer, or continue for ever the slaves of Englishmen. But it was not on speeches that this gallant officer depended to animate his men; but on his noble carriage, his serene confidence, and cool direction of the movements to be made, according to the emergencies of the occasion.

On the memorable 12th of July, 1691, the English army approached, in the orderly march and firm array which became them, as veterans who had learned the art of war in the campaigns of Flanders. Their General viewed the position of the Irish, was struck with its strength, and would have postponed his attack till the 13th, in order to ascertain more minutely the position, but for an affair of outposts, which precipitated a general action. The English had pushed on a party of cavalry to reconnoitre the right of the Irish, a skirmish had ensued, and alternate retreats and advances swelled the number of combatants, until a great portion of the left of the English were drawn into the engagement. It then became a question with the English officers, whether they should fight the battle then, or draw off the troops engaged. General Mackay's opinion, to press on a battle, lest the Irish should retreat during the night, prevailed. In this posture of affairs, the left wing of the English pressing on the right of the Irish, while the centre and left remained still disengaged, the decisive action of Aughrim commenced. "A party of our foot (writes Story) marched up to their ditches, all strongly guarded with musketeers, and their horse advantageously posted to sustain them. Here we fired one upon another for a considerable time, and the Irish behaved themselves like men of another nation, defending their ditches stoutly, for they would maintain one side, till our men put their pieces over at the other, and then having lines of communication from one ditch to another, they would presently post themselves again, and flank us. This occasioned great firing on both sides, which continued on the left an hour and a half, ere the right of our army, or centre, engaged, except with their cannon, that played on both sides." Thus, for a long time, the Irish maintained their hedges with great valour, and repulsed the enemy on every attack, until the English, by superiority of numbers, were at length enabled to extend their left, so as to threaten to outflank the Irish right. St. Ruth, viewing the battle from the hill, thereupon ordered a battalion from the second line of the left to the point of attack; but the orders were mistaken, and a battalion of the first line, in front of the bog near the castle, was detached to the extremity of the position. The English centre, taking advantage of the opening, plunged into the bog in front, waded the river to their waists, and reached the hedges, the foremost of which they carried under a heavy fire; but being charged by the Irish horse, through the openings contrived for that purpose, were soon after repulsed, with great slaughter, and driven into the middle of the morass, two of their principal officers being taken prisoners; and the fortune of the battle seemed to turn in favour of the Irish. The spirit of these brave veterans, however, being raised by the conviction that they had to do with men no less resolute than themselves, the conflict was renewed with extreme valour, so that no assaults were ever made with greater fury, or sustained with greater obstinacy, than those which ensued, especially on the foot, who not only maintained their posts, and defended their hedges, but repulsed their enemies many times, and took several prisoners of distinction, insomuch that they looked upon the victory as, in a manner, certain; and St. Ruth was transported with joy to see the foot, of whom he had so mean an opinion, behave themselves so well, and perform actions worthy of the best discipline. The conflict had now lasted two hours; the right wing of the Irish remained firm in its position, the centre was victorious, and the left untouched; but the English horse, who had hitherto been held in check by the battalion that guarded the pass to the castle of Aughrim, finding it undefended, took courage, and carried the causeway: while, at the same time, the infantry, by the help of hurdles, got over the bog, and began to form in front of the Irish left. St. Ruth, who watched with eagle eye every movement, seeing disorder in that quarter, and being informed of the cause, put himself at the head of his reserve of cavalry, "which being extreme good, would have dispersed the few squadrons of the enemy, who as yet were but forming," and galloped down the hill opposite to the English batteries facing his centre, exclaiming, "They are beaten." At this moment he was struck by a cannon shot and fell dead from his horse. His fall was like that of Turenne at Salsbach, of Tilly at Nordlinghen—it was the death of the soul of the army. Had he lived, the general opinion is, that his admirable disposition, coolness, and bravery, would have gained the victory. He had been in Ireland one month and four days only, and in so short a time never had affections between officer and troops been so powerfully excited. His admiration of the constancy of the Irish, in their resolution to maintain a war upon such unequal terms, having such a formidable power against them, and so little aid from France, often broke out in expressions full of sympathy; and these had won him the love of the people in an inexpressible degree. His cotemporaries, who had witnessed his great mind, his cool and calculating science, his heroic courage, never ceased to deplore his loss. Cut off in his early bloom from high command in the French armies—from honour and glory—from the renown which accompanied Turenne and Luxemburg, Villans and Vendome—from a monument on St. Denis, or in the Invalides—his mortal remains lie hidden and unnoticed on the hill of Kilcommodon. No storied stone commiserates his early doom; the peasant often brushes the morning dew off the turf under which he lies, but knows not that he treads o'er the grave of a hero.

When St. Ruth fell, a cloak was thrown over his body, to conceal the disaster; but the first squadron of the Guards, paralyzed by the loss of this great man, halted. The stroke reached the remotest squadrons with electric rapidity. The whole of the cavalry stood aghast, exposed to the fire of the English battery on the other side of the bog. D'Usson and De Tesse, next in command, at a distance, ignorant of the fall of the commander-in-chief, could not give immediate directions. The English cavalry, in the mean time, formed under the castle of Aughrim, charged, and at once broke the second line of the left of the Irish, weakened by the detachment of the battalion sent to the right in the early part of the engagement. After standing thus paralyzed for a few minutes the whole of the Irish cavalry became seized with a panic terror, and fled from the field, taking the road to Loughrea. The infantry on the right and centre for some time maintained their ground, but, attacked in front and rear, they were shortly broken, and fled in all directions, taking, for most part, to the bogs, to avoid the exterminating swords of the cavalry, who gave no quarter. The humanity of the foreign officers, after some time, checked the slaughter; 450 prisoners, comprising many gentlemen of rank and fortune, who, probably, were not sufficiently alert to take refuge in the bogs, were made prisoners. Night stopped the pursuit. The Irish lost 4,000 men(*a*); the English, according to Story, 1,700 killed and wounded(*b*); but, as partizans generally magnify the loss of their opponents and diminish their own, the killed and wounded of the English may fairly be set down as about 2,000 men. Quincy states them as 2,700(*c*).

De Ginkle's army remained some days encamped in the neighbourhood. They collected their dead and gave them military interment. The bodies of the Irish, lacerated by dogs and mangled by birds of prey, became objects of horror and contagion. For half a century after, the heights of Kilcommodon were whitened with their bones, a remarkable instance of the barbarous practices of civil war, in which even polished nations deem themselves exempted from the ordinary calls of humanity. An affecting incident is related of a greyhound belonging to an Irish officer, which watched his master's remains by night and day, as long as the surrounding

---

(*a*) " Les Irlandois dont l'infanterie avoit fait des marvelles perdirent dans cette occasion environ trois ou quatre mille hommes. M. de St. Ruth y fut tuè d'un boulet de cannon, après avoir donné toutes les marques d'un grand homme, et d'un grande capacitè."—Quincy, vol. ii. p. 462.

(*b*) Story.

(*c*) Quincy, p. 462. Clarke's Memoirs of James II. vol. ii. p. 458.

carcases supplied him with food; and, although the dogs of the country frequented the field, and became fierce from devouring human flesh, the greyhound would never suffer them to approach the dead body of his master. He thus continued till the January following, when a soldier accidentally going that way, the dog, fearing he came to disturb his charge, flew at him, and the soldier shot him. By incidents of this kind the detailed horrors of civil war are sometimes relieved. The mind delights to rest on even the better qualities of the brute creation, after so many repulsive examples of the ferocity of men.

The achievement of this great victory was not followed up with any commensurate activity by De Ginkle. Whatever success had hitherto attended his standard was the result, rather of pressure from circumstances, than of any military genius of his own. He had been forced by his council of war into the storming of Athlone, and into the fight at Kilcommodon; and now, instead of pushing on for Limerick, he considered that the regular routine of war required him not to leave Galway in his rear, though its maintenance was evidently dependent on that of the former and more important place. He accordingly marched on Galway, and consumed seven days in that movement, though the place was only thirty miles distant. Galway had a garrison of seven regiments, some good outworks, and a few great guns,

(a) Story, p. 147.

and might have held out, so as to give time to repair the fortifications of Limerick, to reorganize the army, and perhaps to prolong the war until the rains of winter should have driven the English to their quarters ; but disunion, treachery, and selfishness, betrayed the defence. Lieutenant-General D'Usson was for holding out, but Lords Clanrickard, Dillon, and Enniskillen, who had great influence with the garrison, wishing to save their estates, and make terms for themselves, sacrificed their public duty to their personal interests, and before the coming up of the enemies' cannon, which was yet in Athlone, and without which there was no forcing the place, advised a surrender, and Ulic Burke, and other officers, basely deserted, and discovered to the besiegers the weakest parts of the outworks.

Baldearg O'Donnell, whose name has been already mentioned as an Irish partizan of Spanish birth, was at this time in Mayo, whither he had retreated after the battle of Aughrim. He had received directions to march on Galway, for the purpose of strengthening the garrison, and was now advanced as far as Cong on his way to their relief, when the English, guided by Burke and other deserters, passed the fords on the river of Galway, and intercepted all communication with the town. O'Donnell might now have cut off the supplies of the English, broken up the roads, alarmed their quarters, and done many effective services; but he remained inactive and stationary at Cong.

This Hiberno-Spaniard, who, in the descent of three generations of foreign intermarriages, had degenerated from the illustrious race of the Kinel Connel, possessed neither the spirit of his Irish progenitors, nor the pride of his adopted countrymen. Before the disaster at Aughrim, his folly had speculated on the revival of the power of the O'Donnells in his own person, and the recovery of their former possessions. There was a prophecy that an O'Donnell with a red spot on his cheek, would revive the glories of the Kinel Connel, emancipate Ireland from British thraldom, and restore their forfeited estates to the ancient natives. When in the service of Spain he had been designated as the hero of this prophecy, being marked with a peculiar blemish on his face (whence his Irish soubriquet of *Bealdearg*, or "Redmouth"), and had been invited over to Ireland in 1690, as the expected deliverer. He was most probably the grandson of Caffre O'Donnell, the brother of Rory, Earl of Tyrconnel, who fled to Spain in 1607. He landed at Kinsale, when James was on his flight, and got letters of recommendation from the abdicating monarch to the Lord Lieutenant. He was appointed to the command of the new levies in Ulster, but without money, clothes, arms, or ammunition; an ignorant rabble, degraded by superstition, dupes to fortune-tellers, with the idle retainers and followers of the Kinel Connel, flocked to his standard, and 8000 undisciplined troops gave some apparent strength to the cause of James, but produced weakness and disorganization by plunder and insubordination. They lived at discretion, ruined the inhabitants, and prevented the regular troops from receiving supplies which they would otherwise have had from the people. Tyrconnel had neither the means nor inclination of checking these disorders. He dreaded the native Irish, encouraged insubordination in O'Donnell's forces, drafted some of the recruits into the regular troops, and left the rest to guard the fords of the Shannon. He also encouraged jealousy between Baldearg and Gordon O'Neal, the son of Sir Phelim O'Neal, a very gallant officer, the reputed chieftain of the great rival sept of O'Neal.

(a) The O'Donnels, who remained in Ireland after the flight of the Earl, lapsed to poverty, and but few of them have preserved any authentic traces of their descent. Ignorance, and money, and the shameless compliances of dishonest heralds, have framed pedigrees for them, that have no foundation. Rory O'Donnel, first Earl, is represented as having had a son, grandson, and great grandson, second, third, and fourth earls of Tyrconnel, whereas Rory's only son died without issue, in the flower of youth. The alleged great grandson is stated to have had a daughter, married to Brian Ballagh O'Morcha, who died 100 years before such a person could have been born. On the failure of issue in Rory O'Donnel, the title of Tyrconnel devolved on his brother Caffre, who fled also to Spain. Caffre was married to Rose O'Doherty, sister of Sir Caher O'Doherty, who, after the death of Caffre, married Owen Roe O'Neal, and was buried, with her eldest son, Hugh O'Donnel, in the Irish Franciscan convent of Louvain. The second son, Caffre Oge O'Donnel, on the death of his father, became Earl of Tyrconnel; on his death, the title devolved on his son Hugh, a distinguished officer in the service of Spain. The writer of those pages has in his possession a silk

Baldearg's inactivity at Cong was the result, not
of want of ability, but of treachery; he was in communication
with De Ginkle, had proposed desertion,
and only delayed going over till the terms should be

handkerchief, with a Latin thesis on divinity printed on it, dated
at Salamanca, A.D. 1672, dedicated to this Hugh O'Donnel. This
Hugh O'Donnel, in my mind, was the identical Balldarag O'Donnel
who came to Ireland in 1790. The O'Donnels of the present day,
or their genealogist, have no memorial or knowledge of his pedigree
or origin. Neal Garbh, the supposed ancestor of the O'Donnels
of Larkfield, Greyfield, Newport, and Oldcastle, had betrayed
Hugh Roe; had killed Manus, his brother, with his own hand; afterwards
betrayed the English, was found guilty of high treason,
and died in the Tower of London, under sentence of death. He had
a son, called Naghten; whether he died without issue I know not;
but the O'Donnels of the present day cannot, by grants, inquisitions,
or other memorials, trace their pedigree for five generations.
I am sorry that they should be reduced to derive their descent
from such a traitor as Neal Garbh. The descent from Colonel
Manus O'Donnel and Hugh Boy O'Donnel, fictitious sons of Neal
Garbh, are manifest fabrications, Neal Garb having had no sons
of that name. Five generations are said to have intervened from
the death of Neal Garbh, in 1610, to the death of Lewis O'Donnel,
in 1810, a period of 200 years; another manifest proof of fiction.
Of the O'Donnels in the service of France and Spain, no notice is
taken by their genealogist, nor of Connel O'Donnel, the head of the
family in 1689, who was Lord Lieutenant of the County of Donegal.
He was the father of Hugh O'Donnel, of Larkfield, called
Earl O'Donnel by the common people, and who died in 1754. He
had three sons: Connel, a Field Marshal in the Austrian service,
who, on Downs being wounded, commanded the Imperial army
at the battle of Torgau; John, also a General in the same service,
and Constantine, the grandfather of the present Hugh O'Donnel,
of Greyfield.

adjusted. He had demanded an earldom, the estates of his family, and a sum of money to buy over his followers. It was not in the power of the General to concede the Earldom, or the restoration of the forfeited lands, but what he could he did; he bestowed on the traitor a commission in the English service, and a sum of money. As, however, the fidelity of traitors is always doubtful, in order to fix him in the new interests, his desertion was published in the *Dublin Gazette*, and his treachery made known to the Irish. Upon such a mind, disgrace and infamy could have little effect; but the fear of assassination, often the lot of traitors, induced him to complain of the publication of a treaty intended to be secret, until the men should be gained over, and until time and circumstances should extenuate his infamy. 1,200 men only adhered to him: with these he joined an English corps under Lord Granard, and aided in the reduction of Lough-Glynn, Ballymote, and Sligo. After the capitulation of Limerick he and a Colonel Wilson were the only deserters who were continued in the commission of colonels in the pay of William. O'Donnell proffered his services in Flanders. The opportunity was past in which his services were useful. Distrust invariably accompanies traitors; contempt pursues them with increasing reproaches; the troops under their command lose all confidence in them; at the military mess they are wounded by sarcastic allusions to perfidy and dishonour, which they cannot resent; O'Donnell's proffered services in Flanders were rejected by the calculating caution and prudence of William. The spirit of treachery that had induced desertion in Ireland, might induce the delivery of an important post in Flanders to the French. The stain of Popery, also, marked him out as unworthy of trust; for, base though he was, it does not appear that he abandoned the faith of his fathers. A renegade in Turkey might acquire station and confidence, but, in free countries, employments seldom remunerate the disgrace of a mercenary change of religion: the stain of such an apostacy is indelible. A resolution of the Parliament of England against the employment of Papists in the army, deprived O'Donnell of his commission, and consigned to poverty, during the remainder of his life, this base betrayer of his sovereign.

It is painful to enumerate the instances of desertion with which this period of our history is unhappily so rife; but the historian would neglect a duty who failed to animadvert on the infamy of some men of rank, who, in these base transactions, set the example. Lord Clanrickard, inheriting neither the courage nor the loyalty of his ancestor, the great Earl of St. Albans, compounded his honour for personal security; and, quitting the service of James, remained at Galway, though, by the capitulation, he was at liberty to march to Limerick. Lord Riverston, who had been raised, from an humble reputation at the bar, to a judgeship and a peerage, by the favour of James, calculating on the failure of the Irish, long before their affairs became desperate, endeavoured to secure his fortune and rank, by communicating the secrets of his office, as Secretary at War, to the generals of William. Daly, also promoted to the Bench, meditated treachery under the mask of fidelity; and kept up a correspondence with William's government, for several months before the battle of Aughrim, in which he proposed the surrender of Galway. When the English army approached Dunsandle, his residence, conscious of his treachery, and apprehensive of punishment—or, perhaps, to cloak his communications with the enemy—he desired that a party should be sent to him, seemingly to force him from his habitation. Others of the officers openly deserted, or kept up a secret correspondence, apprizing the enemy of the preparations, state, and condition of the army; but the common soldiers, uninfluenced by the example of officers—undismayed by reverses—continued steady to their colours, and maintained a purity of principle and a steadiness of attachment to their king and country, almost unexampled in the history of civil wars.

From the fall of Galway, the peace party in the Irish camp derived new vigour, and corresponded with the enemy, to ascertain the terms they might procure. Tyrconnel saw, in this anxiety, the germ of a ruinous peace; and that the existing dissensions were pregnant with submission without favourable terms. Though bent with age, and inert from corpulency, he assumed no inconsiderable degree of activity in the repairing the fortifications of Limerick, establishing magazines, and enforcing discipline. He formed an entrenched camp under the cannon of the place, and made the officers and soldiers (first shewing the example himself) take an oath of fidelity, embracing a resolution to defend His Majesty's rights to the last, and never to surrender without his consent. He despatched an express to St. Germain, to beg speedy succour, or leave to make terms. In all these measures he was powerfully seconded by Lord Lucan, " whose intentions were always right, and zealous for the King's service;" but their efforts were unhappily counteracted by treachery and discord, on which the English general relied more than on the number and valour of his troops.

In the midst of these preparations, on the 11th August, Tyrconnel, after a dinner with Lieutenant-General D'Usson, the commander-in-chief, was seized with a fit of apoplexy. He came to his senses and speech, and languished, without any hope of recovery, till the 14th of that month, when death put an end to his sufferings. James, in his Memoirs, gives him the credit of endeavouring, during his illness, to procure union among the conflicting parties; but Burnet says, he advised all those who came to see him on his deathbed, to submit to William, and make the best terms they could; and he also mentions, that he advised

(a) Clarke's Memoirs, vol. ii. p. 462.
(b) Burnet, vol. ii. p. 80.

the French not to send any more troops to Ireland. His friends gave out that he was poisoned by Sarsfield and the French, a calumny which the high character of the former, and the chivalrous spirit of the latter, fully refuted. His enemies more justly ascribed his death to chagrin, and a broken constitution.

Tyrconnel was the Founder, in a great degree, of the Irish Brigade—his character is an important part of their history. It has been handed down to posterity in such various colours, and flattery and malignity have had such a share in distorting and misrepresenting it, that a fair portrait of this singular personage has never been presented to the public. He was the eighth son of Sir William Talbot, a barrister. Born to no inheritance but his talents, he obtained a commission in the Irish army after the insurrection of 1641. He afterwards went to Spain with the troops exiled by Cromwell, and thence to Flanders, following the fortunes of the exiled Stuarts. He there ingratiated himself with the Duke of York, by a handsome figure, insinuating address, and chivalrous loyalty. After the Restoration, by Court favour or play, he was enabled to purchase large estates in Ireland. Here he became enamoured of Miss Elizabeth Hamilton. Paintings of Aurora, or poetic descriptions of the goddess of Spring, could give but a faint image of that celebrated lady. The Graces had put a finishing hand to the symmetry of her figure, and to the elegance of her movements. The vivacity of her eyes, the rosy hue of her countenance, her sparkling wit, the charms of her conversation, the purity of her mind, the elevation of her sentiments, captivated every person that came within the sphere of her attractions. Talbot saw and loved, and his perseverance in this amour gives a good example of the ardour and energy of the man in all the affairs of life. The Duke of York's favour, an ample fortune, the prospect of a peerage, promised success to his addresses. Refusals, coldness, and contempt, could not relax his ardour. He endeavoured, but failed to emancipate himself from the charms which Venus, in the form of this enchantress, had thrown round him. The frost of reserve, and avowed partiality for Phillibert, Count de Grammont, only added fuel to the fires with which he was consumed. He called to his aid his two brothers, one the celebrated Peter Talbot, Almoner to the Queen, and a great matchmaker, the other a secularized friar, who, according to Count Hamilton, retained the licentiousness of his order, and the reputation attached to it. Grammont's uneasiness at the superior fortune and influence of his rival, was relieved by a quarrel between Talbot and Ormond, occasioned by the ardour of the former in espousing the cause of his plundered countrymen, and in endeavouring to procure restitution of their estates to many who had been deprived of them by open violence, or the forms of law in the Court of Claims. Though he occasionally received gratuities from those whom his influence rescued from poverty, their gratitude or policy abstained from imputations of corruption. He stood alone in the breach against the assaults of power, and religious persecution. Ormond, the great plunderer and persecuter of these times, expressed his dissatisfaction in terms of haughtiness and insult; Talbot's pride retorted in terms of asperity, and afterwards refused an apology, rejected terms of reconciliation, and he was sent to the Tower. Released from confinement by the influence of friends, he renewed his addresses. The success of his rival did not cool his friendship for the house of Strabane, and in every vicissitude of his fortunes his early love seemed to influence his partiality for the brothers of Miss Hamilton. Raised to the peerage, and to the Lord Lieutenancy of Ireland, by imprudent zeal for his master he injured his cause; appointed Roman Catholic Sheriffs and Lord Lieutenants for almost every county in Ireland, many of them paupers, without birth, education, or property; and excluded Protestants from all power and situations of trust and emolument, so as to alienate the whole body. He had, it is true, great difficulties to encounter. In the race for petty posts, honours, and emoluments, the ambition, vanity, and hunger of a party, spoliated at the Restoration, had no bounds, knew no restraints, and in the rage of disappointment thwarted his measures, exulted in his difficulties, and exaggerated his defeats. Yet he was not altogether devoid of conduct or moderation. He would not deprive the Protestant clergy of their churches or livings, nor admit the Catholic bishops into the House of Lords.

Talbot inherited the hatred and contempt of the

English of Ireland for the native Irish. Like most men who rise from humble beginnings, he was haughty, proud, and imperious. Courage he possessed in a high degree, had distinguished himself by numerous acts of bravery in the wars of Flanders, and had been a volunteer in the famous naval engagement between Van Tromp and the Duke of York. His ambition was unbounded; his avarice considerable, but this, indeed, was more the passion of his Duchess than his own; his friendships were said to be inconstant, but they appear to have been steady. To the connexion between England and Ireland he was unalterably attached. To this attachment, after the affair of the Boyne, and to the desire of preserving his estates, he sacrificed his loyalty to James, his own safety, and the hopes and prospects of his party in Ireland. The English praised him as a lover of peace, yet confiscated all his estates, which, if he had lived a month longer, would have been preserved by the treaty of Limerick. Tyrconnel died without issue male, and his nephew inherited his title of Earl, the dukedom being entailed on the male issue only. The Earl pined in poverty, a poor dependant at the Court of St. Germain; his son attained the rank of a lieutenant-general in the armies of France, but died without issue, and in him the earldom of Tyrconnel in the Talbot family became extinct.

On Tyrconnel's death D'Usson, the senior officer, assumed the command at Limerick; but Sarsfield attended to all the details, superintended the repair of the fortifications, the providing ammunition and stores, and watched the motions and defeated the designs of the peace party: his vigilance and activity admitted of no relaxation; his ardour inspired the troops with confidence, and dissipated the dismay produced by the disaster at Aughrim.

But activity and zeal could not counteract discord, treachery, and desertion. Henry Luttrel, Sarsfield's bosom friend and partisan, had a principal command in the cavalry, and had been ordered to meet the garrison of Galway at Six-mile Bridge; here this base traitor entered into a negotiation with the English officer commanding the escort to betray Limerick; and as the enemy approached, kept up a treasonable correspondence, with that intent. His practices were kept secret, and remained undiscovered, until a letter, addressed to him by Sebastian, the secretary of De Ginkle, was, through mistake of the messenger, put into the hands of Sarsfield. It revealed the treason(*a*). Luttrel had many connexions and adherents; he had been a powerful and zealous partizan of Sarsfield on former occasions. In the existing relaxation of military discipline, it might have been dangerous to arrest, and illegal, in the absence of the king, to execute the sentence of a court-martial. Between prudence and personal friendship on one side, and duty on the other, Sarsfield's firmness was put to a severe trial; but his sense of

(*a*) Story, p. 189.

duty and honour triumphed over the solicitations of personal feeling. Luttrel's arrest, a bold and decisive measure, stamped the loyalty of Lord Lucan with a zeal not to be damped by personal friendship, nor relaxed by personal danger. Luttrel was tried by court-martial, found guilty, and reserved to abide the king's pleasure. The surrender of Limerick saved him from an ignominious fate, but reserved him for an untimely death some years after, by the hand of an assassin, an enthusiast probably, who sought to avenge the wrongs of his country in the blood of the traitor. His memory has ever since been infamous and hateful in the recollections of the Irish people: this retribution has even been extended to the name of his family, who long endured the execration earned by their base ancestor. The death of Henry Laws Luttrel, the second Lord Carhampton, the last of his descendants, obliterated from the Irish peerage the stain of an earldom purchased by services so odious; but time cannot erase the original blot from the pages of Irish history.

On the 21st of July, Galway had been surrendered, and though all the rules of war prescribed an immediate march to Limerick, to prevent the re-organization of the Irish army, and the repair of its fortifications of that city, Ginkle did not approach it till the 15th of August, calculating, probably, upon effecting, by the treachery and desertion of the Irish officers, what William had failed to accomplish by force and skill, and with a better appointed army.

From the 15th to the 25th was consumed in tampering, publishing proclamations of pardon, encouraging desertion, and procuring information. A commission had been found in Tyrconnel's papers, appointing Sir Alexander Fitton, Sir Richard Nagle, and Francis Plowden, who were of the peace party, Lords Justices. These civilians could have little fluence amidst the din of arms, and Sarsfield's energy and resolution had determined the garrison to defend the works to the last extremity. Accounts from France also, announced great preparations at Brest to send reinforcements to Ireland. De Ginkle thus found, when the rainy season was at hand, that he must venture on a siege, difficult in its operation, and doubtful in its issue. His orders, probably, were, to hazard it under all circumstances. On the 27th, 28th, and 29th, the English, therefore, began to erect their batteries, and on the 30th they opened their fire, which was returned by the Irish, with fewer guns, but with steadiness and resolution.

At the same time, eighteen English ships came up the river, within cannon shot of the town. The united fire of this fleet, and of the batteries, soon reduced both the English and Irish towns to a heap of ruins. But although the breach was practicable, the besiegers delayed giving the assault, relying on the effects of dissension within the town, it being notorious that great divisions prevailed, some of the principal officers seeking an accommodation, and others resolved to die in the breach rather than surrender

On the 7th, 8th, and 9th of September the English plyed their great guns and mortars incessantly, but neither the fires in the town, nor the thunder of the batteries, which were mounted with forty pieces of heavy cannon, could relax the efforts of the garrison, who were constantly employed in extinguishing the fires, raising breastworks behind the breaches, returning the enemy's shot, and making sallies to destroy the trenches; so that on the 13th De Ginkle was constrained to dispatch Colonel Earl to King William to apprize him of the difficulties of the siege, and the probability of his being compelled to raise it. But desertion prevailed to a great extent, and communications were kept up with the disaffected in the town, whereby the English general had information of the state, and expectations, and disunion of the garrison.

Brigadier Clifford, an officer of Dragoons, was suspected of treachery, but owing to the disunion among the principal officers, was continued in command of 1500 horse, to guard the passes of the Shannon; for Lieutenant-General D'Usson, the governor, had ordered the Irish cavalry out of the town to the Clare side of the river, on which side it was open for reinforcements and provisions; calculating justly that as long as the enemy remained on the opposite bank, they could have no chance of succeeding in face of a garrison so resolute and provided. De Ginkle, seeing the difficulty in the same point of view, resolved on posting a portion of his army on the opposite bank, in which attempt he was favoured by the negligence or treachery of Clifford. During the night of the 15th of September the English threw a bridge of boats across the river, two miles above the town, and about three miles distant from the camp of the Irish horse, commanded by Lieutenant-General Sheldon. At daylight the English were passing over. Clifford was not very forward in the matter: he brought down his dragoons on foot, made some show of opposition, and then fell back without giving Sheldon the slightest notice of the passage, intending, probably, that he should be surprized and cut to pieces, but Sheldon, by great address, and by stopping the enemy at a narrow pass, effected his escape to Six Mile Bridge. But a fair and impartial court martial could scarce be formed amidst the existing heats and contentions. It was proved that Clifford had had notice of the enemy being at work at the bridge; he admitted negligence, pleaded innocence, and was honourably acquitted.

But though the besiegers had crossed the river, and erected a fort to secure their new position, this division of their army into two bodies, connected by a temporary bridge, made their situation extremely perilous. The portion on the right bank of the river might be overwhelmed before it could receive succour from the left, and *vice versâ*. A council of war, on the 17th, decided that the siege should be turned into a blockade—that the resources of the garrison should be cut off, and a surrender expected from famine. With this view the heavy cannon were removed on board ship from the trenches, and the crews of the ships of war directed to destroy the harvest on the Clare side. The removal and embarkation of the great guns occupied the 19th and 20th; and, for the purpose of destroying the harvest, a large body of horse and foot were ordered to the right bank of the river on the 22nd. On their approaching the works opposite Thomond Gate, a sally of 800 picked men, under Colonel Lacy, was ordered to check their approach. This was effected with great valour and good success for a time, till, overpowered by a continued supply of both horse and foot, Lacy was forced to give way. He, however, rallied again, and re-possessed himself of the ground he had lost; but the enemy—still bringing up fresh troops—forced him to retire towards the gate, which the mayor of the town, as it is said (apprehending that the English might come in, pell-mell with them), imprudently shut against his own people, whereby the greatest part of them were cut to pieces.

Quincy states, that the order to shut the gates was given by the governor, D'Usson, and such an error appears not unlikely to have been committed by that officer. To his mistakes, more the result of indolence than of want of spirit, may be ascribed most of the chief disasters of the campaign. The surprise of Athlone. where he was governor, had found him asleep. On the fall of St. Ruth at Aughrim, being next in command, he had suffered the battle to be lost for want of orders. At Galway he had made a hopeless defence, instead of marching direct on a tenable position at Limerick; and now, at Limerick, on a sudden and groundless apprehension, Quincy reports that he gave the order for this fatal measure of closing the gates, which exposed Lacy's corps to be cut off under the very walls, and so disheartened the garrison as to precipitate the negotiation for a surrender, which, if it had been delayed for but a few days, the result might have been a total alteration of the whole complexion of the King's cause in Ireland. A capitulation was now openly discussed. The promised aids from France had not arrived. The French officers, disgusted at the want of discipline— having no common interest with the natives—and wishing to return to their own country—were the strongest advocates for submitting. Sarsfield, brave, generous, attached to his country, chivalrous in loyalty, conscious of the bravery of his countrymen, urged that the works were untouched, the winter at hand, the town suplied, and the French fleet hourly expected. But these representations were met by the selfish arguments of the French, and the interested suggestions of those traitors in the camp, who had been bought over by the gold and promises of the enemy; and a formal resolution to surrender was put in their council, and carried. The constancy of Sarsfield now gave way: he apprehended, probably, that some of the gates or works would be betrayed to the enemy; that the whole garrison would be involved in the horrors of a town taken by storm; and that no terms could, in that event, be made for the religion or nation. Overpowered by such considerations, he ultimately acquiesced in the wishes of the majority. But the native troops still held out for defence. They had every thing to lose, and nothing to gain, by accommodation; they had no estates to secure; the Acts of Settlement and Explanation had not restored to them any portion of their former forfeitures; and they doggedly relied on the oath taken by the army not to surrender without James's permission. An appeal was thereupon made to the Archbishops of Armagh and Cashel, then in the Irish camp at Six Mile Bridge. These ecclesiastics, apprehensive of the extirpation of their religion, in case of Limerick being taken by storm, replied that the King's permission might be presumed, considering their extreme want, and the impossibility of apprizing the King of it in time for deliverance. D'Usson and the French officers, eager to return to France, urged treating with the enemy; so that by the absolution of the bishops, the desertion of the foreigners, and the clamour of the Anglo-Irish, no resource remained to the native Irish, who were thus compelled into a negotiation for terms at a time when they had reason to expect a French fleet, and great supplies of arms, ammunition, and clothes.

On the night of the 23rd of August a cessation of hostilities was concluded, and on the day following was continued for three days. Lord Lucan and

General Wachop proposed to treat for the nation at large, and for that purpose required to send to the Irish horse camp for the bishops and peers who were there, to aid in the negotiation. Sarsfield had already proposed an indemnity for the past, free liberty of worship, enjoyment of estates, admission to all employments, civil and military, and equality with the Protestants iu all corporations. De Ginkle was fully aware of the heats and divisions of the Irish camp, and though directed by William to conclude the war on any terms, he rejected these proposals, calculating that discord and treachery would induce the acceptance of terms less advantageous. On the 28th, Sarsfield, Wachop, the two Archbishops, Colonel Purcell, and three Barristers, Sir Garret Dillon, Sir Theobald Butler, and John Browne of Westport, men of limited knowledge and confined capacities, negotiated the articles of surrender. Any degree of tact in diplomacy would have secured their estates to the whole of the Irish, as well to those in arms, at home and abroad, as to the representatives of those who had been killed in the progress of the war; but the officers were skilled in military matters, not in civil affairs; the ecclesiastics were versed in theology, but were simple in the affairs of the world; the lawyers, who had never attained eminence, might have shewn some talents for declamation in the Courts, but were utterly incompetent to manage the concerns of a nation. In violation of all decency and common justice they allowed in the second of the articles the exclusion of all prisoners of war from the enjoyment of their estates, and also of all persons beyond seas, unless they returned within eight months, and took the oath of allegiance to William.

Had the Irish Commissioners relied, as they ought to have done, on the numbers and resolution of the garrison, the approach of the rainy season, and the expected succours from France, they might have had the whole nation included in the terms. The second article of the Treaty consigned many illustrious Irishmen to poverty and perpetual exile. The capacities and courage of some of them were crowned with fortune in foreign service, but many others pined in misery, aggravated by the recollection of former opulence, and humbled by the indifference and contempt which invariably pursues the fallen gentleman. The names of a few whose estates were thus sacrificed, through the incapacity of the Irish Commissioners, will excite the sympathy of the reader, even after a lapse of 150 years : Richard Duke of Tyrconnel; his nephew, Richard Earl of Tyrconnel; Donough Earl of Clancarty ; Lords Clare, Galway, Galmoy, Enniskillen, Slane, Lucan, Kilmallock, Mountcashel, Brittas; Sir William Talbot, Sir Neal O'Neal, Sir John Fitzgerald, Sir Patrick Trant, Sir Richard Nagle, Sir Luke Dowdal, Sir Terence Dermott; James Lally, of Tullanadaly; Richard Fagan, of Feltrim; Nicholas Darcy, of Platten; besides many others of less note: the Goolds, Galways, Murroughs, and Coppingers, of Cork; the

Cheevers's of Drogheda; the Savages of Down; the O'Haras of Antrim; the Bagots of Carlow; the Barretts of Cork; the O'Flynns and O'Conors of Roscommon; the Nugents of Dardistown; the O'Garas of Coolavin. They had committed no offence—were guiltless of treason or rebellion—they had fought for their legitimate King, and now suffered the penalties of treason, because they had not recognized the authority of an English convention to substitute a foreign invader for him whom their principles taught them to regard as the lawful sovereign of the British Islands.

The civil stipulations of this famous treaty have so often been made the subject of discussion, that I need not here dwell on what is now generally admitted to be their manifest intention, and their undeniable violation. The military provisions are what most concern the reader, who would trace the further progress of the Irish in arms, and in the pursuit of glory. These articles run as follows:

" I. That all persons, without any exceptions, of what quality or condition soever, that are willing to leave the kingdom of Ireland, shall have free liberty to go to any country beyond the seas (England and Scotland excepted) where they think fit, with their families, household stuff, plate, and jewels.

II. That all general officers, colonels, and generally all other officers of horse, dragoons, and footguards, troopers, dragooners, soldiers of all kinds that are in any garrison, place, or post, now in the hands of the Irish, or encamped in the Counties of Cork, Clare, and Kerry, as also those called rapparees or volunteers, that are willing to go beyond seas as aforesaid, shall have free leave to embark themselves wherever the ships are that are appointed to transport them, and to come in whole bodies as they are now composed, or in parties, companies, or otherwise, without having any impediment, directly or indirectly.

" III. That all persons above-mentioned that are willing to leave Ireland and go into France, shall have leave to declare it at the times and places hereinafter mentioned, viz., the troops in Limerick, on Tuesday next in Limerick ; the horse at their camp on Wednesday, and the other forces that are dispersed in the Counties of Clare, Kerry, and Cork, on the 8th instant, and on none other, before M. Tameron, the French intendant, and Colonel Withers; and after such declaration is made, the troops that will go into France must remain under the command and discipline of their officers that are to conduct them thither: and deserters of each side shall be given up, and punished accordingly.

" IV. That all English and Scotch officers that serve now in Ireland, shall be included in this capitulation, as well for the security of their estates and goods in England, Scotland, and Ireland (if they are willing to remain here), as for passing freely into France, or any other country, to serve.

" V. That all the general French officers, the intendant, the engineers, the commissaries at war, and of the artillery, the treasurer, and other French officers, strangers, and all others whatsoever, that are in Sligo, Ross, Clare, or in the army, or that do trade or commerce, or are otherways employed in any kind of station or condition, shall have free leave to pass into France, or any other country, and shall have leave to ship themselves, with all their horses, equipage, plate, papers, and all their effects whatever; and that General Ginkle will order passports for them, convoys, and carriages by land and water, to carry them safe from Limerick to the ships, where they shall be embarked, without paying any thing for the said carriages, or to those that are employed therein, with their horses, cars, boats, and shallops.

"VI. That if any of the aforesaid equipages, merchandize, horses, money, plate, or other moveables, or household-stuff, belonging to the said Irish troops, or to the French officers, or other particular persons whatsoever, be robbed, destroyed, or taken away by the troops of the said general, the said general will order it to be restored, or payment to be made according to the value that is given in upon oath by the person so robbed or plundered: and the said Irish troops to be transported as aforesaid: and all other persons, belonging to them, are to observe good order in their march and quarters, and shall restore whatever they shall take from the country, or make restitution for the same.

VII. That to facilitate the transporting the said

troops, the general will furnish fifty ships, each ship's burthen two hundred tons ; for which, the persons to be transported shall not be obliged to pay, and twenty more, if there shall be occasion, without their paying for them; and if any of the said ships shall be of lesser burthen, he will furnish more in number to countervail; and also give two men of war to embark the principal officers, and serve for a convoy to the vessels of burthen.

VIII. That a commissary shall be immediately sent to Cork to visit the transport ships, and what condition they are in for sailing: and that, as soon as they are ready, the troops to be transported shall march with all convenient speed, the nearest way, in order to embark there: and if there shall be any more men to be transported than can be carried off in the said fifty ships, the rest shall quit the English town of Limerick, and march to such quarters as shall be appointed for them, convenient for their transportation, where they shall remain till the other twenty ships be ready, which are to be in a month; and may embark in any French ship that may come in the mean time.

IX. That the said ships shall be furnished with forage for horse, and all necessary provisions to subsist the officers, troops, dragoons, and soldiers, and all other persons that are shipped to be transported, into France; which provisions will be paid for as soon as all are disembarked at Brest or Nants, upon the coast of Brittany, or any other port of France they can make.

" X. And to secure the return of the said ships (the danger of the seas excepted), and payment for the said provisions, sufficient hostages shall be given.

" XI. That the garrisons of Clare-castle, Ross, and all other foot that are in garrisons, in the Counties of Clare, Cork, and Kerry, shall have the advantages of this present capitulation; and such part of those garrisons as design to go beyond seas, shall march out with their arms, baggage, drums beating, ball in mouth, match lighted at both ends, and colours flying, with all the provisions, and half the ammunition that is in the said garrisons, and join the horse that march to be transported; or if then there is not shipping enough for the body of foot that is to be next transported after the horse, General Ginkle will order that they be furnished with carriages for that purpose; and what provisions they shall want in their march, they paying for the said provisions, or else that they may take it out of their own magazines.

" XII. That all the troops of horse and dragoons that are in the Counties of Cork, Kerry, and Clare, shall also have the benefit of this capitulation; and that such as will pass into France, shall have quarters given them in the Counties of Clare and Kerry, apart from the troops that are commanded by General Ginkle, until they can be shipped; and within their quarters they shall pay for every thing, except forage and pasture for their horses, which shall be furnished gratis.

"XIII. Those of the garrison of Sligo that are joined to the Irish army, shall have the benefit of this capitulation; and orders shall be sent to them that are to convey them up, to bring them hither to Limerick the shortest way.

"XIV. The Irish may have liberty to transport nine hundred horse, including horses for the officers, which shall be transported gratis: and as for the troopers that stay behind, they shall dispose of themselves as they shall think fit, giving up their horses and arms to such person as the general shall appoint.

"XV. It shall be permitted to those that are appointed to take care for the subsistence of the horse, that are willing to go into France, to buy hay and corn at the king's rates wherever they can find it, in the quarters that are assigned for them, without any let or molestation, and to carry all necessary provisions out of the city of Limerick; and for this purpose the general will furnish convenient carriages for them, to the places where they shall be embarked.

"XVI. It shall be lawful to make use of the hay preserved in the stores of the County of Kerry, for the horses that shall be embarked; and if there be not enough, it shall be lawful to buy hay and oats wherever it shall be found, at the king's rates.

"XVII. That all prisoners of war, that were in Ireland the 28th of September, shall be set at liberty on both sides; and the general promises to use his endeavours, that those that are in England and Flanders shall be set at liberty also.

"XVIII. The general will cause provisions and medicines to be furnished to the sick and wounded officers, troopers, dragoons, and soldiers of the Irish army, that cannot pass into France at the first embarkment; and after they are cured, will order them ships to pass into France, if they are willing to go.

"XIX. That at the signing hereof the general will send a ship express to France; and that besides he will furnish two small ships of those that are now in the river of Limerick, to transport two persons into France that are to be sent to give notice of this treaty; and that the commanders of the said ships shall have orders to put ashore at the next port of France where they shall make.

"XX. That all those of the said troops, officers, and others, of what character soever, that would pass into France, shall not be stopped upon the account of debt, or any other pretext.

"XXI. If, after signing this present treaty, and before the arrival of the fleet, a French packet-boat, or other transport-ship, shall arrive from France in any other part of Ireland, the general will order a passport, not only for such as must go on board the said ships, but to the ships to come to the nearest port, to the place where the troops to be transported shall be quartered.

"XXII. That after the arrival of the said fleet, there shall be free communication and passage between it and the quarters of the above said troops; and especially for all those that have passes from the chief commanders of the said fleet, or from Monsieur Tameron, the intendant.

"XXIII. In consideration of the present capitulation, the two towns of Limerick shall be delivered and put into the hands of the general, or any other person he shall appoint, at the time and days hereafter specified, viz., the Irish town, except the magazines and hospital, on the day of the signing of these present articles; and as for the English town it shall remain, together with the island, and the free passage of Thomond-bridge, in the hands of those of the Irish army that are now in the garrison, or that shall hereafter come from the Counties of Cork, Clare, Kerry, Sligo, and other places above mentioned, until there shall be convenience found for their transportation.

"XXIV. And to prevent all disorders that may happen between the garrison that the general shall place in the Irish town, which shall be delivered to him, and the Irish troopers that shall remain in the English town and the Island, which they may do, until the troops to be embarked on the first fifty ships shall be gone for France, and no longer; they shall entrench themselves on both sides, to hinder the communication of the said garrisons: and it shall be prohibited on both sides, to offer any thing that is offensive; and the parties offending shall be punished on either side,

"XXV. That it shall be lawful for the said garrison to march out all at once, or at different times, as they can be embarked, with arms, baggage, drums beating, match lighted at both ends, bullet in mouth, colours flying, six brass guns, such as the besieged will choose, two mortar-pieces, and half the ammunition that is now in the magazines of the said place: and for this purpose, an inventory of all the ammunition in the garrison shall be made in the presence of any person that the general shall appoint, the next day after these present articles shall be signed.

"XXVI. All the magazines of provisions shall remain in the hands of those that are now employed to take care of the same, for the subsistence of those of the Irish army that will pass into France: and if there shall not be sufficient in the stores for the support of the said troops, whilst they stay in this kingdom, and are crossing the seas, that upon giving up an account of their numbers, the general will furnish them with sufficient provisions at the king's rates; and that there shall be a free market at Limerick, and other quarters, where the said troops shall be; and in case any provisions shall remain in the magazines of Limerick when the town shall be given up, it shall be valued, and the price deducted out of what is to be paid for the provisions to be furnished to the troops on ship-board.

"XXVII. That there shall be a cessation of arms at land, as also at sea, with respect to the ships, whether English, Dutch, or French, designed for the transportation of the said troops, until they shall be returned to their respective harbours; and that, on both sides, they shall be furnished with sufficient passports both for ships and men: and if any sea commander, or captain of a ship, or any officer, trooper, dragoon, soldier, or any other person, shall act contrary to this cessation, the persons so acting shall be punished on either side, and satisfaction shall be made for the wrong that is done; and officers shall be sent to the mouth of the river of Limerick, to give notice to the commanders of the English and French fleets of the present conjuncture, that they may observe the cessation of arms accordingly.

"XXVIII. That for the security of the execution of this present capitulation, and of each article therein contained, the besieged shall give the following hostages .... And the general shall give ......

"XXIX. If before this capitulation is fully executed, there happens any change in the government, or command of the army, which is now commanded by General Ginkle; all those that shall be appointed to command the same, shall be obliged to observe and execute what is specified in these articles, or cause it to be executed punctually, and shall not act contrary on any account.

"In faith of which we have subscribed our names, the 13th of October, 1691. *Signed*—Dussen, Le Chevalier de Tesse, Lucan, Wachop, and La Tour-Montfort. Charles Porter, Thomas Coningsby, Baron Ginkle."

Pursuant to these provisions, the victorious English entered these, the last entrenchments in which native valour was ever, from thence hitherto, to display itself, in any way worthy of military notice, on Irish ground; while the remains of the royalist army withdrew to the Clare side of the river, where they had the mortification of witnessing the arrival of the French squadron, commanded by M. Chateau Renaud, which hove into sight the 23rd of October, ten days only after the treaty had been executed.

The Irish troops, preparatory to making their election between the service of their conquerors and expatriation, rendezvoused at their respective quarters, the greater number at the horse camp near Quin Abbey, in the County Clare, where M. Tameron, the agent of the French court, was in attendance to receive the names of such as preferred an honourable exile in the service of Louis. The names of the officers, probably, were alone to be given, it being arranged that the election of the privates should be indicated by their filing off in separate parties at a place appointed in their parade.

Great efforts were now made to seduce the Irish soldiers from their colours, and prevent their availing themselves of the option given them by the treaty, of taking service with foreign powers. Henry Luttrel, discharged from arrest, Nicholas Purcell, the Burkes, Brigadier Clifford, and others, joined in endeavouring to enlist them in the English service; and De

Ginkle, by a proclamation, gave leave to the troopers and dragoons to sell their horses, offered payment for their arms to such as would give them up, and quarters and subsistence to all who might be inclined to serve under King William. He also, with the Lords Justices Porter and Coningsby, went to view the Irish foot, being 15,000 men, and, through Adjutant-General Withers, held out the superior advantages of the English above the French service. The disgrace of serving a foreign power against the interests of their own country was urged in the most impassioned manner. The general's proclamation was distributed in all directions, and perpetual exile denounced against those who should go to France. But all these representations of benefits to be conferred, of increased pay, rations, and clothing, and of the royal favour, proved of no avail against the exhortations of Sarsfield, Wauchop, and their own clergy, who, from the head of each battalion, promised the restoration of their fallen Church, and spoliated territories, through the aid of the great Louis, and of the magnanimous and warlike French nation. They appealed to their loyalty to God and their King; inflamed their hatred against the enemies of their creed and race; animated them with hopes of a triumphant retaliation, and pointed to the glory that would surround their names, if, through their constancy in such an hour of trial, the Church and kingdom should be restored to their ancient splendour and stability: added to this were, doubtless, all those representations of the contempt and scorn they would incur among their own countrymen by deserting, which have ever been at the command of popular orators, and which have at all times had so powerful an influence over the minds of the Irish. So great was the effect of these appeals, that when the King's Guards, a noble corps of 1400 men, came to the place assigned for separating, the whole body, with the exception of seven men, marched for France. This was an inexpressible mortification to Ginkle, who had made the greatest efforts to retain this splendid regiment in the service of his master. The same took place, in a greater or less proportion, in all the other corps. The principal defections to the English were from Wilson's, Lord Iveagh's, Clifford's, Luttrel's, Purcel's, Lord Dillon's, and Hussey's regiments; but in all, amounting only to 1046 men. These recreants were mustered near the general's quarters, and regaled with bread, cheese, brandy, tobacco, and a fortnight's subsistence, to steel them against the reproaches of their countrymen, and drown any reproaches of conscience or honour that might induce them to return to their colours. Some also deserted from the garrisons in Clare and Kerry, particularly from O'Reilly's, Nugent's, Cormack, Felix and Gordon O'Neal's, Geoghegan's, Burke's, and Magennis's regiments, seduced by the influence of officers, who sought favour from the Government by corrupting their soldiers. But the whole could not have exceeded 3,000 men, who, when their companions were embarked for France, received the treatment which deserters deserve, and usually meet with. Under pretext of their being pillagers and marauders, they were broken and disbanded, with the exception of 1400 men, formed into two regiments, under the command of Baldearg O'Donnel and Wilson, both of whom, shortly after, experienced the same usage, and incurred greater disgrace, in the stipulation of wages for treason, and in the humiliation of dismissal.

On the 23rd October, just ten days after the city had been handed over to its new occupants, Chateau Renaud's fleet, consisting of five men of war, and 18 ships of burthen, laden with stores and ammunition, appeared in the mouth of the Shannon, and, when too late, shewed what might have been effected, but for the fatal precipitancy of resolves prompted by personal interests and animosities. The arrival of this squadron, a few days sooner, would have saved the town, prolonged the war for another year, called forth all the energies of the nation, and disciplined the valour of the natives. The only advantage derived from the appearance of the fleet was the insertion, into the articles of capitulation, the words: " all such as are under their protection in said counties," contained in the original draft, but omitted in the first engrossment, and of vast importance to the Irish.

Some angry communications took place between

De Ginkle and Sarsfield with respect to the shipping of the troops to France, the former endeavouring to obstruct, and the latter to facilitate the embarkation. In spite of these obstructions, however, Sarsfield succeeded in embarking the whole of the levies, the principal command being intrusted to Lieutenant-General Sheldon. Their departure, still spoken of by the people as the " Flight of the Wild Geese," marks one of the most mournful epochs in our sad history. It was indeed a memorable and mournful spectacle: women and children, severed from their husbands, and the ties of nature rent asunder. The parting sails were pursued by moans and lamentations, that excited even the sympathies of the English and foreign troops, and still find a mournful echo in the breasts of the Irish people. It is said that the weather was unusually gloomy, as if the sun itself had been unwilling to behold so sad a spectacle, of fathers torn from their children, husbands from their wives, and, more touching still, of brave men torn from the bosom of their native land, to fill the world with the fame of their valour, and the glory of that nation which they were never again to revisit.

CHAPTER VIII.

FINAL FORMATION OF THE IRISH BRIGADE IN THE SERVICE OF FRANCE, AND CAMPAIGNS TILL THE PEACE OF RYSWICK.

THE expatriated Irish arrived in four divisions; one of 4500 men, under Sarsfield, Lord Lucan, who landed at Brest, the 3rd December; another under the command of Generals D'Usson and Tesse, numbering 4736 rank and file, besides officers, conveyed at about the same time, by the squadron of M. Chateau Renaud; a third under Wauchop, about 3,000 in number, in English transports; and lastly, the residue of the King's guards, making altogether, including various smaller drafts of those who followed the exiled monarch's fortunes (and, probably, including a considerable number of English and Scotch loyalists), the total number, as it is said, of 19,059 men and officers.

Upon the arrival of the troops at Brest, James wrote to General Sheldon, that he was well satisfied with the behaviour and conduct of the officers, and the valour and fidelity of the soldiers, and how sensible he should ever be of their services, which he would not fail to reward, when it should please God to put him in a capacity of doing so.

These brave men were now to experience the caprices of new masters. Their original formation, as they had at first been raised by their respective colonels, was no longer recognized; regiments were reduced and consolidated, and many brave officers and men of rank, who had raised regiments at home, at the sacrifice of the last remains of their estates, found themselves reduced to the rank of subordinates in other corps. Had these arrangements been left to James himself, it is probable the lingering sense of generosity in his bosom would have prompted a greater degree of respect to the feelings of men who had testified so noble a devotion to his cause. But, though these troops were nominally termed the forces of the King of England, their whole reorganization was conducted under the immediate control of the French court. And first, the pay of the troops was limited to that of the ordinary soldiers of the French army, being considerably less than that paid to other mercenaries. Then, in the distribution of commissions, great causes of dissatisfaction arose. Generals were reduced to the rank of colonels, colonels to that of captains, captains to that of lieutenants; and many of the old Irish gentry, who had staked their all in the contest, had raised, equipped, and clothed regiments to the ruin of their fortunes, were left, without commissions, to serve as volunteers.

The old natives experienced the greatest injustice in this arrangement. Sir Neal O'Neal had raised a regiment of dragoons; Gordon, Henry, and Felix O'Neal, three regiments of infantry; Edmond Buoy O'Reilly, of Cavan, Arthur Oge M'Mahon, of Monaghan, Magennis of Down, Oliver O'Gara, of Coolavin, Conel O'Donnel, of Tyrconnel, Roger O'Cahan, of Donegal, Connaught M'Guire, of Enniskillen, Hugh O'Rorke, of Breffny, Arthur Oge M'Mahon of Monaghan, had also respectively raised regiments of foot, all of which were incorporated with others, without any regard to the rank, sacrifices, services, or destitution of their colonels. The soldiers, who were enrolled by, and attached to, the ancient lords of their country, murmured in private, but submitted to these wrongs with the same resignation they had shewn in enduring the privations and sufferings of the previous campaign—privations which have rarely had a parallel in the annals of war. In fortified towns, during sieges, soldiers submit to food sufficient for bare subsistence, but these sieges are of short continuance. The Irish soldiers, during whole winters, had subsisted, without any pay, at times on horseflesh, at other times on half a pound of bread per day; had been clothed in rags, bareheaded and bare-footed, quartered in huts inundated with water, with scarce any covering but the canopy of heaven, benumbed by the cold, diseased by the moisture of a wet climate, and without fuel to preserve animal heat. They had made these sacrifices to their king and country; and when their officers and great men were deserting, true to their colours, and faithful to their engagements, had never swerved from the fidelity they had sworn to, and now following the fortunes of their king, they submitted to the sacrifices he required, in exile and adversity. Noble and generous men, taken from humblest life, you want but an historian to rescue your fame from the calumnies of your conquerors, and to elevate you to a level with the soldiers of the republics of antiquity!

Such, however, as the reception of the Irish in France was, it might have been even less favourable, but for a mistaken idea conceived by Louis, that by terminating the war in Ireland, he accomplished the double purpose of recruiting his armies, and putting an end to the heavy drain on his treasury, caused by the operations in that country(a). The campaign of the next two years developed the mistake. He then found that the diversion in Ireland had occupied 40,000 of the best of William's forces, who were now transferred to the continent, and gave such a preponderating influence to the Allies, as checked the career of the French, and exposed their frontier provinces to ravage and desolation. The vi-

(a) "L'abandon de l'Irelande donne une augmentation des troupes au Roy et lui epergna les grandes depenses de secours qu'il auvoit d'y envoyes par la suite." Quincy, vol. ii. p. 472.

gour and wisdom of Louis the Fourteenth's youth were impaired by the imbecility of declining years. Mistresses directed his councils, and, too often, minions without merit headed his armies. The Irish war did not afford patronage to his ministers, nor plunder to his parasites. It had, therefore, been neglected, and the value of the lost opportunity was only discovered when too late to do more than deplore the oversight. But although no services on the continent of Europe could make amends for this fatal error, which concentrated the efforts of the Allies on the most vulnerable points of the French monarch's dominions, he was yet to reap as great an amount of benefit from the devotion of his new servants, as, probably, any potentate ever yet did from the valour and fidelity of his soldiers. The new comers were formed into twelve regiments. We have already mentioned the Brigade of Mountcashel, consisting of *Mountcashel's*, *Clare's*, and *Dillon's*. The residue, being the bulk of the so celebrated Irish Brigade, were regimented as follows:

Sheldon's Horse.—Dominic Sheldon, an Englishman, Colonel; Edmond Prendergast, Lieutenant-Colonel; Edmond Butler, Major;—two squadrons, four companies, six lieutenants, six cornets.

Galmoy's Horse.—Lord Galmoy, Colonel; Renè de Carne, a Frenchman, Lieutenant-Colonel; James Tobin, Major. This regiment comprised the same number of squadrons, companies, and officers as the former, and the two were known in the French service by the names of the *King* and *Queen's* regiments.

King's Regiment of dismounted Dragoons.—Viscount Kilmallock, Colonel; Terence O'Carroll, Lieutenant-Colonel; De Sallis, a Frenchman, Major; consisting of one battalion, formed into six companies, each of 100 men, officered by one captain, two lieutenants, two cornets.

Queen's dismounted Dragoons.—One battalion, comprising the same number of companies, officers, and men, as the King's, and commanded by Lord Clare, Colonel; Alexander Barnewal, Lieutenant-Colonel; Charles Maxwell, Major.

King's Regiment of Guards.—Two battalions, consisting of six companies, each of 100 men. William Dorrington, an Englishman, Colonel; Oliver O'Gara, Lieutenant-Colonel; John Rothe, Major; twelve captains, twenty-four lieutenants, twenty-four sub-lieutenants, fourteen ensigns.

Queen's Regiment of Guards.—Simon Luttrel, Colonel; Francis Wachop, Lieutenant-Colonel; James O'Brien, Major;—same complement of men and officers.

Marines.—Same number of battalions, companies, men, and officers. Lord Grand Prior, brother to the Duke of Berwick, Colonel; Nicholas Fitzgerald, Lieutenant-Colonel; Edmond O'Madden, Major.

Regiment of Limerick.—Same number of battalions, companies, men, and officers. Sir John Fitzgerald, Colonel; Jeremy O'Mahony, Lieutenant-Colonel; William Sherry, Major.

Regiment of Charlemont.—Gordon O'Neal, Colonel; Hugh M'Mahon, Lieutenant-Colonel; Edmond Murphy, Major;—same complement of battalions, men, and officers.

Regiment of Dublin.—John Power, Colonel; John Power, Lieutenant-Colonel; Theobald Burke, Major;—same complement of battalions, companies, men, and officers.

Regiment of Athlone.—Walter Burke, Colonel; Owen M'Carthy, Lieutenant; Edmond Cantwel, Major;—same complement of battalions, companies, men, and officers.

Regiment of Clancarty.—Roger M'Elligot, late Governor of Cork, Colonel; Edward Scot, Lieutenant-Colonel; Cornelius Murphy, Major;—same complement of battalions, companies, men, and officers.

Besides these there were two companies of King James's body guards, each of 100 men, and three *Free Corps*, viz., *Hay's*, *Browne's* and *Rutherford's*, each consisting of a company, commanded by a captain, a lieutenant, a sub-lieutenant, and an ensign. Of supernumeraries from Ireland four companies were formed, each of 100 men, two of which were added to Clare's and two to Mountcashel's; thus raising these regiments to 1800 men each. These, by a new arrangement, were formed each into three battalions. They had lost, in the two last campaigns, a vast number, both of the men who formed it originally, and of the recruits sent to it by Lord Tyrconnel. In each of the regiments a vast number of persons who had been officers in Ireland, but had not interest enough to get commissions in the new modelled corps, served as volunteers, and were supported by the generosity of their more fortunate countrymen. They were consoled by the consciousness that their misfortunes flowed not from treachery to their king or country, but from generous loyalty and devoted patriotism.

To understand the distribution of the Irish in the subsequent campaigns, it may be necessary to take a short review of the position of the French monarch's affairs at this time. The war in which the brigade of Mountcashel was engaged, had been terminated by the treaty of Nimeguen. The interval of repose which followed this treaty was, however, of short duration, its terms having been almost immediately infringed, and its spirit violated, by Louis. By the treaty of Nimeguen, the territory of Alsace had been ceded to France, in right of which Louis set up numerous claims to detached portions of territory, alleged to have formerly belonged to Alsace, but which had for a long time been enjoyed by various independent princes and monarchs. To ascertain his right to these appurtenances, he erected chambers of inquiry at Metz and Brissac, before whom his advocates affected to investigate the rights of, among others, the Elector Palatine, the King of Sweden, the King of Spain, and several of the prince bishops of the Rhine. His next act of aggression was to seize on Strasburg, a free city, which his troops occupied by violence; while on the same day, Cassal, the principal town of Montferrat, admitted a French garrison without resistance. Following up these infractions by a demand of the town of Alost, in the Spanish Netherlands, which was alleged to have been omitted from the treaty by mistake, and this being resisted, Louis next proceeded to march an army into Flanders, under the command of Crequi, who laid siege to Luxemburg. These hostilities, interrupted for a time by the invasion of the Emperor's territory by the Turks, in 1682, were resumed with increased vigour in the following year, when a large French force entered Flanders, under the Marshal Humieres; and in 1684 another of Louis's armies, commanded by the Marquis Bellefond, crossed the Pyrenees, and assailed the Spanish garrisons in Catalonia. The death of the Elector of Cologne furnished the pretext for the last of this series of aggressions, which led to the formidable league, against which Louis was contending when the expatriated Irish entered his service. The Pope and Emperor, with whom the nomination legitimately lay, bestowed the vacant electorate on one of the princes of Bavaria, while Louis insisted on intruding his nephew, the Cardinal Furstemberg, and on the refusal of the Papal See to accede to this violent usurpation, seized on Avignon. That the design of these various unjustifiable aggressions was to provoke a war on the German and Flemish frontier, it seems impossible to doubt, as well as that the end aimed at was to extend the French frontier to the Rhine and the sea, that constant object of ambition to enterprizing French monarchs; but if the blind ambition of Louis had permitted him to foresee the coalition of European powers, in which the resistance to his rapacity was to eventuate, it may well be questioned whether even he would have coveted a conflict with enemies so numerous and powerful as now menaced him on every side. The great instrument in bringing about the treaty of Augsburg, which united the Emperor, the King of Spain, the States of Holland, Sweden, Bavaria, the Princes of the Germanic Confederation, and the Duke of Savoy, in an alliance against the ambitious projects of France, was William, Prince of Orange, who, immediately on the conclusion of the treaty, became, by so extraordinary a combination of events, the powerful and warlike King of England. In the same year that had witnessed the abdication and flight of James, the war, which had hitherto been confined to Flanders and Catalonia, burst with terrible fury over the frontier of the Rhine. The French forces, under the command of the Marshal de Duras, spread their devastating masses over the three ecclesiastical electorates, seized Mayence, Triers, Spire, Bonn, Heidelberg, Kaiserwert, Manheim, and Philipsburg, while the confederate army, commanded by the Duke of Lorraine and the Elector of Brandenburg, offered an ineffectual, though vigorous opposition. This tide of success, flowing on with an irresistible force over the Palatinate, met with its first check in Flanders, where the Prince of Waldeck, commanding the army of the Allies opposed to Humieres, and having associated with him the famous Earl of Marlborough, defeated the French in a conflict attended with a loss of two thousand killed and wounded, at Walcourt.

While these operations were carried on in the north, a large and well appointed army, under Marshal Catinat, had been despatched to the south-eastern frontier, to turn back the tide of invasion threatened on the side of Savoy. Catinat, advancing through the vallies of the Maritime Alps, had seized on the strong town and citadel of Pignerol, and pitched a fortified camp at Susa, in the Piedmontese territory, whence the way lay open to Turin. In this neighbourhood he had already drawn the Duke of Savoy into several disadvantageous trials of his strength, and at the time of the arrival of the Irish had made himself master of all the western Piedmontese frontier.

Thus, when the expatriated battalions of Limerick arrived in the dominions of the French monarch, they found that territory encircled by a blaze of war, on the Pyrenees, on the Alps, on the Rhine, on the Flemish plains, and on the ocean, where the fleet of M. Tourville awaited orders for the intended descent on England, which was to replace the exiled

James on the throne of his fathers, and restore his faithful subjects to their estates, their liberties, and their country.

Among scenes of such excitement it was that the newly formed corps marched, in the month of May, 1692, out of their winter quarters in Brittany and Normandy, for Brest, to form part of the invading army of England; but they had scarce arrived, when the squadrons of De Tourville were utterly destroyed by the combined English and Dutch fleets, led on by Russell, off the heights of La Hogue, an event which consigned these brave men to perpetual exile, and sealed their doom never to return to their native shores. However, there was abundant occupation for their arms elsewhere; and the miscarriage of the English expedition enabled Louis to prosecute the war on his other frontiers with increased activity.

They were now ordered to march for the Rhine, where the French army, under the Marshal Lorges, who had succeeded Duras, laboured under the incapacity of their General, and the superior numbers of their opponents. The French were encamped at Turkeim, thirty miles to the west of Manheim, with intent to cover the left bank of the Rhine from invasion. Nine battalions were detached under Milac, to Alloy, near Manheim, to watch the motions of the enemy. The commander in this service was soon after superseded by Feuquieres, an active, vigilant, and intelligent officer.

The Germans, by a curve in the river, and an island, had been enabled to construct a bridge at Sandheim. Feuquieres despatched messenger after messenger to apprise De Lorges of this movement, and of the impossibility of his feeble corps, 5,000 men, giving any effectual opposition. De Lorges, notwithstanding, remained motionless in his camp, and when apprised of the passage, which any degree of activity on his part would have prevented, ordered Feuquieres to retreat on Phillipsburg, to cross the Rhine there, and mark out a camp for him in the rear of the Germans. This order would, if executed, have separated the two corps, and exposed them to defeat in detail. Feuquieres, either pressed by the Germans, was unable, or, seeing the danger, was unwilling, to comply with the orders. He fell back upon Spire, possessed himself of the town, and bridge over the Spirebach, and made a resolute stand to give De Lorges time to come up in force. Here he maintained his position against 30,000 men, who, finding their efforts in that quarter fail, pushed a strong detachment to the village of Dudenhaven, two miles distant from Spire, took possession of the bridge there, and left four Swedish battalions and some artillery in possession; scarce an obstacle remained to their getting in the rere of Feuquiere's corps, and cutting off all communication between it and the main body of the French army. A branch of the Spirebach, a carabine shot distant from Dudenhaven, was still to be passed; it was nowhere fordable, but a bridge over it lay opposite to the old tower of Dudenhaven. An Irish battalion, one of those just arrived from Brest, detached by De Lorges, possessed itself of the tower, after a rapid march, and by an incessant fire of musquetry, prevented the Swedes from passing the bridge. Their obstinate defence gave time to the whole French force to come up. Both armies, divided by a deep and impassible stream, assailed each other with incessant discharges of musquetry and artillery. Cavalry could not act, nor could either come to close quarters. The Germans made several efforts to pass the bridge, but were as often arrested by the fire of the Irish(*a*).

During the whole of the night the engagement continued; at the dawn of day the Germans, perceiving that they had the whole of the French army before them, reinforced by the Irish, made a precipitate retreat. The Swedes flung away their arms and fled in the utmost disorder. De Lorges, though pressed by Feuquieres to follow the Germans, and cut off their retreat, suffered them to retreat unmolested.

The French army was now enabled to act on the offensive. It was composed of some of the finest troops in Europe, disciplined, courageous, and eager

(*a*) Feuquiere's Memoirs, vol. i. p. 172. Quincy, vol. ii. p. 555. Les battalions Irlandois qui arriverent a propos dans les temps firent un tres grand feu et obligerent les enemies apres un asses long resistance d'abandoner l'eglise et chateau de Dudenhaven.

for enterprize. The Irish forming a great portion of it were well armed, clothed, and fed, in a condition very different from that in which, in their own country, their spirits were broken, and their boldest efforts marred, by want of supplies and ammunition. Distinguished achievements were, accordingly, looked for, and the French court expected that the army would winter on some of the circles on the right bank of the river; but the incapacity of De Lorges deprived the inferior officers of every opportunity of distinguishing themselves, and the common soldiers of displaying their courage. The summer was spent in long marches, without object, and in besieging small towns, such as Psforzeim, incapable of defence, and not worth retaining the possession of. Instead of quartering his army in the Dutchy of Wirtemburg, De Lorges re-crossed the Rhine, and placed his troops in winter quarters on the French territory.

While the main body of the Irish were engaged in these services, under De Lorges, on the Rhine, the King's Guards earned some distinction under Luxemburg, who had succeeded Humieres, at Roumont, near Namur, where 10,000 of the troops of Neubourg, and Zell, and Cologne, attempted to surprise and cut off a detachment under the Marquis of Harcourt, who had approached a detachment of 4000 of their troops. A river separated the parties. The German dragoons dismounted to favour their skirmishing in some brushwood close to the river. Harcourt led the Guards, and the dragoons of Asfield across the stream, and placing himself at the head of the first company of the Guards, and Monsieur de St. Fremont at the head of the second company, charged the foe with such vigour, that they were instantly broken, and fled, abandoning 800 of their horses to the victors, 300 dead on the field, and 500 wounded(a).

During these proceedings the Brigade of Mountcashel was engaged in brilliant services with Catinat on the Piedmontese frontier. Before proceeding to detail the gallant exploits of these veterans at Guillestre and Embrun, it will be necessary to devote a few words to the then posture of affairs on that side of the French King's dominions.

At the commencement of this year's campaign in Piedmont, the allied armies there had been reinforced by 20,000 Austrian veterans, trained in the wars of Hungary. This superiority induced an attempt to invade and ravage the southern provinces of France. The Carthaginians had made the gorges, chasms, and precipices of Mount Genevre passable to horses and elephants. The Romans had often scaled Mount Cenis and the Little St. Bernard, and had brought over them military engines of enormous magnitude. But all these

(a) Quincy, vol. ii. p. 546. "M. D'Harcourt se mit a la tete de la premiere compagnie des gardes du Roy d'Angleterre et Mr. de St. Fremont a la tete de la seconde ; alors ils chargerent les ennemis avec tout de vigueur, qu'ils furent renverses presque aussitot."

passes were now guarded by formidable works, artillery, and troops. The main body of the French, under Catinat, would dispute the approaches by the valleys of Susa and Oulx. The mountains westward of Mount Genevre had never been attempted by an army : winding pathways through them, hanging over precipices some thousands of feet in depth, were known only to the Vaudois, who practised their ancient religion in these Alpine solitudes, braving persecution, and vindicating their native hills with a degree of courage and perseverance unequalled in modern times.

The Vaudois, settled for centuries in the vallies of St. Morbind Pragela, had long groaned under the Piedmontese government, having endured persecution under it more like that of the Moors under Ferdinand and Isabella, than any other modern instance of such cruelties, and far surpassing even the oppression of the Irish under the government of Elizabeth. The history of the Inquisition in Piedmont is a continued record of the cruelties inflicted on this unfortunate race. Driven to desperation, they set at defiance the denunciations of the clergy, the fires of the Inquisition, and the sword of the Savoyard government. The court of Turin, finding its inability to crush the heroism of this noble race, now tolerated their religion in the midst of barrenness and glaciers, where the avarice of ecclesiastics could exact no tithes, and selfish zeal for religion disdained hopeless missions and the inadequate wages of doubtful conversions. Though animated with profound hatred to their persecutors, the Vaudois had been softened by the gold of England, and now regimented themselves on the side of the Allies.

These Vaudois now became the allies and guides of the forces of Victor Amadeus, and conducting them through defiles where the men could pass only in single files, descended the ravines and slopes which led into the French territory. The valleys of St. Martin, Lucern, Queras, the gorges of Monte Viso, St. Martin, and the Col de Cerveres, where traversed by small divisions in succession, where they would have been overpowered by the slightest opposition. If Catinat had detached the Irish, who were accustomed to mountain warfare, to oppose this invading force, he would have saved Dauphiné from a devastation of Hungarians, more terrible than the destruction of the Palatinate by the descendants of the Franks. But he remained immoveable and inactive in his impregnable camp at Susa, dreading an attempt on the fortresses gained in the former campaign, and refusing to believe in the possibility of scaling mountains unattempted before.

The several divisions, as they emerged from the different defiles, were collected on the heights near Guillestre by the Duke of Savoy, as commander-in-chief, having under him Eugene, Commerci, Caprara, Schomberg, Ligoner Governor of Milan, and others of the most distinguished generals in Europe. Their artillery had been delayed by the difficulties of the passes, but this small town at the confluence of the Durance and the Guill, surrounded by an old wall without a fosse or outworks, defended by 200 Irish and 600 armed peasants, was not expected to offer any obstacle to their progress. Guillestre guarded the defile along the Durance, through which the invading army should pass, and its capture was besides essential for the security of artillery and convoys. To the French it was of the utmost importance to retard, to the Allies to accelerate their march. The former would have time to garrison Briançon, Embrun, Grenoble; the latter, by rapid advance, would surprise these several posts, and thus open the road to Lyons and Marseilles. The feeble garrison was accordingly summoned to surrender at discretion, with a menace of no quarter in case of resistance. A refusal to surrender was the signal for an assault. The Austrians, trained in the wars of Hungary, eager for prey, and for the sack of a place remarkable for its fairs, mounted their ladders with the resolution of men unconscious of danger, and eager to put to the sword the few who opposed them; but the resolution, coolness, and steadiness of the Irish, defeated these veterans, who were precipitated headlong from the top of the walls, and repulsed, with loss, to their quarters. A second escalade was hopeless, and a siege in form was deemed necessary. A train of battering artillery, sent from Coni, was delayed some days by the difficulties of the defiles and the repairs of the roads. Batteries were at length erected, the old walls crumbled after an incessant fire of three days, and the garrison was forced to surrender at discretion. This defence was of incalculable importance to France. In the interim Catinat threw supplies and garrisons into Besancon and Queiras, and the Marquis of Larrè, 1600 Irish and 1400 French into the important town of Embrun, which commands, lower down, the defile of the Durance, famous for the passage of Hannibal, being the very route traversed, two thousand years before, in the opposite direction, by that greatest master of the art of war(*a*).

(*a*) Where Hannibal passed the Alps, and his route to them, have long been subjects of controversy among the learned. The Mons Jovis, or the Alpis Pennina, the modern Great St. Bernard, was, by many of the ancients, supposed to be the pass, and the ascent from Martigni the route of the Carthaginians. The similarity of the Celtic words *pen*, from which these mountains derive their name, and *Pœni*, gave rise to this mistake. Hannibal should have passed the Isere, and the Arve, the Col de Balme, the Tete Noire, the countries of the Centrones and the Varagri, to reach this pass, which, for the first time, was attempted by a great army, in our own age, and effected by the genius of the mighty Napoleon. Neither Livy nor Polybius mention these nations; and it is strange that Pliny should have fallen into this error. " Inter geminas Alpium fauces Graias atque Pœninas. Hic Pœnas Graias Herculem transisse memorant." Lib. iii. c. 17. Others have maintained that he ascended the valley of the Isere, passed over the Alpis Graia, now the Little St. Bernard, and descended into the country of the Salassii, now the Valley of Aosta. Livy expresses his surprise at these mistakes: "Miror ambigi, quinam Alpes Annibal transierit et vulgo credere Pænino, at queinde nomen ei jugo Alpium inditum, transgressum." L. 21, c. 28. Hanni-

Embrun is situated on the platform of a rock that projects into the stream of the Durance, from an impending mountain which commands it on the side of the river; it has neither walls nor works, being protected by the depth and rapidity of the stream, and the steepness of the rock, 150 feet perpendicular. The mountains on the opposite side rise to an immense elevation, and are inaccessible to artillery. The roads leading to it from Gap are accessible only to horsemen, from Guillestre, only to the rude cars of the country. On that side an old wall, with stone bastions and towers, protected it. But the mountain over it, covered with underwood, afforded great facilities for attack and shelter. On the night of the 27th of July the allied armies opened their trenches, and on the 28th pushed their approaches. The indefatigable Victor Amadeus, spent the night in the trenches, encouraging his men, and exposing himself to the incessant and terrible fire of the garrison. On the night of the 29th the be-

bal's route is laid down with great exactness by Livy. He proceeded by the left bank of the Rhone, to the country of the Tricastini, then wheeling to the right along the boundaries of the Vocantii, entered the territories of the Tricasii, now the valley of the Durance, and must have passed that river, near Embrun, have ascended Mount Genevre to the Col du Corunne, and descended by the valley of the Dacia, into the plain of Piedmont. Livy's words are: "Quum jam Alpes poteret non recta regione iter instituit, sed ad levam in Tricastinos flexit, inde per extremam oram Vocantiorum tetendit in Tricovisos, haud unquam impedita via, prousquam ad Druentiam flumen pervenit," L. 22, c. 31.

siegers pushed their works quite close to a half moon, which the exertions of the garrison had constructed, from which they kept up an incessant fire, and had torches lighted, in apprehension of an assault. Several of the allied generals were killed, and some wounded. On the night of the 29th three several sallies were made, at midnight, at two o'clock, and at daylight, in which 200 of the besiegers were killed, and several of their works destroyed; but these disasters were soon repaired by numbers, and the assiduity and encouragement of the commanding officers. On the third of August a practicable breach was made, when Larrè at last hoisted the white flag, his garrison and ammunition being quite exhausted. This siege is remarkable in the Annals of Europe; for though its duration was short, it was fatal to persons of great distinction, and memorable for the extraordinary bravery of the garrison: 1300 of the assailants were killed, as many more, probably, wounded, and, among the latter, Prince Eugene, Prince Commerci, the Marquis Leganes, the Marquis Vongeir, the Marquis Bernay, and several others. The capitulation marked the obstinacy of the defence, and the esteem of Prince Eugene for the gallantry of the defenders. The terms were, that the garrison should not serve for six weeks against the Allies, should be escorted to Pignerol by the shortest route, preserving their baggage, and that the king's property should remain in Embrun.

The defenders of Guillestre and Embrun were

the troops sent by James to France, at the commencement of the Revolution war. Had these men defended Athlone, Galway, or Limerick, the contest might have terminated very differently. Brave to excess, devoted to their country, and in the highest state of discipline, what might they not have achieved in defence of their homes, their families, and their native land! Even the new levies that defended these towns evinced great resolution; but their commanding officers had estates to preserve, and by articles of capitulation, not warranted by want of ammunition, or breach, bartered their country for their properties. The privates, like their countrymen at Guillestre and Embrun, would, if supported by their officers, have held out to the last extremity.

These two sieges terminated the campaign of the Allies for this year; during their continuance Grenoble, Quieras, Besançon, were effectually secured, and the plunder and devastation of the country about Embrun, and of some of the adjoining open towns, were the only operations of the rest of the campaign. Gap was sacked, and given up to the flames; from thence to Suteron, and all around, for 20 square miles, was ravaged; towns, villages, gentlemen's seats, were all destroyed; the devastation of the Palatinate was avenged, though the German soldiery lamented that they could not retaliate on the tombs of St. Denis the outrages of the French in the electoral sepulchres at Heidelberg. Churches, monasteries, and nunneries were alike committed to the flames, and when peace was at length restored to this part of Dauphinè, plunder and fire had left no subsistence or shelter to the inhabitants. But Provence, Languedoc, the Lionnois, and the rest of Dauphinè, were saved from like desolation, by the bravery of the Irish at Guillestre and Embrun. The approach of September announcing the approaching snow storms, dictated the prudence of a retreat to the plain of Piedmont, before the passes should become impracticable, and Victor withdrew to the eastern side of the Alps.

The Irish who served this year in Piedmont, under Catinat, comprised nine battalions of Mountcashel's brigade; three of Clare, two of the King and Queen's dismounted dragoons, two of Limerick, and two of the Queen's infantry. Great superiority of cavalry gave the Allies the possession of the plain of Piedmont. Catinat having again shut himself up in his entrenched camp in the valley of Susa, left the Duke of Savoy at liberty to besiege fort St. Bridget, a post of great strength, connected with the citadel of Pignerol by a covered way, by which the garrison might, at all times, be relieved, or effect its retreat. After fifteen days' open trenches, the garrison retreated from a mound of ruins, blew up the covered way, and got safe into the citadel. From the 20th of September to the 1st of October, Pignerol sustained the fire of 80 pieces of cannon and 15 mortars. Catinat, by this time, had received a great reinforcement of cavalry, from the army of Germany, and at length put himself in motion, on the 1st of October, for the relief of Pignerol. Two valleys lead from the high Alps into the plain of Piedmont; the former, that of Susa, watered by the Doria, the latter, that of Pragela, separated by a chain of mountains, lifting their summits to the clouds, and usually, in the month of October, covered with snow, is traversed by the Cluson. The outlet of the valley of Susa, at some distance to the east of Pignerol, opened into the plain of Turin, that of Pragela debouched close to the works of the place. The pass of Fenestrelle, into the valley of Pragela, was open to Catinat; but steep precipices, deep chasms, and pathways, practicable only for the chamois of the hills, rendered it almost impassable for a cavalry fatigued by a march of four hundred miles, and for artillery and baggage; to surmount such obstacles the mighty mind of the great Napoleon was alone capable of conducting such a march. Catinat's movements along the banks of the Doria indicated his plans to intercept the communication between the Allies and Turin, to cut off their supplies, and force them to an engagement, or to abandon the bombardment of Pignerol. The Duke of Savoy, fiery as a war-horse, exulted in the prospect of an engagement, and panted for the combat. Calling a council of war, not for advice, but to sanction his intended operations, he informed them they should continue the blockade on the side of Pragela, wait for Catinat in the plain, and, after routing his army, return to the siege; they could then easily destroy the French in the defiles, and winter in Dauphiné and Savoy, at the expense of their enemies. Prince Eugene, and the Duke of Leinster (Schomberg), advised the guarding and shutting up the passages from the valley of Susa, which would compel the French to pass the Col of Fenestrelle, a march which could not fail to harass them to excess, and represented, that if they were allowed to emerge into the plain of Turin, they would intercept the communication of the Allies with their magazines, and starve them into a battle, or into relinquishing the blockade of Pignerol. But the suggestions of flattery prevailed over the council of independence, and the parasites and sycophants who were about the Duke's person overruled the prudent advice of these generals. Catinat was allowed to descend into the plain, in the rere of the besieging army, without opposition, where he courted an engagement by insults and injuries, which he calculated would excite the passions of Victor Amadeus. With this view he pillaged and destroyed all around, not sparing the Duke or his ministers, and consigning their palaces, furniture, paintings, and works of art, to the flames. The Duke, in a rage, published a proclamation that no quarter should be given to such barbarians, and, drawing off from the environs of Pignerol, marched eastward, and pitched his camp at Marsiglia, between the Cesola and Nun, which were then dry, and were no protection to his flanks. Prince Eugene advised him to extend his right to the rapid stream of the Sangone, to protect his left by the rising grounds of Piosasco, and to await the charge of the French in that formidable position, where his right and left would be equally secure. In his eagerness for a pitched battle Victor rejected this advice also. His courage bordered on temerity, his resolution on obstinacy; his confidence never calculated chances, always anticipated success, and opposition suggested to his impetuous temper views which were groundless and imaginary. " No," he said, " this position between the Cesola and the Nun, as the channels are dry, will afford a retreat, without difficulties, to Saluzzo and Villafranca on the Po, in case of failure;" and so he adhered to his original position.

Catinat, with the eye of a lynx, perceived the blunder of the Allies, and immediately possessed himself of the heights of Piosasco; four pieces of cannon on that eminence flanked the left wing of the Duke, and the French marched out of their camp in order of battle. The Duke, when too late, perceived the excellence of Eugene's advice, but the opportunity was lost, and an effort to possess himself of the hill failed. Catinat placed the cavalry on the right and left of each wing. The King's and Queen's Irish dragoons, 1400 men, commanded by Sarsfield, Lord Kilmallock, were on the right; Clare's infantry, 2000 men, on the left, and the regiments of the Queen and Limerick, 2600 men, under Wauchop, in the centre. The valour and discipline of these troops led to this division, in order to strengthen the different corps, and to animate them by the example of veterans, deemed the *elite* of the French army. The French right, with fixed bayonets, and without firing a shot, received the discharge of the German infantry, who fell back unable to meet the discharge of the Irish dismounted dragoons. These, in their turn, were assailed by the German cavalry, but stood firm as a wall, and attacking the horse with fixed bayonets, drove them off in the utmost disorder. The French cavalry then charged and broke the line of the Allies, and the battle became no longer doubtful, as the flank of the centre of the Allies was left exposed by the irretrievable defeat of their right. On this occasion the Irish dragoons performed prodigies of valour, and had most of their officers killed. On the left the conflict was terrible, and the issue doubtful for a considerable time. The French regiments of Conde, Catinat, and the Marines, in the first line, after an obstinate resistance, were broken, but Clare's three battalions, and Grancè and Perche, two French battalions, charged the German regiments of Wurtemburge, Saxe, Melburg, and Lorraine, with fixed bayonets, and restored the battle. The cavalry and infantry of both armies were now mixed in terrible affray. Clare's three battalions presented a phalanx which remained impenetrable, and at length the Germans were broken and trampled under foot by the French Gens d'Armes, and fled from the field in the utmost disorder. The German centre, commanded by Prince Eugene, was, in the mean time, engaged with the

French centre, and, animated by the heroism of its chief, his coolness and resolution nearly balanced the reverses of the wings. Wauchop now led the infantry of the French centre, of whom 2,600 were Irish, three several times to the charge, desperately endeavouring to break the centre of the Allies, consisting of the French refugees, and the veteran corps of Carrara, Carafa, Montecucoli, and Stadel. Three times these assaults were repulsed; but, after four hours' conflict, and that chiefly with the bayonet, the centre of the Allies being exposed on its flanks by the rout of the wings, the prince, with the consummate address and skill which marked his whole military carreer, threw his battalions into a square, presenting fronts on all sides, received several charges with fixed bayonets, the more murderous because made by such active and impetuous troops as the French and Irish, and retiring with unbroken ranks, though leaving a large proportion of his troops stretched on the field, carried off his corps of the army across the Po(a).

Such was the battle of Marsiglia, in the gaining of which the Irish had undoubtedly the principal share. Quincy, and other French writers, have not done them justice, but the Memoirs of Catinat make some amends for their silence. The King and Queen's dragoons suffered most. Turenne O'Carrol, of the

(a) Quincy, vol. ii. pp. 690, 691. Histoire du Prince Eugene, vol. i. p. 176.

King's, Maxwell, Wauchop, and Fordun, of the Queen's, were killed, also Lord Clare, colonel of Clare, and the number of other officers killed and wounded was in proportion to the number of the Irish troops engaged, amounting, in the whole, to 6000 men.

Prince Eugene rallied the allied army at Montcallier, and Catinat ravaged the plain of Piedmont, levied contributions where he could force them, and destroyed and burned wherever poverty debarred plunder. But though he had great talents for a field of battle, Catinat possessed none for those less exciting but equally important arrangements which secure or improve victory; and being obliged to repass the mountains in November, reaped little fruit from his great victory(a).

This year is also memorable in the annals of the Irish Brigade for the death of Patrick Sarsfield, Earl of Lucan. He had been instrumental in bringing over a great part of the Irish army to the service of France, and had the command of the troops destined for the invasion of England. After the destruction of the French fleet off La Hogue, the Irish troops marched to Alsace. Sarsfield, in 1692–3, was ordered to join the French army in Flanders, under the Duke of Luxembourg, and lost his life, at the

(a) Feuquiere's Memoires, vol. ii. p. 109. They excuse Catinat for not besieging Coni, and abstaining from wintering in Piedmont, on the grounds of his not getting supplies and ammunition from France.

head of a French division, on the plains of Neerwenden. If it had pleased God to suffer him to fall at the head of his countrymen, we would look back with less regret on the fate of this gallant soldier; but there was no Irish corps in the army of Luxembourg, and Sarsfield fell leading on the charge of strangers. His contemporaries long deplored the loss of this gallant officer, and his memory is still cherished with enthusiastic admiration in his native country. We have already sketched his character as a citizen and a subject; as a military man he does not rank as high as some even of his own countrymen. In the science of war, Hugh, the famous Earl of Tyrone, and Owen Roe O'Nial, far surpassed him. He had neither their skill, experience, or capacity. As a partizan, and for a desultory warfare, Sarsfield possessed admirable qualifications; brave, patient, vigilant, rapid, indefatigable, ardent, adventurous, and enterprising; the foremost in the encounter, the last to retreat; he harassed his enemy by sudden, unexpected, and generally irresistible attacks; inspiring his troops with the same ardour and contempt of danger with which his own soul was animated. His valour prolonged the contest in Ireland, and if he had but possessed a corresponding degree of military skill, might materially have altered the issue of the contest. A saying attributed to him at the close of the Irish war, was spoken of much in Europe. Some reflections having been cast upon the conduct of his countrymen, during the contest, by some of the

English officers of William's army: " Exchange but kings," said he, " and we will fight it over again." By the capitulation of Limerick, his estates were secured to him on condition of submitting, and swearing allegiance to William. Romantic loyalty, the sense of honour, and perhaps the hope of retrieving the fortunes of his country, prompted him to abandon his possessions, and to reject the tempting offers of William. No general was ever more beloved by his troops. Their extraordinary attachment to him impelled them to follow his fortunes, as well as those of their sovereign, and induced many to forego the important advantages they had gained by the capitulation of Limerick.

In Germany the French army, commanded by the Marshals Bouflers, De Lorges, and Choiseuil performed little. The conduct of the generals did not correspond with the valour of one of the finest armies that had ever taken the field. It approached the Imperial camp at Hailbron, on the Neckar, and, finding Prince Lewis of Baden's camp impregnable, recrossed the Rhine at Fort Lewis, Philipsburgh, and Altenheim. Lord Mountcashel served as Lieutenant-General in this corps of the grand army, having under him his own regiment, consisting of three battalions, Dublin, Charlemont's, and the Marines, in all nine battalions, about 6000 men. The grenadiers of Picardy, Auvergne, and Mountcashel, partook in the reduction of Beringheim, on the Neckar, the only achievement of the French in Germany this year.

In Spain, one battalion of the Queen's infantry,

and one of Dillon's, served under the Marshal De Noailles in Catalonia, and though the campaign was not of any brilliancy, they maintained their character of being worthy to be reckoned among the *elite* of the French army. At the siege of Rosas, the grenadiers of Dillon carried the counterscarp, and the place surrendered in three days after.

The campaign of the ensuing year was in no way memorable. The nations of Europe were exhausted by the continuance of the war. Their ardour was cooled by the equipoise of successes and reverses; resources were every year diminishing, and the agricultural population nearly destroyed. Even the foreigners in the French armies, 30,000 Irish, 15000 Swiss, and the Swedes, Germans, Danes, and Scotch, who could not be less than 6,000, did not afford sufficient supplies for the demands of destruction. The fields lay waste, the vines failed, famines ensued, and sickness and desolation saddened the wide extent of the French territory.

Catinat retained the nine battalions of Irish which had contributed so much to his fame and victories, but his army was reduced to 20,000 men, and the subsidies of England had arrayed 45,000 in the plain of Piemont, to crush his feeble corps. Shut up in the valley of Susa, with only the passes of Mount Cenis and the Little St. Bernard to secure his retreat into Savoy and Dauphine, he was sorely harassed by the Vaudois, his detachments intercepted, his supplies cut up, his communications obstructed by the boldness and constancy of their attacks, and his very quarters rendered insecure. These hardy sons of the mountains bordering on the valleys of Susa, Pragela, and La Perouse, were stimulated by hatred against the French persecutors of their brethren in Languedoc and Provence, victims to the revocation of the edict of Nantz, and martyrs to their common religion. Catinat, planning their destruction, now sent his nine battalions of Irish to hunt them in their fastnesses(*a*). These men, accustomed to chase the red deer of the mountain, to traverse bogs and morasses, and to climb the eagle's nest, on the summits of the steep precipices of their own country, eagerly took up the pursuit of the Vaudois in the unknown and lonely defiles of the Alpine hills, where deep chasms and narrow pathways, fit only to afford a footing to the chamois and the wild goat, led to the retreats of brave and desperate men; where every rock afforded cover for a deadly aim; where the re-percussion and echo of distant discharges of musquetry from concealed enemies magnified their numbers; where deep caverns and hollows, concealed by treacherous snows, or frail glaciers, swallowed the unwary adventurers in fathomless abysses. On this perilous excursion they displayed their wonted bravery, agility, perseverance, and endurance of privations. They scaled the highest rocks, plunged into the mountain streams, evaded the avalanches of stones

(*a*) Quincy, vol. ii. p. 656.

and trees which the Vaudois rolled down, beat them from their entrenchments, pursued them into the wildest recesses, and carried terror and dismay into the heart of the mountains; plundered, pillaged, destroyed, and burned what they could not carry off, and returned to the camp, driving before them herds and flocks, the only wealth of the foe they had nearly extirpated. The memory of this destructive incursion has rendered the Irish name and nation odious to the Vaudois. Six generations have since passed away, but neither time nor subsequent calamities have obliterated the impression made by the waste and desolation of this military incursion.

This diversion was of incalculable service to the French arms. The Duke of Savoy fluctuated between the sieges of Coral and Pignerol. His army, double in numbers to that of the French, but depressed by the misfortune at Marsiglia, marched and countermarched, without any fixed plan. The passes of the mountains had been left open to the French by the total defeat of the Vaudois. Catinat might receive reinforcements, and the Allies were obliged to send large detachments, under the Marquis de Pareille, to prevent the utter extermination of their mountain allies. The Duke's former presumption had now lapsed into timidity, and, though pressed by Prince Eugene, he would neither venture on a siege, nor on an engagement. The French, though far inferior in numbers, had now virtually the superiority which they maintained during the remainder of the campaign, and for which they were undoubtedly indebted to the achievements of the Irish in the early part of it.

The campaign of 1694, on the Rhine, was not rendered memorable by any decisive operations. Lord Mountcashel acted as Lieutenant-General under the Marshal de Lorges, and several of the Irish battalions served under him, though they appear not to have been in action during the summer; but the Queen's dismounted dragoons, so distinguished in the former campaign in Piemont, joined the army in Spain, and at the battle of the Ter exhibited the same cool, steady, and invincible bravery, which they displayed at Marsiglia. The Spaniards were strongly entrenched on the right bank of the Ter, having deep and dangerous fords of shifting sands in their front. A party of the French horse, 800 foot, and the Queen's dragoons, plunged into the river under a close fire of artillery and musquetry from the Spanish intrenchments. Nothing could stop the impetuosity of the assailants. Though the water was breast-high, and the bottom of the channel soft and unstable, they reached the opposite bank with surprizing rapidity, and stormed the Spanish lines with irresistible valour. The intrenchments were carried by assault, and the whole Spanish army was put to the rout. The capture of the two strong fortresses of Gerona and Palamos were the fruits of this victory. Lord Mountcashel's death in 1795 made room for the advancement of Colonel Lee, an officer of distinguished reputation, who afterwards attained the rank of Lieutenant-General, and by whose name Mountcashel's regiment was thenceforth known.

Exhausted by a long war the belligerent powers seemed incapable, on both sides, of any further continuance of active exertions, and the campaign of this year languished without any memorable engagements or sieges. The regiments of Lee, Charlemont, and Dublin, were attached to the army of the Rhine, under the orders of the Marshal De Lorges. The summer was spent in marches and countermarches, and the troops retired early to their winter quarters. The campaign in Piemont was equally barren of memorable events. Twelve Irish battalions formed the chief strength of this army, commanded by Catinat, who, from his great inferiority of force, remained fixed during the whole campaign in a fortified camp.

In Spain, Lord Clare, at the head of the Queen's dismounted dragoons, was very active in several encounters with the Spanish Miguelists, and chiefly contributed to the raising the siege of Castlefollet.

In the campaign of 1696 the greater part of the Irish were employed in actual service. Five battalions of Lee's and of the Royal Marines, and the Queen's regiment of cavalry, were attached to Marshal Boufler's army on the Meuse. The regiments of Dublin and Charlemont were under the Marshal Choiseuil in Germany. Clare, Limerick, Athlone, the Queen's guards, and the King's dismounted dragoons, in all ten battalions, fought under the orders of Marshal Catinat, and in Catalonia, Dillon's regiment and the Queen's dismounted dragoons served under the Duke de Vendòme. In Germany or on the Meuse, the Irish were not engaged in any affair of importance, but in Piemont they distinguished themselves at the obstinate siege of Valency. In one of its sallies the garrison bore every thing before them, until checked by Clare's regiment, who finally repulsed, and pursued them to the palisades. In Catalonia the Queen's dragoons had a commendable share in the brilliant action of Ortavie, and 200 of Dillon's regiment, at the little village of Colfilla, repulsed 4000 Spaniards, in two well-contested assaults.

During 1697 nearly the whole of the Irish troops in the service of France were employed in Germany, Flanders, and Catalonia, but the campaign was spent in negociations rather than in military operations. The siege of Barcelona was the most memorable event of the campaign. That important city was obstinately defended by the Spaniards. The regiments of Clancarty and Dillon, the Queen's guards, and dismounted dragoons, formed part of the besieging army. The sallies from the town were vigorous, incessant, and successful. The French lost near 10,000 men, and their success was problematical until the Irish regiment of Dillon dislodged the Spaniards from the neighbouring hills, whence they had been enabled occasionally to throw succours into the place, and to incommode the besiegers. The capture of the city followed, and with it the termination of the war, by the treaty of Ryswick, ratified in the month of September.

CHAPTER IX.

SERVICES DURING WAR OF THE SPANISH SUCCESSION.

THE war of the Spanish succession again called the Irish Brigade into action. All Europe was engaged in this memorable contest in 1701. In the conflict of claims, consequent on the death of Charles the Second of Spain, the Emperor of Austria, and Elector of Bavaria, with their allies, the Dutch and English, were again opposed to Louis, who in this new turn of the political machine, found himself for some time on the same side with his former opponent, Victor Amadeus, Duke of Savoy.

On the slopes of the Tyrolean Alps a cloud was collecting, and threatening to burst in thunder on the Rhine or the Po. The eyes of all Europe were fixed on an army of 40,000 men, encamped on the sides of Mount Brenner, waiting for a general to direct its course. The appointment of Prince Eugene of Savoy to the chief command, and the march of this formidable body towards the sources of the Eisack, and into the valley of Adige, dissipated the suspense which

(a) Feuquiere Memoires, vol. ii. c. 31. Vic du Prince Eugene, vol. i. pp. 286, 287. Quincy, vol. iii. p. 466.

hung over its destination. At Raveredo it halted, was there joined by the commander-in-chief, and spread out its wings on the adjoining heights, in the form of a crescent, as if preparing to take its flight for the plains underneath, and to pounce on its prey, where it lay in a state of torpid security, covered by rapid streams, and concealed in deep intrenchments. The Prince was awed by the difficulties which nature presented in inaccessible mountains, narrow defiles, and mighty streams, guarded by the vigilance and activity of a numerous army, directed by a general of the greatest renown. The stream of the Adige, the second river of Italy, rising in the glaciers of Mount Brenner, precipitated its waters in a tortuous course, through narrow defiles, over fragments of rocks, and masses of avalanches, that rendered artificial bridges, at short distances, necessary to transport waggons and artillery. In many places chasms were filled up and hills levelled into valleys, so that the discipline, toil, and endurance of the Roman legions seemed to be revived in the Hungarian battalions of the eighteenth century. Had Catinat taken possession of some of the Trentine territory, equally rugged and impracticable, even the genius of Eugene might have failed in the effort to penetrate into Italy. But Catinat was cramped by orders from his court not to commence hostilities, and by the perfidy of officers, some envious of his fame, others in correspondence with the Austrians, who betrayed the secrets of his councils to Eugene, and urged him to confine himself to the defence of the right bank of the Adige, from the narrow defile of the Chuesa, under Monte Baldo to the Canal Bianco, formed by the junction of the Adige and the Tartaro, and thence to the Po. Catinat objected that the line of the Adige was too extensive, contained great sinuosities, would weaken his forces into small divisions difficult to collect, and exposed to defeat in detail. The Mincio, he suggested, issuing out of the Lake of Garda, and flowing in a direct course to the Lakes of Mantua, and thence to the Po, with the two fortresses of Perchiera and Mantua, presented a short and admirable line of defence upon which the army might be concentrated, and from which detachments might be sent to cut off the communication of the enemy, with its magazines in the Trentine. But the majority voting for the line of the Adige, Catinat yielded, which caused the ruin of the French arms in Italy in 1701. The same mistake produced nearly the same effects in 1796, when it needed all the genius of the great Napoleon to retrieve the error of operating on the line of this river; and the incapacity of Alvinzy, at the head of one of the finest armies that ever descended into the plains of Italy, revived the glories of the great Eugene, after a lapse of a century.

The Adige runs parallel with the Lake of Garda, along its whole extent, passes through Verona and Porto Legnago, and joins the Tartaro, at the Veronese Marshes. Issuing from Verona, it forms a great curve convex to the East, and thus presents a line of nearly seventy miles for defence. At Rivoli, in the narrow defile between the Lake and the Adige, great entrenchments were formed, and a portion of the French army stationed there. Verona, with the line above and below it, was guarded by another body; a third occupied Legnago; a fourth was placed at Carpi and Castagnova; and a fifth at Ostiglia, on the Po(*a*). To concentrate these forces at a given point, in a country intersected by rivers, canals, and marshes, would not take less than four days(*b*).

With eagle eye, the Austrian general perceived the feebleness of the French line, avoided Verona and Legnago, marched, with the secret approbation and diplomatic remonstrance of the Venetian government, unmolested through the territory of Vicenza, by a rapid movement passed the Canal Bianco, with a great portion of his army, surprized, overwhelmed, and destroyed the French division at Castagnova and Carpi, drove the division at Legnago before him, forced the French to abandon their intrenchments at Rivole and Verona, and, as if by magic, annihilated their whole line of defence on the Adige, possessed himself of the plain between the Mincio and that river, and forced Catinat to take shelter under the cannon of Mantua.

Four Irish regiments of foot, Galmoy's, Burke's, Berwick's, and Dillon's, with Sheldon's horse, formed

(*a*) Quincy, vol. iii. 468. (*b*) Feuquiere, vol. ii. c. 31.

part of the army which now retired behind the Mincio, and which even the impregnable works of Mantua were deemed insufficient to cover. Courier after courier was now dispatched to the Duke of Savoy, who, as generalissimo, joined in a few days after with 10,000 men. Upon the approach of the Germans, the line of the Mincio was abandoned. Eugene crossed it without opposition, attacked Castiglione, took the garrison prisoners, and became master of the country between the Mincio and the Oglio. At court, these disasters, the result of perfidy in their own council of war, and of the transcendant talents of Eugene, were ascribed to the incapacity of Catinat; and the imbecility of Louis, and influence of Madame de Maintenon, substituted Villeroy as commander-in-chief. Catinat sacrificed his pride on the altar of his country, and served as second in command, under a general, whose skill and talents he considered below mediocrity(a).

Eugene had, by this time, cleared the banks of the Adige and the Mincio, as far as Mantua, forced the French beyond the Oglio, levied contributions beyond the Po, and made the French garrison of Castiglione prisoners. Villeroy arrived at the French camp at Antignano, on the 24th of August, with great reinforcements, passed the Oglio, and approached the German army strongly entrenched. Eugene had

(a) Vie du Prince Eugene, vol. i. pp. 291, 292. Quincy, vol. iii. pp. 461, 462. Ib. Order of Battle, 474. Feuquiere's Memoirs, vol. ii. p. 223.

been apprised of an intended attack(*a*). Sovereign princes cannot bear equality; and the Duke of Savoy, disgusted with the familiarity of a French minion, who called him "Savoy," already meditated defection to the Austrians, apprehensive of the conquest of Italy by the Gallo-Spaniards. In the gratification of wounded pride, and the policy of fear, he had the meaness of apprising Prince Eugene of the intended attack by 45,000 men, double the force under his command.

The annals of warfare do not exhibit a more admirable disposition to meet the coming tempest. Chiari, a Venetian fortress, on the road between Brescia and Ponte D'Oglio, having a fosse and bastions, was at once forcibly occupied by the Prince. To the right of Chiari were two rivulets, running from east to west, and on the left two other rivulets from north to south. Several houses, scattered and detached on the left, rendered the approach of an army, in order of battle, extremely difficult. The prince placed some battalions in these houses, drew an intrenchment from the fosse of Chiari to the rivulets on the left, covering his centre and left, and threw back his right behind Chiari and the rivulets on the right. The Imperialists were, in a great degree, concealed in the houses, intrenchments, and the little fort of Chiari, so that the French did not

(*a*) Vie du Prince Eugene, vol. i. pp. 290, 291. Uniscaglia Memorie Islaviche, p. 87.

estimate their force at above 6000 men; but their reconnoitering parties ascertained that their whole force was stationed there, and reported the strength of the position. Catinat advised a retreat, deeming the position impregnable, but Villeroy ordered an immediate assault. Catinat heard the orders thrice repeated, and then, turning to his officers, said, "we must obey." He commanded the centre, Villeroy the left, and the Duke of Savoy the right. The Irish Brigade, Burke's, Dillon's, Galmoy's, and Berwick's, led on the attack on the right, with the regiments of Auvergne, Anjou, Normandy, and Vendome. These were the *elite* of the French army; and French impetuosity and Irish valour carried the houses and the intrenchments adjoining to the fosse of Chiari; but when they attempted the fosse, a shower of balls from the ramparts and bastions overwhelmed them. Whole files were extended on the ground, and the slaughter was dreadful.

The Duke of Savoy, whether to conceal his treachery, or led by innate bravery, performed all the duties of a soldier and a general; exposed his person in the midst of the conflict, exhorted, animated, and in person brought on the Irish and French battalions repeatedly to the assault. The perseverance of these gallant veterans was beyond example. Lord Galmoy, of the noble house of Butler, particularly distinguished himself. The German regiments of Guillistern, sallied from the intrenchments, carried the houses that had been originally lost, and after a contest of four hours, Villeroy, finding his centre and left had not even the success of his right, ordered a retreat. Catinat seemed to court death in the centre, led on the French infantry repeatedly to the assault, was always received by a deadly fire from behind the parapet: Villeroy himself on the left, was not more successful, and in the ill-judged, and disastrous engagement, 5000 men were sacrificed by the incapacity and obstinacy of the general. The loss of the Irish surpassed that of any of the other regiments: two of their colonels, and several other officers killed, and many more wounded, attested their matchless bravery in this most sanguinary conflict. The French retired unmolested, and continued for two months within two cannon shot of the Prince's camp, hoping to draw him out of his impregnable position. But Eugene's prudence prevented an encounter in the plain with double his numbers. In November, the French re-crossed the Oglio, Galmoy's brigade, and that of the Marines, covering the passage. The Germans, with ten pieces of cannon, come up too late to effect any disorder in the rear guard, and the Oglio again separated the armies.

War had desolated the territories of Bergamo and Brescia. The Imperialists appeared to have no resources during the winter, but retreat into the Tyrol, and the abandonment of Italy. The Venetian government opposed their wintering on the Adige; and the line of the Oglio was guarded by an army superior in numbers. The mind of the Prince, fertile in resources, resolved, in the depth of winter, to pass the Mincio and the Po, to take up his quarters in the territories of Mantua and Modena, and to subsist his army on plunder and contributions. Another Hannibal seemed to have started up at the end of the seventeeth century, as skilled in military science, as fertile in *ruse de guerre*, and as capable of maintaining armies in an enemy's country, without any supplies from his own. He besieged the fortified post of Canelo, on the Oglio, in the middle of December, when the ground was covered with snow, and took it without any effort on the part of the French to relieve it. He next destroyed the French bridge at the Terre D'Oglio, captured all the towns in the dutchy of Mantua, except Godo and Mantua, strengthened the garrison of Ostiglia on the Po, gained over the Princess Pico, surprised the French garrison in her capital (Mirandola), and with the secret connivance of the Duke of Modena, took possession of the important post of Bersillo on the Po, so that Eugene was now master of the whole course of that river, from below Cremona to Ferrara, and of the Mincio, from its junction with the Po to Mantua. Mantua itself, and Girta, he blockaded, intercepted all the communication of the French, beat up their quarters, and carried on a winter campaign more successful than his operations during the preceding summer(a).

(a) Quincy, 480. Manuscript Memoir of the Irish Brigade.

In one instance, however, Eugene met with a reverse, occasioned by the bravery of Sheldon's cavalry. On the 10th of December, the Marquis de Tesse dispatched four regiments of cavalry, under Count Clermont, from Mantua, to take possession of Burgoforte, at the confluence of the Mincio and the Po. Prince Eugene having spies every where, had information of all the movements, even the most minute, of the enemy. He detached Count Merci with 1200 horse and 200 dragoons on foot, to intercept Clermont's detachment, who, being charged by superior numbers, broke and fled in great disorder. Sheldon's horse being then *en route* to the quarters appointed for them, fell in with the runaways, drew up, received and repulsed the heavy charge of the pursuers, and being aided by the rallying squadrons of the French, charged the Germans with irresistible weight, broke and cut them down, giving no quarter, on account of some former cruelties of the Germans. Merci throwing himself into the arms of the officers, escaped the merciless swords of the troopers, and was shortly after exchanged for the governor of Canelo.

This achievement acquired great glory at the time for Sheldon's horse. A number of reduced officers were attached to it as volunteers. These gallant gentlemen, exiles from their native land, reduced to French half-pay, scarce sufficient for subsistence, preferred the activity and *eclat* of a camp to the indolence and obscurity of a French provincial town. The hospitality of their native country was revived at the mess of the Irish regiments. As the Irish peasant shares with the beggar, his supper and his nightly bed, the officers of Sheldon's shared with their poor countrymen their rations and quarters, and these latter evinced their gratitude by undaunted courage, and heroic efforts to advance the glory of the regiment. On the occasion in question the volunteers surpassed all former exertions; and Louis, to mark his satisfaction at the distinguished manner in which they acted, raised their pay to an equality with that of officers of infantry of the same rank(*a*).

But indolence and effeminacy at this period began to paralyse the activity of the French. Their martial order was relaxed by the fine climate, delicious fruits, and seducing luxuries of the finest country of the globe. Milan, Pavia, and Cremona, became Capuas. In the feasting and carousing of their winter quarters, all discipline was relaxed; the vigilance requisite in face of an enterprising enemy was omitted; no outposts, guards, or videttes, protected from surprise; and dances, theatrical exhibitions, and entertainments, absorbed altogether the attention of a gay and licentious soldiery, who indulged, to the fullest extent, their natural propensities, mirth, amour, and social ease. The clarion, or the drum, seldom recalled the image of war, and peace seemed to slumber un-

(*a*) Manuscript Memoirs of the Irish Brigade.

disturbed, in the midst of hostile squadrons, and ravaging incursions into the heart of Lombardy.

Cremona, on the left bank of the Po, near its junction with the Adda, was the centre of the French forces, their head quarters, and from its strength, supposed to be beyond surprise. The place was large; had a citadel, rampart, and outworks, a bridge of boats across the Po, with a *tête du pont*, and a bastion to protect it. A Spanish governor had the command: Lieutenant-General Count De Revel, had the superintendence of the French garrison, 8000 strong, in itself an army, and under the immediate inspection of Villeroy, who lodged in the town. A large portion of the army lay under the Marquis Crequi, between the town and Alessandria, so that the place appeared beyond the reach of *a coup de main*, or surprise. Security, and love of pleasure, had, as has been observed, induced the garrison to forego the precautions prescribed by the rules of war. No patroles scoured the neighbourhood; no rounds on the ramparts, or through the open streets, secured the vigilance of the sentinels and *corps de garde;* and except the squares, the gates, and the *tête du pont*, the rest of the town, ramparts, bastions, and outworks, were wholly neglected. Of the whole garrison, sunk in every species of licentiousness and

(a) Vie du Prince Eugene, vol. ii., from p. 6 to p. 8.
(b) Quincy, vol. iii., from p. 612 to 627.

revelry, the two Irish regiments of Burke and Dillon, stationed near the Po gate, alone observed the rigor of military discipline, and were alone found regularly under arms, on parade, or at the posts assigned to them. They had not been corrupted by example, nor debauched by the luxuries of a country, in which they were perfect strangers, of which they spoke not the language, and from the excesses of which their humble means and low pay, as well as unrefined manners, and uncouth appearance, probably excluded them.

Eugene had information of all these disorders, and, prompted by the opportunity, planned the surprise of Cremona. If he succeeded he would annihilate the main force of the French, insulate Mantua, and possess himself of the whole Duchy of Milan. The plan developed the genius of the hero: but Irish valour, and the fortune of war, marred its execution. An aqueduct conveyed the ordure of the streets of Cremona into the fosse. It was a Roman work, lofty and broad, resembling the sewers of ancient Rome; and went under the house of an ecclesiastic called Cassoli, close to the gate of St. Margaret. Eugene's spies noticed it, gave him a plan of the whole town, of the situation of the *corps de garde*, of the lodgings of the general officers, of the security and revelry of the garrison. He instantly tempted the avarice of Cassoli, knowing that the love of money was often the first passion of man devoted to celibacy. A patriotic desire for the expulsion of the Gallo-Spaniards might be an additional incentive, and may have reconciled his conscience to the infamy of treachery and a bribe. The bait took, and Cassoli introduced a body of German soldiers, armed and disguised, through the aqueduct, and concealed them in his house till the treason was matured and exploded. He also, through his associates outside, procured the introduction of others, who entered as peasants; and so sunk was the garrison in the inebriety of pleasure, that the slightest knowledge of a matter, seemingly so difficult to keep secret, never reached any of the officers.

On the 30th of January, the Imperial troops at Urliano, and along the Oglio, and in the Modenese, were all in bustle, as if bent on some great enterprise. Villeroy, suspecting an attack on Crequi's corps, along the right bank of the Oglio, or on Placentia, by the troops in the Modenese, never dreamt of Cremona, and after visiting the posts on the Oglio, returned, on the evening of the 31st, to Cremona.

The gate of St. Margaret, near Cassoli's house, had been closed up with mason work, and wholly neglected, having neither guard nor sentinel. At three o'clock in the morning of the 31st, the concealed troops broke down and opened this gate of St. Margaret to the Imperial cavalry, and Eugene forthwith possessed himself of the great and little square and Town House, and put the guards at the different posts to the sword, while the soldiers were asleep, and the officers slumbered after the revels and orgies of the night. Eugene had ordered the Prince of Vaudemont, with a large body from the Modenese, to attack the *tête du pont*, at day break; and upon the success of this attack depended the success of the enterprise. The Count De Merci, on entering the gate of St. Margaret, proceeded, with 250 horse and some grenadiers, by the ramparts, at full speed, to take possession of the Po gate, where thirty-five Irish were on guard, who were not asleep on their posts like others of the garrison, and perceiving an enemy approach, sheltered themselves behind a barrier, in form of a pallisade, and staggered the approach of the Germans, with a well directed and deadly discharge. Merci then ordered his grenadiers to screw bayonets, and push them between the bars of the pallisades, so as to dislodge the guard; but when they were at an halbert's length from the barrier, they perceived they were anticipated by the Irish, whose bayonets already projected from every opening, while their muskets sent forth a continued and galling fire. Merci, in vain, endeavoured to bring up his men to this well defended post. Disheartened by the fall of so many of their comrades, they fell back, but mounted the rampart adjoining, and carried a battery of seven twenty-four pounders, which protected the Po bridge; but which, unfortunately, had not men of equal resolution with those at the palisades to turn them on the enemy.

The regiments of Burke and Dillon were quartered near the Po gate. Mahony, a reformed officer, in the absence of Lieutenant-Colonel Lake, commanded

Dillon's; one of the Burkes the other. Mahony, a great martinet, having ordered his men to parade at day-break, had thrown himself into bed, ordering his valet and host to awaken him a little before the first light: hearing the trampling of horses in the street, he now started up, complaining of not being awakened as he had ordered, but was told, that the troops, whose march he heard, were not his own; but the Imperial cuirassiers. Mahony immediately ran out, and watching his opportunity, safely reached the barracks. There the drums beat to arms; the men, in their shirts and small clothes, with their muskets and cartouche boxes, in an instant turned out, and fell into their ranks, marched for the Po gate, and arrived at the moment when Merci got possession of the battery. Without delay they attacked his troops in flank by the ramparts, and in front by the streets leading to the gate, with such fury, and a fire so destructive, that the infantry of the Germans gave way, and Merci brought up the cuirassiers to support them; but the infantry, broken and routed, fell back on the cavalry, who being charged by the Irish with fixed bayonets, were thrown into disorder, and forced to fly, leaving Merci mortally wounded, while the infantry were fain to seek shelter in the neighbouring houses. Thereupon the Irish took possession of a Franciscan convent opposite, from whence they kept up an incessant fire on the enemy, where they had sheltered themselves. This contest was most obstinately continued, from break of day to noon. The Irish, exhausted by hunger, fatigue, and cold, being in their shirts, and without food, during a conflict so contested and protracted, still maintained the attack, until the French at length, recovering from the panic of the surprise, rallied, and having got together, carried the church of Santa Maria Nuevo, Cassoli's house, and some of the intrenchments. The streets and squares now became the scenes of repeated and murderous conflicts, the combatants yielding and advancing alternately, while the horrid image of a field of battle was presented in the midst of a populous city. Blood flowed in every street; mangled bodies of men and horses, bloody sabres and bayonets strewed the squares, the streets, and ramparts. The cries of the wounded, the moans of the dying, the shouts of the combatants, the thunder and smoke of the artillery and musquetry, the crackling of the flames of houses set on fire, and the lamentations and dismay of the citizens, presented a theatre of horrors, such as no pen could describe, no imagination could reach.

Of the French, the Chevalier D'Entragues, Colonel of the regiment des Vaisseaux, was the first officer who attended to his duties, and at daybreak had been on horseback, and had his regiment on parade. Alarmed by the firing at the Po gate, and shouts that the enemy were within the city, he had led his battalion to the square, where he was joined by several officers, half dressed. When within musket shot of the Imperial grenadiers,

"You are welcome, gentlemen," cried D'Entragues, " you have deranged our toilets, but we will do you all the honours in our power." His bravery was equal to his gallantry, he received the fire of the grenadiers, charged the cuirassiers with fixed bayonets, and forced them to a precipitate flight. The Imperial infantry in the Town House now arrested the career of the French by a destructive fire from the windows; under this fire the brave D'Entragues fell. The consternation of the French at the fall of their heroic colonel, left the enemy in possession of the square. Villeroy, roused by the firing, jumped out of bed, burned his papers, proceeded to the square, and arriving just as D'Entragues received his death wound, was himself borne down by the cuirassiers, trampled under foot, and in danger of being killed, when rescued by Francis M'Donnell, an Irish officer of the regiment of Bagni. Villeroy whispered, " I am the Marshal Villeroy; I will make your fortune, bring me to the citadel; you shall have a pension of 2,000 crowns annually, and a regiment." M'Donnell replied, he had hitherto served with fidelity; he would never be disgraced by perfidy; he preferred honour to fortune, and hoped to attain, by honourable services in the Imperial army, the rank offered to him in the French, as the reward of treachery. He conducted the Marshal to the most distant *corps de garde*, and was again tempted by a bribe of 10,000 pistoles; but M'Donnell's honour was beyond the reach of corruption, and he gave up his prisoner to General Stharemberg.

Lieutenant-General the Marquis de Crenant, next in command, at the head of a few soldiers, attacked the cuirassiers, was mortally wounded, and General the Marquis de Mongon, was unhorsed, trampled on, and made prisoner. The whole circuit of Cremona, with the exception of the Po gate near it, the Irish barracks, and the citadel, was, by this time, in the hands of the Germans. The principal officers were taken or killed; and General the Count de Revel, and the Marquis de Praslin only remained, who, seeing the hopelessness of maintaining the body of the place, raised the cry of "Frenchmen, to the ramparts."

The Prince of Vaudemont, led astray by his guides, having wandered about for five hours, approached the *tete du pont* at the time Merci was most hotly engaged. The officer in the redoubt abandoned it, and a serjeant volunteered to cut away and burn the bridge, which was effected under a heavy fire. The party rejoined Mahony's corps, and prevented the entrance of the Imperialists on that side. Frustrated altogether, Eugene had no hopes of success remaining, but to tempt the fidelity of the Irish. Mac Donnell was selected for the purpose. He approached with a flag of truce, and, having procured a suspension of the combat, is said thus to have addressed the soldiers of the Brigade:

"COUNTRYMEN,—Prince Eugene sends me to say to you, that if you will change, you shall have higher pay in the Imperial than you have had in the French service. My regard for my countrymen in general, and especially for brave men like you, induces me to exhort you to accept these offers. If you should reject them, I do not see how you can escape certain destruction. We are in possession of the whole town except your part. His Highness waits my return only to attack you with his whole force, and cut you to pieces, if you do not accept his offers."

" Sir," replied one of the Irish officers, " if your general waits only your return to cut us to pieces, he shall wait long enough; we will take care you shall not return. You are my prisoner. You come not as the deputy of a great captain, but as a suborner. We wish to gain the esteem of the Prince by doing our duty, not by cowardice or treachery, unworthy of men of honour."

The combat was instantly after renewed. The Irish faced on all sides, played the battery they had recovered on the Prince of Vaudemont's corps on the other side of the Po, and having cleared the ramparts, and beaten the enemy out of the adjoining houses, and having left 100 men to guard the battery, proceeded through the streets to the gate of Mantua, to wait the further orders of the Count de Revel.

In their progress they were attacked by 200 grenadiers in the street leading to the Mantua gate: these they drove before them to a *corps de garde*, having a much more considerable force. There they experienced a fire so terrible, as would have repelled any troops but such as were determined to conquer or die. But heedless of danger, they rushed with fixed bayonets on the foe, and in an instant broke, and forced them to a precipitate flight.

Aware of the unconquerable spirit of this band, Eugene had recourse to a *ruse*, of which his mind was ever fertile, to induce them to lay down their arms : He sent Prince Commerci to Villeroy, to get an order from him to the Irish to cease the conflict; " you have seen," said he to the Marshal, "in traversing the town, that we are masters of it; but there is still some firing on the ramparts, which must compel us to put to the sword the few who are still resisting." Villeroy replied he was a prisoner, and had no power to give orders; the shooters on the ramparts might do as they pleased.

Having no other resource, Eugene now detached a large body of cuirassiers to crush the Irish in one desperate effort. Mahony, perceiving the approaching storm, fell back on his former position at the Po gate. The ground was level some distance from the houses, so that the squadrons could charge without breaking. Friburg, Lieutenant-Colonel of the cuirassiers of Taaff, who succeeded Merci in the command, wheeling a portion of his cavalry to the left, fell impetuously on their rere; but the Irish having formed in square, poured in a deadly fire, which brought men and horses to the ground, and threw such disorder into the whole body that they fled, riding through their own infantry as they came up to their assistance: no effort of their officers could rally them, nor did they stop till they reached the Square Sabbatine, fancying the Irish to be still at their heels. A reinforcement of infantry arrived at this moment. Friburg, enraged at the cowardice of the runaways, attacked, with this fresh body of infantry, the front, flank, and rere of the Irish, and putting himself at the head of his own regiment, the cuirassiers of Taaff, resolved to perish or crush them. The fury of the charge bore down bayonets and ranks. Friburg exulted in the midst of the broken ranks of Dillon. Mahony seized the bridle of his horse and cried out "quarter for Friburg." The officer replied, putting spurs to his charger, "this is not a day for quarter [meaning that he would give no quarter to the Irish] do you your duty, I will do mine." He had scarcely uttered the word when a musket ball laid him prostrate on the ground, a lifeless trunk.

The fall of Friburg turned the fate of the conflict. Cavalry and infantry fell into disorder. The Irish ranks began to reform after their temporary derangement, and finally the Imperialists were repulsed, and fled with the utmost precipitation, leaving the Irish in possession of their post, exhausted by hunger and eight hours' incessant combat, but finding in the glory they obtained, and the victory they achieved, strength sufficient to bear up against fatigues and privations, above almost the endurance of nature. Their loss, exceeding a third of their number, attested the obstinacy of the contest, and their unparalleled heroism. Burke's regiment lost in this affair seven officers and forty-two soldiers killed, and nine officers and thirty soldiers wounded; of Dillon's one officer and forty-nine soldiers were killed, and twelve officers and seventy-three soldiers wounded, in all 223 out of 600. Mahony, apprehensive of an attack on the battery, did not proceed to the gate of Mantua, as ordered. His apprehensions were well founded; a still larger body of the enemy soon after returned to the charge. Mahony retreating to the battery, turned the guns against the assailants, who were overwhelmed by a deadly salvo fired into their columns at a distance of a few yards, and again fell back, broken and discomfited. They then took post on some heights, on the angles of bastions, and other places of shelter, but night was descending, and Prince Eugene gradually drew off his men, and retreated by the same way he had entered, having lost 2000 men, in killed and wounded. Thus ended the surprise of Cremona, one of the most remarkable events in modern warfare. A garrison of 7000 men, in a town strongly fortified, surprised in their beds, obliged to march in their shirts, in the obscurity of night, through streets filled with cavalry, meeting death at every step; scattered in small bodies, without officers to lead them, fighting for ten hours' without food or clothes, in the depth of winter, yet recovering gradually every post, and ultimately forcing the enemy to a precipitate retreat.

Mahony was sent to Paris with the despatches,

carrying intelligence of this glorious achievement. In relating the various conflicts he did not mention the Irish. "You have said nothing," observed the King, "of my brave Irish." Mahony replied, "they fought in conjunction with the other troops of your Majesty." A memorable instance of the modesty of merit, or of pride, conscious of merit and disdainful of vainglory. Such transcendant services deserved and obtained the rewards of wealth and distinction. Mahony had a pension, and was raised to the rank of colonel; as were also Wauchop and Connock of Burke's. The captains of Burke's had an increase of pay of 23 sous per day; the lieutenants twelve; and the other officers and soldiers in the same proportion. Four other regiments of Irish, then in Lombardy, had a like increase of pay. Dillon's, having had higher pay from their arrival in France, received only a gratuity.

Marshal Vendôme was, upon Villeroy's being taken prisoner, appointed to the command of the army in Italy(*a*):—a general differing, in many respects, from Villeroy, as enterprising and courageous as the favourite, but endowed with traits of heroism as well as with sagacity to penetrate and defeat the designs of his opponents. In a field of battle, by his example, his intrepidity, his gestures, his animating voice, by his *coup de œil* reaching every point, he imparted at once strength, animation, and order to his army. But though possessing genius for great projects, and

(*a*) Camp De Vandosme.

energy to carry them into execution, Vendôme was deficient in vigilance to guard against surprises, and in firmness to enforce rigid discipline.

Five Irish regiments of infantry, Clare, Galmoy, Dillon, Burke, and Albemarle, and Sheldon's horse, had their share in the glory and renown of the ensuing campaign. Eugene, with an army vastly inferior, retained the field, but was obliged to raise the blockade of Mantua. Vendôme detached a considerable force to besiege Caneto. Dillon's and Burke's regiments, commanded by Mahony, and by Burke of the house of Clanrickard, composed part of these troops. Caneto, after a stout resistance, surrendered. Prince Eugene, inferior in forces, encamped between Mantua and Borgoforte, the armies being within cannon shot of each other, Eugene still on the defensive, but watching, with eagle eye, an opportunity to assume the opposite part. His communications with Germany were cut off by the capture of Castiglioni, but he obtained supplies of provisions, by bridges over numberless canals and rivers, from the Veronese. The generals were not complimentary to each other. Eugene nearly succeeded in carrying off Vendôme by surprise. Vendôme in return saluted the Prince's tent with a salvo from all the batteries, which endangered his life, and killed some of his attendants(a).

The French army, reinforced, and now under the nominal command in chief of the King of

---

(a) Quincy, vol. ii. p. 642. Ib. p. 647. Ib. p. 669.

Spain, soon after broke up, passed the Po towards Corale Maggiore, to come on the rere of the Prince's army, and cut off his supplies: where he lay with his front covered by the fosse Maedra, his left by the fortress of Borgoforte, and his right by intrenchments to guard against the sallies of the garrison of Mantua. In the skill with which his works were erected, Eugene equalled Pirrhus and Farnere. His camp on the fosses leading from the lake of Mantua to the Po, has been the wonder of all military men. Vendôme viewed it, found it impregnable, and spent two months foolishly watching an opportunity to surprise an officer whose eyes never winked, vainly thinking to intercept the communications of the Prince with the Modenese. 3000 of the Imperial cavalry were thereupon detached under Visconti, to watch the motions of the Gallo-Spaniards, and took post on the Christallo, near Santa Victoria, calculating upon the precipitous banks of this mountain stream, as a sufficient safeguard against surprise or attack. Vendôme, observing this, selected the best of his regiments of cavalry, and among the rest, Sheldon's horse, to surround and attack the corps of Visconti. The Imperialists were taken by surprise, whilst their horses were at grass; and though their resistance was such as might be expected from troops of their skill and spirit, they were nevertheless overwhelmed, and driven into the Sassoni, a river in their rere, where most of those who were not cut down, were drowned. Sheldon's horse had a principal share in this brilliant affair, in which Sheldon himself was wounded.

The Gallo-Spanish army, after this success, marched on to Luzara, a small town with a fosse and an old tower, on the right bank of the Po, which here forms an angle intersected by the canal of Zero, running from below Luzara to St. Benedetto. The Imperial general, having been forced to abandon the blockade of Mantua, took post at Borgoforte, at the confluence of the Po and the Mencio. Another general, with such inferior forces, being exceeded by many thousands, as brave as his own, would have retired by the Veronese to the defiles of the Upper Adige; but Eugene, relying on the resources of his own mighty mind, resolved to meet the coming tempest, aware of its fury, and relying on his skill to weather it out. Here it will not be amiss to give characters of the generals opposed to each other, because much of the success of military operations depends on the conduct of the leaders, more, perhaps, than on the bravery of the troops: such troops as the Irish Brigade required only science in their leaders to achieve whatever could be effected by intrepidity and perseverance. The storming of a breach, or a battery, the passing of rivers, scaling precipices, and charging with the bayonet, were the characteristics of their battalions, in the armies of the most military nations of Europe.

Vendôme inherited the intrepidity of his grandfather, Henry IV.; careless of danger, hot and impetuous in a field of battle, plunging into the midst of the fight when his troops yielded, to animate by his example, and restore confidence by his personal exposure; yet judicious and calculating, and, when not engaged in the midst of the combatants, surveying every part with serenity, sustaining weak points by reserves, throwing in additional battalions to break the enemy's line when yielding, and availing himself of every mistake of his opponent, and of every chance which the fortune of war presented to him. In other respects he was deficient in the qualities of a great commander. In courting the love of his troops, he allowed marauding, and corrupted the discipline of his camp. On a field of battle he shone like a meteor in a clouded sky; his white plumes and scarlet mantle careering in the midst of smoke and fire, moving death and dismay in their rapid course; but when the thunder ceased to roll, and his fiery spirit had no longer the excitement of the conflict to sustain its energy, his soul languished in indolence and repose. He slumbered when his enemy watched; his want of vigilance exposing him to surprises and defeats. The attachment and heroism of his troops often retrieved his mistakes, and often extricated him from difficulties insuperable to his genius. He was slow in penetrating the designs of his enemy; but when they flashed upon him, they electrified all his energies, and the hero and the general were alike conspicuous in the impetuosity of his attack and the skill of his evolutions. In private life he was haughty to his equals, condescending to his inferiors, improvident, extravagant, heedless of private engagements, negligent in the ordinary decencies of personal appearance. Affability of manners, benevolence of disposition, disinterestedness, and love of glory, stamped him as an inheritor of the virtues of his grandfather, Henry IV. Pride, hatred, or revenge had no part in his noble nature, and his prodigality, and indulgence to the vices of others, were the only foibles that clouded the purity of his elevated mind.

Eugene surpassed him in military genius, equalled him in bravery, and rivalled him in the affections of the soldiery, though rigid in discipline, and inexorable in punishing disorders. The love of the one sprung from affability, familiarity, and connivance at their excesses; that of the other in gratitude for ample supplies, for never-failing care of the sick and wounded, and for that confidence in the commander, which genius alone can call up in the breast of the soldier. In enterprize and activity, no comparison can be instituted between these great men. In stratagems, surprises, marches, passages of rivers, encampments, the art of creating resources in the enemy's country, and of turning, with inferior forces, a defensive into an offensive war, Eugene far surpassed the level of his age, and rises to a comparison with Hannibal or Napoleon, the two greatest generals of ancient and modern times. Napoleon, indeed, by the rapidity of his marches, multiplied his forces, beat his enemy in detail, and triumphed over enemies often five times as numerous as his own. But he exhausted his soldiers by fatigues too great for nature to sustain. Eugene, on the contrary, spared his troops, took advantage of canals and defiles, and cast up intrenchments to cover them; never exposing them, but when chance favoured, or necessity required. He effected much by espionage, intrigues, and bribery; but more by great genius, matchless valour, inviolable secrecy, bold conception, and heroic execution. As a military character, Eugene was all virtue : a single vice does not stain him as a warrior in the pages of the historians of his age. In one respect Vendôme and the Prince approached each other. They were both descended from houses equally illustrious. The princes of Maurun and Bourbon exhibited constellations of glory for 800 years. They both commanded armies equally brave and equally disciplined, both were nearly of the same age, and the resemblance is only lost in the superior talents of the great Eugene. Such were the great commanders who were now about to measure arms on the plain of Luzara.

Below Luzara, two dikes restrain the overflowing of the Po, both running almost parallel with the river, the smaller one close to the stream; the larger half a mile distant, the intervening space being planted with underwood and trees. The Prince passing the canal of Zero, and finding by his spies that the French army had reached Luzara, summoned the castle to surrender, and was answered by a discharge of musketry, as his troops were pitching their tents, piling their arms, and preparing supper. Thereupon, he formed his army in order of battle under the embankment at the larger canal, made his infantry throw themselves on their faces to avoid the shot from the castle; and went to view the French encampment in the midst of the plain on the other side, which was interspersed with small canals and cuts for irrigation, and planted with scattered trees. The French had neither out-posts, videttes, nor cavalry, to scour the country; not dreaming that the Imperial army, which they fancied was still in the Serraglio, on the other side of the Po, lay within musket shot, and in battle array(*a*). A French officer, by mere chance, mounted the bank at the time Prince Eugene was reconnoitering, saw the Imperial infantry on their bellies, gave the alarm, and the whole of the French army was in bustle. They had scarce time to form a front line; the necessity of the event did not suffer the formation of a second: another half hour would have been accompanied with an irretrievable defeat, had the enemy remained undiscovered. The Prince, however, was delayed by some changes in his order of battle(*b*). Observing the Irish regiments, whom he distinguished by their scarlet uni-

(*a*) Memoirs de Feuquieres, vol. ii. pp. 129, 130, 1. 134.
(*b*) Memoirs du Prince Eugene, vol. ii. p. 87.

forms, moving on the left of the French, he justly calculated on the nerve of the enemy being stationed in that quarter. And such was the fact. Berwick's formed part of the brigade of Piedmont, and Galmoy's was attached to the Marines, on the extreme left; Bourke's to that of Anjou, Albemarle's to that of Brittany, and Dillon's to Grancey's(*a*), in the centre: all these being the *elite* of the French army, whom Vendôme, not having had time to form a second line to support his first, and having no hope of sustaining the shock of the Imperialists, except in the bravery of the troops had placed in his van.

The Prince had been eye-witness of the valour of the Irish at Guillestre, Embrun, Marsiglia, Carpi, and Cremona. The *elite* of his own army in his order of battle marching from the Serraglio, had been brigaded on his left. It was now necessary to change them to the right wing, and the troops of the right *vice versa*. The renowned regiments of Nigrelli, Herberstein, Stharemberg, Guttenstein, and the dragoons of Lorrain, now moved to his right, headed by the gallant Commerci, the bravest of the brave, the Pappenheim of the Imperial army(*b*). The Prince himself led the centre, and the Prince of Vaudemont the left. His finest regiment of cuirassiers (Taaff's) were in reserve on the right.

(*a*) Quincy, vol. iii. p. 638.
(*b*) Histoire du Prince Eugene, vol. ii. p. 93.

Two causes contributed to save the French from irreparable defeat, namely, the accidental discovery of the Imperial army, and the scarlet uniforms, indicating the position of the Irish. The first put them on the alert, the second delayed the attack of the Imperial army, until Vendôme had time to put his army in order of battle. A second line he was not able to form, but supplied this defect by great bodies of reserves, to sustain any yielding point, and bear down when an opportunity should offer. Tessi guided his left, himself the centre, and the King of Spain the right. Sharp-shooters and skirmishers lined the bank of the canal in front. The position of the Gallo-Spaniards, and their superiority in numbers, notwithstanding the surprise, seemed to put them beyond the reach of defeat. Commerci, at the head of the veterans of the wars of Hungary, plunged into the fosse, dissipated the skirmishers like chaff before the wind, advanced without firing, within pistol shot, and poured a volley into the French left, where every ball told, and in an instant the ground was strewn with the bodies of the slain. The Irish and French likewise reserved their fire, and so terrible was their discharge, that whole files of the Imperialists fell prostrate, so that had it not been for the heroism of Commerci, in the thickest of the fire, exhorting, reproaching, and animating, they would have turned their backs and taken shelter behind the embankment. But, inspired by their chief, in the midst of a truly tremendous fire, those brave veterans pushed on till taken in flank by the regiments of Piedmont, Berwick, the Marines, and Galmoy's, whilst the brigade of Grancey, comprising Dillon's, the regiments of Perche and Sault, stood firm as a wall in front; and here their course was checked. Commerci still urged on, though whole ranks were extended on the ground, but, at this moment, a musket ball struck him to the earth, and death cut off this youthful commander, in a career of glory, scarce surpassed in the war of the Spanish Succession. On his death the Imperialists gave way. Prince Leichtenstein, Bagni, and Guttenstein then brought up the second line, restored the battle, and pushed back the pressing battalions of the French behind the fosses where they were originally posted. Here the Imperialists were for a moment stopped by a dreadful discharge of musketry, but pushed on, animated by the example and exhortations of their officers, till again repulsed by the fire of the French and Irish, and the disadvantage of the ground. The cavalry on both sides stood spectators of this conflict. Mounds of bodies, dead and dying, presented a spectacle of carnage and blood most horrible. After performing prodigies of valour, the Imperialists, on both their first and second lines, were repulsed. Eugene, who performed all the duties of a soldier, and displayed the skill of a consummate general, brought up a reserve of three Danish battalions, under General Boinembourg, rallied the broken battalions, and once more assailed the left wing, which he burned to break, containing, as it did, the chosen troops of the whole French army(a). The combat now recommenced with more fury than ever. The Irish and French, exhausted by fasting, fatigue, and fighting, notwithstanding the most desperate efforts, maintained their position, and preferred death to giving an inch of ground. The French writers state, that these valiant troops, having lost most of their officers, fell back five hundred paces, unable any longer to bear up against the reserves and fresh troops of the Imperialists. This account is incorrect. The regiments of Lord, Perck, and Grancey, and Dillon's, only fell back, and left the regiments of Piedmont, Berwick, the Marines, and Galmoy's, separated from Burke's, Brittany's, Albemarle's, and the other regiments forming the French centre. The Imperialists now demanded a suspension of a few moments, to find and carry off the body of Commerci, a request which the chivalrous spirit of the French immediately granted. The body of the hero being found, the battle was renewed with excessive fury. The most strenuous efforts were now made to break the Irish attached to Piedmont and the Marines(b), comprising Berwick's and Galmoy's regiments. These devoted heroes, who formed the key of the French left, had to sustain the impetuosity of the whole of the Imperial right wing, reinforced by

(a) Umiscaglia, p. 128. (b) Quincy, vol. iii. p. 669.

the Danes, and a fresh body of infantry, led on by the gallant Leichtenstein. Attacked in front, flanks, and rere, they still stood firm and immoveable, though unsupported by a second line or reserves, separated from their centre, and both their flanks uncovered. As rocks resist the waves of the sea, so they threw off the repeated charges of the Imperial bayonets. It was a sublime and marvellous spectacle, to behold these compact battalions pouring forth death from their files at one moment, at the next presenting a forest of bayonets, and rushing to meet the assault of whole battalions. Vendôme, hastening to the left, now endeavoured to rally the battalions that had fallen back, and sent his aide-de-camp, Janet, for the corps of reserve; but this officer went astray, and the utmost Vendome could do, was to maintain his ground. In the meantime, the brigades of Piedmont and the Marines were enveloped in a circle of fire, which they returned as destructively as they received it. Montandre, the colonel of the Marines; Jallet, colonel of Galmoy's; the Marquis de Renel, colonel of Piedmont, were killed; and most of the remaining officers lay on the ground dead or wounded. Leichtenstein also received a mortal wound, and several other Imperialist officers of superior rank lay before the unbroken battalions, in the midst of a terrible carnage. Night descended in utter darkness, but the combat still raged. The obscurity was illumined by continued volleys. When all nature was at rest, the thunder of artillery, the shouts of the combatants, the explosions of gunpowder, the groans of the wounded, and continued flashes of platoon firing, exhibited the horrors of war in its most hideous aspect; the fate of the battle still hanging upon the fate of the brigades of Piedmont and the Marines. In other parts, the battle raged, not contested with so much fury, nor attended with so many viscisitudes. In their first attack on the French right, the Germans had failed. The French cavalry had some even and unintersected ground for evolution, whereby they had at first been enabled to break the Imperial infantry; but the heavy counter-charge of the Imperial cuirassiers was irresistible. Crequi was killed at the head of the French infantry, which gave way, and Vendôme arriving at the moment, plunged into the midst of the combatants, crying out, "my children, we must die before we lose the victory(a);" but the utmost he could do was to maintain his ground, not to regain what he had lost. The centre of both armies were equally engaged in furious conflict, and maintained their respective positions without any superiority on either side.

At one o'clock in the morning, hunger and fatigue had relaxed the powers of destruction; utter darkness intercepted the erring aim, the generals could give no directions, and friends and foes were equally indistinguishable. The murderous

(a) Histoire du Prince Eugene, vol. ii. p. 96. Ib. p. 97.

conflict then ceased, the best contested, perhaps, of modern times, for the number of men engaged one of the most sanguinary, and for the valour of the troops and the conduct of the leaders during the engagement, one of the most memorable. Prince Eugene remained master of the field; Vendôme retiring under the walls of Luzara. *Te Deums* sung at Vienna and Paris claimed the victory for each(*a*), and affronted the Supreme Being with conflicting thanks, for the inhuman immolation of his creatures to the ambition of kings.

The loss on both sides was immense; that of the Irish frightful. Most of their officers were killed or wounded; and, of the combatants engaged, though not altogether more than 35,000, 10,000 lay either dead or dying. Prince Eugene undoubtedly gained the victory; but Vendôme's superiority of force enabled him to take a position under Luzara unassailable, almost impregnable. The Prince was obliged to intrench himself within cannon shot of the French encampment; and for two months the operations of both armies were confined to an intermittent cannonade(*b*). Vendôme's superiority enabled him to take Luzara, Guartalla, Bavisello, and Borgoforti, and ultimately to compel the Prince to retire on Mirandola, where his active intriguing spirit formed a plan to surprize Mantua,

(*a*) Histoire du Prince Eugene, vol. i. p. 108.
(*b*) Ib. vol. ii. p. 105.

as he had Cremona; but the attempt was defeated by the discovery of the conspiracy for the introduction of his troops. In December, both parties retired to their quarters. Lieutenant-Colonel Barnwell, of the house of Trimbleston, with Galmoy's, to Regiolo; Mahony, with Dillon's, Burke, with his regiment, to Guallieri; the rest of the Irish were mixed up in the other quarters with the French.

During the campaign of 1703, Sheldon's horse served in the army of the Rhine, and highly distinguished themselves at the battle of Spire. Marshal Tallard was besieging Landau, when the army of the Empire, under the Prince of Hesse Cassel, crossed the Spirebach to raise the siege. Tallard marched out of his lines to give battle, without waiting for reinforcements, which were not far from him under General Precontal. He soon came in sight of the enemy, drawn up in order of battle, with his right leaning on Spire, and his left on a branch of the Spirebach. The French, not having had time to form in order of battle, were in danger of being utterly defeated. Their right wing deployed, but their left had not arrived, and the Germans might at once have taken the ground destined for the French right, and so have utterly destroyed their centre and left; but the Prince did not avail himself of the error. The French cavalry, with their usual impetuosity, on the left, attacked the German infantry, but were repulsed with great slaughter, and threw their own infantry into disorder. Tallard now thought the battle irretrievably lost; but the Germans did not pursue or improve their advantage with sufficient promptitude; and the French left, gaining time, again formed in order of battle. At the same time, Precontal arrived to support the left wing of the French; and Sheldon's horse, by a desperate charge, broke the enemy's cavalry on the right, then charged their infantry, and so gave time to their own left to rally. A desperate engagement ensued, the Germans defending themselves with great obstinacy, but they were ultimately broken, and forced to take shelter in Spire, and under the cannon of Phillipsberg. In this action Sheldon was again wounded, and was raised to the rank of a Lieutenant-general(a).

In Germany, under Villiars, the regiments of Lee, Dorrington, and Clare, maintained the character of the Irish. Villiars had formed a junction with the Elector of Bavaria near Ulm, and the combined army was opposed by a superior force under Prince Lewis of Baden. This celebrated Prince had acquired fame in the Turkish wars; but his laurels faded on the Rhine and the Danube. The imperial city of Augsburg having received him within its walls, he now, with an intrenched camp in front, pos-

(a) Quincy, vol. iii. p. 125. Manuscript Memoir of the Irish Brigade.

sessed a decided advantage over the superior forces of the Elector. But he divided his army, placing 20,000 men under the command of General Stirum, with directions to pass the Danube and take post at Hochstadt. Villiars had left 14,000 men in the lines of Dellingen, on the Danube, under Lieutenant-General D'Usson, whilst with his main body he remained near Donaworth, lower down, so that Stirum had to cross between these two positions, both occupied by the enemy. Villiars resolved to attack him with the combined forces; and D'Usson had orders to take such measures as would bring him in front of the enemy at day-break, where he lay encamped at the foot of the heights of Gremen, on the left bank of the Danube, and to give the signal by three cannon shots, to apprise Villiars, who was to return the same signal. The Marshal left Donaworth at midnight, but did not arrive at Gremen till eight o'clock in the morning. D'Usson, having been punctual, gave the signal, but mistook three cannon shots fired by the enemy to call in their foragers, as the counter-signal agreed on. He had just time to form in order of battle, when the whole force of the Germans came upon him, and forced him back into the lines of Dellingen with considerable loss. The Elector and Villiars had by this time approached, and marched against the victorious Germans, who faced about, and formed in a new order of battle behind the stream of the Gremen, more usually called Plentheim,

*

or Blenheim, afterwards the scene of so great a battle.

After a march of eight hours, and the passage of two rivers, the French were exhausted, and, marching in column, it took some time to range them in order of battle. The regiment of Dauphine being pushed on in advance, to gain time for the infantry to occupy the ground in the centre; the Irish, led by Lord Clare, took their position "with incredible alacrity to come to blows." The right wing of the French, commanded by the Elector and the Marshal, made a furious attack, and were repulsed by the steady fire and obstinate resistance of the German left. Stirum now began to retreat from a force so superior. General Lee, with the Brigades of Dauphine and Bourbon, attacked him with great spirit, but these brigades were broken, and the enemy's retreat seemed secure, the efforts of the Marshal D'Arco on the left, with the French cavalry, having equally little effect. The French infantry, from fatigue, were unable to overtake or pursue. Their artillery and cavalry were all that could be directed against those firm battalions, which for two hours continued unbroken and invincible. At last, by a forced and rapid march, the Irish Brigade and that of Artois overtook, charged, and broke them, and commenced a horrible carnage, which continued in the woods during the whole of the following night. The Imperialists had 3000 killed, and left 4500 prisoners, 32 pieces of artillery, and all their baggage, in the hands of the Gallo-Bavarians. This victory was chiefly achieved by the valour and activity of the Irish(*a*).

A second battalion was raised for Berwick's regiment at Arras, in 1703, which was ordered to Spain in 1704. These battalions were separated until 1707, the first serving in Italy, and the other in Spain(*b*).

Some of the Irish officers were promoted, a mark of great merit, as the French nobility, by favour, engrossed all advancement. Lee, Sheldon, Dorrington, and Galmoy, were raised to the rank of Lieutenant-Generals; Charles O'Brien, Lord Clare, Fitzgerald and Bourke, to that of Major-Generals(*c*).

French intrigue had by this time gained over to the Gallo-Spanish cause, the Elector of Bavaria. But this acquisition was counterbalanced by an equal loss, in the withdrawal of the Duke of Savoy, who, offended and disgusted, deserted the Bourbon, and joined the standard of Austria. Prince Eugene was removed to the command in Hungary, and Stharemberg left to direct the operations of a very diminished army in Italy. Dillon's, Berwick's, and Albemarle's, remained under Vendôme, and performed important services during the whole of this campaign. Vendôme had orders to

(*a*) Quincy, vol. iii. p. 133 ; Maffei's Memoirs.
(*b*) Manuscript Memoir of the Irish Brigade.
(*c*) See France Militaire, vol. ii. p. 315.

march into the Tyrol by the Trentine, to form a junction with the Bavarians, who invaded it on the German side. In a few days the Electoral troops became masters of Kuffolein, Rottenburg, Innspruk, Emberg, and Rheuth, all the strong fortresses of the country(a). The nobility and clergy, always the first to yield their necks to the yoke, submitted tamely, swore allegiance to the Bavarian prince, sung Te Deums for his victories, and offered up thanksgivings to the Almighty for having visited them with the plagues of war and conquest. But the peasants, the hardy sons of the mountains, long attached to the mild government of the house of Hapsburg, with very different feelings heard their hills and valleys resound with the tumult of hostile invasion, and saw their chalets invaded by marauders, and their winter subsistence carried off as plunder, or contributions to the Bavarians, a people whom border animosities and national rivalship had long rendered objects of hatred. The same causes will invariably reproduce the same events, and in our own times we have seen the noble race of the Tyrolese, inspired by the same attachment to a prince of the house of Lorraine, as animated their fathers to a sovereign of the house of Austria, gather in armed bodies on their hills, rush to the field of war, and revive the memory of those scenes, which elevated the glory of the Alpine shepherds

(a) Umicaglia, pp. 181, 182, 183.

as high as the pinnacles of their mountains, and expanded their fame to the most distant portions of the globe. Abandoned by the nobles and clergy, the peasants fled to their most inaccessible recesses. Their mountains blazed with fires, the usual signal of invasion, the roll-call of the national militia. The slopes of Mount Brenner became another Grulli. Martin Sterzingher, Christopher Kindi, and John Auschinscider, swore they would avenge the wrongs of their country or perish in the attempt. Sterzingher, bailiff of the community of Landech, the Arminius of old, the Hofer of modern times, was cast in the finest proportions of strength and agility,—a master of rustic eloquence, and could inspire his hearers with the passions that animated his own breast. "Countrymen," cried he, "our fathers stood firm against the Swedes, the most warlike of men, and expelled them from their hills. Will you, their sons, yield to the dastardly Bavarians, will you give up Leopold, your Emperor, to become the slave of his rebel subject, who has dishonoured the German name by desertion to Gallic invaders?" These appeals were responded to with enthusiasm. Officers were chosen from among the peasants and substituted for the deserters who had gone over to the enemy. Intrenchments were thrown up, abattis formed, and the rifles that oft arrested the eagle in his rapid flight, and took down the chamois from his cliff, were cleaned and prepared for the coming contest. The steadiness and bravery of disciplined numbers carried the hastily and rudely constructed intrenchments on Mount Brenner; but in descending on the side of Italy, the opposition was so furious, the contest so fierce, and the concourse of the peasants so great, that the Elector, though within a few miles of Vendôme's army, could not advance. He was met by the Tyrolean chasseurs on the banks of the Eisach, opposite to Brixen. The Bishop, more a grenadier than an ecclesiastic, flinging away his breviary, and shouldering his rifle, headed the infuriated peasantry. Irregular, but destructive volleys compelled the precipitate retreat of the Elector, far more rapid than his advance. The best marksmen sought to single him out; and a rifle ball laid prostrate at his feet an officer who was mistaken for himself. Flinging off his dangerously conspicuous uniform, the Elector sought shelter in the dress of a common soldier. Finstermunz was attempted, and proved as fatal as the pass of Morgarten. The deadly aim from behind rocks and banks, left hundreds of the Bavarian officers food for the vultures of the Alpine solitudes, and avalanches of rocks and trees precipitated whole battalions into the deep channel of the Inn. Fame expands on the wings of freedom more rapidly than on those of loyalty. The Tyrolese equalled the Swiss and Catti in bravery and success, but they fought to maintain the mild sway of Austrian despotism, and not, as the latter did, to uphold the free institutions of their country. Arminius and Tell have long been the heroes of the Swiss and German bards; but Sterzingher, the champion of regal authority, is now known only in the Tyrolese annals. The fields fought by the former will live for ever in the memory of mankind. From all countries and climates, the slaves of despotism, the subjects of monarchies, and the citizens of republics, will annually pay their devotions at the shrine of the martyrs of liberty on the defile of Morgarten: for servitude, even in its most degraded condition, worships freedom, and is never so debased as not to aspire to emancipation. But the pass of Finstermunz will be visited by the lonely traveller, for its sublime and solemn scenery only, heedless of the triumphs obtained by the peasants of the Julian Alps, over the organized and disciplined battalions of Bavaria and France.

Happy it was for the Tyrolese that the regiments of Lee, Dorrington, and Clare, were not sent on this expedition; they were attached to Villiars army in Germany. As brave as the Tyrolese, and accustomed, like them, to scale the precipice, to brave the mountain torrent, and to take the deadly aim, they would have gained the summit of the cliffs, and penetrated into the inmost recesses of the mountains. But Berwick's, Dillon's, and Galmoy's regiments, attached to the French army of Italy, soon made the Tyrolese chasseurs feel that they were their equals in bravery, and surpassed them in agility.

Vendôme, unable to perform his orders of effecting a junction with the Elector, expostulated, setting forth the danger of the defiles, the difficulties presented by bad roads, mountain torrents, and a hostile population. But, yielding to peremptory mandates, he left 15,000 men to watch the movements of Stharemberg on the Adige, and with 10,000 more cleared the defiles of the precipitous and lofty chain of Montebaldo, and penetrated into the Trentine. Dillon and his Irish were ordered to clear the mountains on the northern side of the lake of Garda. The passages were closed by intrenchments, constructed by Austrian engineers, and guarded by the peasants and regular militia. On viewing them, they were found impregnable in front, and, in the rere, steep precipices lifted their summits to the clouds, accessible only to the wild animals of the Alps. There the eagle built his nest, the chamois bounded from cliff to cliff, and the bouquelin gambolled in the wantonness of his freedom; but man had never been seen on these inaccessible summits. The Irish scaled these lofty cliffs, and appearing in the rere of the intrenchments, so terrified the armed peasantry, and a few regular troops who were with them, that after a few discharges, they abandoned the intrenchments with the utmost precipitation(*a*).

Dillon caused several fires to blaze on the summit of the mountain, in order to magnify his detachment into a large body in the eyes of the garrison and inhabitants of Riva. The Lieutenant-Colonel

(*a*) Quincy, vol. iii. pp. 161, 162, 163.

commandant having marched out a regular body of troops to reconnoitre, and finding Dillon's detachment inconsiderable, returned to defend the town; but the citizens, apprehensive of the horrors of being taken by storm, shut their gates, and sent a deputation to Dillon with the keys. He entered in triumph. His detachment was regaled with refreshments, and possessed themselves of several pieces of cannon, and considerable ammunition.

Dillon's Irish detachment proceeded on the day following, 4th of August, to ascend a mountain of such formidable aspect, that it was said to be impracticable without divine aid; the abysses were frightful, and the narrow pathways hung on the edges of precipices some thousands of feet perpendicular; no water was to be had there, says the French historian; but the cattle were in such abundance, that a sheep was sometimes exchanged for a tumbler of wine and water(*a*).

Vendôme, on the eastern side of the lake of Garda, was proceeding in a career not less rapid. The strong and important castle of Nago, after four days' siege, surrendered. The castle of Arco held out some time longer; but at length the several divisions of the French army appeared on the right bank of the Adige, opposite to the imperial city of Trent. But here their critical situation, caused by the retreat of the Elector of Bavaria, and by the

(*a*) Quincy, vol. iii. pp. 161, 162, 163.

defection of the Duke of Savoy, dictated a retreat more rapid than their advance.

Upon his return from the Trentine, Vendôme disarmed and made prisoners all the Piedmontese in his army; the French Court having resolved to chastise the Duke of Savoy's defection with the most signal vengeance. The season was too far advanced, but preparations were made to overwhelm him from Dauphiny and the Milanese, on the opening of the campaign of 1704. Dillon and the Irish were quartered in Monferrat on the frontier of Piedmont, and Savoy was taken possession of by the Marshal De Tessè. Stharemberg, at the pressing instance of the duke, was ordered to reinforce him, to prevent his utter destruction. To effect this appeared utterly impossible. The Modenese, the Parmesan, and Placentine were in possession of the French. Thirty rivers and canals were to be passed; the Appennines were covered with snow, and a circuit of 250 miles was to be traversed, from all parts of which roads led, like the rays of a circle, to the centre of the French cantonments. But Stharemberg's orders being peremptory, he relied on the negligence and security of the French, to carry them into execution; and in the last days of October dispatched Visconti with 3000 cavalry(a), to effect a junction with the Duke of Savoy. These troops proceeded in a rapid march across the Secchia, the Taro, the Trebbia,

(a) Quincy, vol. iii. pp. 175, 176, 177.

the Scrinia, the Orba, the Bormida, and the Tanaro; but were overtaken at San Sebastiano by Vendôme, at the head of 300 Spanish horse, four companies of grenadiers, and Dillon's regiment; when a furious encounter took place between the Irish infantry and the imperial cavalry. The Grand Prior, Vendôme's brother, came up with reinforcements; and Visconti, after bravely sustaining the combat, was forced to retreat, and that retreat became a precipitate flight; his men taking refuge in the woods and defiles of the Appennines. Dillon's regiment was sent in pursuit of them; hunted them out of the recesses of the mountains, and forced them to take shelter under the cannon of Savona. Stharemberg himself, on the 24th of December, when he thought the French secure in their quarters, suddenly collected his army, deceived Vendôme by a false demonstration on the Bergamosco and Brisciano, got three days' start of him, passed all the great rivers descending from the Appennines into the Po, traversed mountains covered with snow, passed the narrow defile of Stradella, but was overtaken on the Bormida, and his rere guard sustained a considerable defeat. The Irish had their share of the toils and hardships of this winter campaign(*a*).

Hitherto Louis XIV. had been one of the most successful of the sovereigns of Europe since the days of Charles V. His councils were directed by consummate wisdom, and his armies led by profound

(*a*) Quincy, vol. iii. pp. 175, 176, 177.

skill; but his old ministers and generals had sunk in the course of nature to the grave ; and Villeroy, Tallard, and Marsin, were placed by court intrigue and female devotion in the stations formerly filled by Conde, Turenne, and Luxemburg. Villiars alone could sustain the glory of the French arms, and a misunderstanding with the Elector of Bavaria in a fatal hour removed him from the command of the army of the Danube, and Marsin was substituted in his place.

Austria was open to the invasion of the Gallo-Bavarians, and Vienna in danger of being captured. Marlborough from Flanders, and Prince Lewis of Baden, marched from the lines of Behel into the heart of Germany to crush the Elector(a). Disunion and jealousy thwarted the operations of the Anglo-Imperial army. The Margrave, as a prince of the empire, claimed the command in chief. Marlborough, despising his incapacity, would not act under him; till Eugene compromised their differences by proposing alternate command. Baden wished to negotiate with the Elector. "I came to fight," cried Marlborough, "not to negotiate." On the 1st of July, Marlborough approached the Bavarian intrenchments on the heights of Schellemberg, adjoining the outworks of Donawerth. They were not completed, and were lined by 8000(a) French and Bavarians. It was Marlborough's day of command. He resolved to signalize it by the capture of these formidable intrenchments. His artillery for some

(a) Quincy, vol. iii. 251.

time thundered on the parapets, and his troops advanced to the assault amidst shouts and hurras calculated to strike terror into the hearts of the Bavarians. They mounted the parapet with inconceivable rapidity, but were encountered by heroes. It was the combat of giants. The fury and obstinacy of the assailants and the assailed were unparalleled; they were the bravest troops in the world; and the parapet became the scaffold of the most horrible butchery the imagination can conceive. The Bavarian guards sustained for a full hour the furious assault: the parties on each side plunging their bayonets into the bodies of their opponents, precipitating them from the top of the parapet, or dashing out their brains with the butt ends of their muskets, grasping and struggling with each other in the arms of death, and on the very verge of existence. No other struggle during the war was so bloody. Hell itself could hardly exhibit a scene more horrible. At last when 8000 dead bodies had filled up the fosse, a shout of triumph from the Bavarians proclaimed the repulse and discomfiture of the English and Imperial battalions, who retired behind a ravine close to the intrenchments. Their heads and colours were visible from the mound of bodies in front of the works, from whence the French and Bavarians poured in among them showers of balls and grenades.

Marlborough's fate and fame depended on the

success of this effort. He made every intreaty to bring the troops back to the charge. He and generals Stirum and Goor, the Princes of Hesse Cassel, and Wirtemberg, dismounted, and placing themselves at the head of the troops, shamed them by reproaches into a second assault, more murderous and horrible than the first, exhibiting the same horrible scenes of fury and slaughter. The Duke never spared his men; his object was fame, to attain which he would sacrifice thousands without the slightest sensibility. The English, ever brave, heedless of danger, not disheartened by reverses, and equal to efforts surpassing almost the powers of human strength, on this occasion were brought back to the charge, were followed by the Dutch, and were received with equal firmness by the Bavarians on the mounds of dead bodies, and on the parapet, where the same horrible carnage ensued. Most of the general officers, the Prince of Bevern, Goor, Furstemberg, the gallant Stirum, and several others, were killed. Scarce a general officer escaped being wounded. The modern annals of warfare exhibit no resemblance to it in the fury of the combatants, the numbers killed and wounded, in the proportion of the assailants and the assailed. It is the proudest day in the annals of Bavaria, though the fortune of war rendered it ultimately disastrous; for just as the shouts of the Bavarians for a second time announced the discomfiture of the assailants, the Prince of Baden came up, with 30,000 fresh troops. The commandant of Donawerth, from fear or treachery, withdrew his men from the outworks which touched the intrenchments. Here the assault was renewed. The Bavarians had not troops to man the works. The intrenchments were burned, and the brave defenders were at once overwhelmed by numbers. Lieutenant-General Lee, of the Irish Brigade, brought off three regiments, and escaped through the woods. The remnant of the Gallo-Bavarians were cut to pieces. Such was the fight at the lines of Schellemberg(*a*).

On the same day Tallard passed the Rhine on his route to join the Elector. His and Villeroy's army amounted to 80,000 men. Prince Eugene's, in the lines of Behel, amounted only to 30,000, not in any degree sufficient for their defence. An united attack by the two marshals would have driven the Imperial army before them. Eugene's talent never could have supplied the deficiency of numbers before so brave and active troops as the French; but Villeroy remained inactive, and Tallard consumed ten days in the siege of the unimportant town of Willinghen, from which he desisted on the approach of Prince Eugene, who quitted the lines of Behel, leaving in them 6000 men only, and overtook the Marshal, who had six days' start of him. All this time the Elector, in danger of being overwhelmed by Marlborough, lay in the intrenched

(*a*) Quincy, vol. iv. p. 251.

camp, under the cannon of Augsburg, waiting the junction of the Marshal, which was effected shortly after. Great was the joy, but short the enjoyment of it. Marlborough, who had tempted the Elector, by English money, to abandon the French, and now tempted his attachment to his own subjects, approached the Elector's camp, found it impregnable, and then sent out detachments on all sides to waste, plunder, and burn. The Elector, faithful to his engagements, expostulated only, and appealed to the laws of humanity, which are invariably silenced by the thunder of war.

Eugene had on the left bank of the Danube skirted the march of the French Marshal on the right bank, from Willinghen to Lavinghen, and then pushed on, by Hockstet, towards Donawerth, to join the Anglo-Imperial army. He found that the pride and ignorance of the Margrave of Baden were still thwarting the operations. His great mind, always fertile in expedients, proposed to him the siege of Ingolstat, which, though it would lessen the allied armies, would remove the Margrave from head quarters, relieve the councils of war from his presumption, and leave free scope to his and Marlborough's operations. The Prince, not anticipating the folly of the French in hazarding a general engagement, fell into the snare, and brought off 16,000 to the siege of Ingolstat.

The allied army was still superior in cavalry to

the French, and equali in infantry; but they laboured under a scarcity of provisions, being under the necessity of drawing their supplies from Nordlinghen and Nuremburg. Villiars had in 1703 occupied an impregnable camp between Dillingen and Lavinghen; had the marshals occupied that camp, they would, by means of the bridges in these towns, have been enabled to cut up the communication between the allies and their magazines, without the hazard of a battle, and forced them back to the Rhine and the Meuse.

Prince Eugene's penetration entered equally into the feelings and passions of the generals along with and opposed to him. He calculated that the siege of Ingolstat would not only remove the difficulties presented by Baden's pride, but would tempt the presumption of the Marshals, who, instead of waging a Fabian war, rushed headlong into the precipitancy of Marcellus, broke up from their impregnable post at Augsburg, passed the Danube between Dillingen and Donawerth, and encamped on the plain of Hockstet, in the order of two separate armies, against all the rules of war; Marsin's corps being on the left, with its cavalry on both wings, and Tallard's on the right, in the same disposition as to cavalry and infantry(a).

Marlborough and Eugene, apprised of this move-

(a) Quincy, vol. iv., pp. 272, 273, and 274; Marquis Maffei's Memoirs; Umicaglia.

ment, passed the Danube at Donawerth, and approached the Gallo-Bavarian army, determined to anticipate their desire of a general engagement.

The plain of Hockstet presented a fine position for defence. It is intersected by a considerable stream, forming morasses on its edges, and which runs into an angle of a deep curvature of the Danube. The village of Blenheim on its right bank, close to one of the points of the curvature; and the villages of Oberklaw, of Schonbach, and Litzheim, higher up on the same side, presented admirable outposts of defence. If the French army had been drawn up close to this brook, with its infantry in the centre, its cavalry on its wings, the reserves in the rere, and the villages in front occupied by a few battalions, that could be reinforced or withdrawn, as occasion required, the military experience of Eugene, and the boldness of Marlborough, would have hesitated to attack in a position so formidable. On the 12th of August, these generals, from a rising ground, observed the negligence and incapacity of their opponents; their armies, separately encamped on a rising ground, gradually receding from the brook, and at such a distance as would allow the allies to pass, and form in order of battle.

At two o'clock on the morning of the 13th, the allied armies marched to give battle. Their movements on the left, commanded by Marlborough, were concealed by a wood; the right, commanded by Eugene, were at first mistaken for the Prince of

Baden's corps, then before Ingoldstadt. So negligent were the French, that they had no scouts to ascertain the motions of the enemy; their foragers were all out, and their camp in perfect composure, when the right wing of the Allies was disclosed by the beams of the morning sun, at ten miles distance.

Ignorance, inflated by accidental success, is always presumptuous; and incapacity, elevated to command, is unable to estimate difficulties and risks without calculation. Tallard had gained the battle of Spire by the feebleness of his sight; his vanity claimed it as the achievement of skill. Marsen had never commanded a division. A stranger to adverse and prosperous fortune, he was devoid of experience, and, on the approach of battle, confused. In reverse, he was devoid of courage, the characteristic of Frenchmen, and intent only upon personal safety. When the cloud foreboding the coming tempest appeared, the presumption of the Marshals, one the appointee of court intrigue, and the other of court devotion, lapsed into diffidence and confusion.

Though taken by surprise, they had still time to make some arrangements. The passage of the marshy ground delaying the advance of the Allies, they might easily have formed their infantry on the edge of the brook, or of the marsh adjoining. Tallard, as weak in intellect as in sight, threw twenty-seven battalions and twelve squadrons into the village of Blenheim. They were thus surrounded by the brook, and the curvature of the Danube on three sides, and too far from his order of battle to sustain or be sustained by his line, which had no infantry, except eight battalions of Piedmontese deserters, and was too remote to give any effectual opposition to the passage of the brook. The Irish regiments of Lee, Clare, and Dorrington were posted in Oberklaw, in advance of the right wing of Marsen's corps, also composed exclusively of cavalry. If valour and resolution could have effected the salvation of the French army, it might have been achieved by these regiments; but discipline and resolution, when not directed by science, are as much exposed to disaster as cowardice, which however slow in encountering, is quick in escaping danger. The plain of Hochstadt is a memorable instance of the finest army in the world anihilated by the ignorance of the leaders.

From the edge of the wood, the allied generals beheld the defects of the French order of battle; when the genius of Eugene at once suggested the plan of masking Blenheim, and breaking the French centre. Marlborough approved, and to his resolution and energy was committed its execution. The right of the allies was weakened, to strengthen their left. This alteration took two hours' delay, was concealed by the underwood, and was unnoticed by Tallard. Eugene's right, at twelve o'clock, advanced to the attack, was retarded by the brook, and his march met with the most obstinate resistance. Tallard galloped off to his left, where his presence was not required, leaving his right without orders, or a leader. The English plunged into the stream on their left; by the help of pontoons, fascines, and planks, passed the marshy ground unopposed, except by the French artillery, which was admirably served; formed, as they reached the firm ground, the infantry in front, the cavalry in the rere. Then Marlborough, by a skilful, but unusual movement, the result of a mighty mind, wheeled a portion of his infantry round the village of Blenheim, making a false demonstration, to engage the attention of the troops in the town, and at the same time made a desperate charge on the French centre with his cavalry, supported on each side by bodies of infantry, whose terrible volleys accompanied the charges of the horse. No firmness could stand such an attack, and the French centre was utterly, and almost irretrievably broken. Tallard had by this time returned; he brought up his eight battalions of Piedmontese deserters; but, through cowardice or treachery, they fled upon the first fire, and Tallard himself fell into the hands of the English. The best and bravest of the French troops, shut up in the village of Blenheim, were unable to act. Clerambaule, their commander, in desperation, plunged into the Danube, and was ingulfed in the stream. Still the battle was not irretrievably lost. Marsen's army was victorious; his broken cavalry rallied be-

(a) Cox's Life of the Duke of Marlborough.
(b) Umicaglia.
(c) Quincy, vol. iii. p. 271.

hind, and he might still, under the cover of Oberklaw, by pushing his right in the direction of Blenheim, have extricated the 13,000 *elite* of the army shut up there. But he had no presence of mind or capacity for such a movement, and the men in Blenheim were sacrificed.

The Prince of Holstein was now sent to dislodge the Irish from the village of Oberklaw; four Dutch regiments stormed it. Lord Clare maintained the post with indescribable bravery. The carnage was horrible; Goor's regiment, 500 strong, retired with fifty men only. Prince Eugene attacked the left of the Gallo-Bavarians with his usual intrepidity, and was met with equal valour; three times repulsed, he rallied, and brought his men back to the charge; the carnage was horrible; 160,000 men were engaged in this slaughter; and modern warfare had seen nothing equal to it, in the fury of the combatants, and in the number of slain.

Marlborough sought to drive the French cavalry off the field altogether, in order to capture their infantry; but Oberklaw still held out; the Irish posted there annoying the English in flank, and enabling the broken cavalry of the French to rally behind them. The place was therefore repeatedly, but vainly, assaulted by the English and Dutch, notwithstanding the intrepidity of the English, who long sustained a tempest of balls and grenades. They covered the field with their bodies, yet remained firm, not yielding an inch of ground, and held the troops in the village almost in a state of siege.

Marsen still maintained his position, and repulsed Eugene four several times. Had he fallen back on the centre and right, he might have extricated the infantry shut up in Blenheim, and restored the battle; but he had no genius for war, and should have spent his life in courts, not in camps, should have joined in the devotions of Louis and Madame de Maintenon, instead of leading the gallant veterans of Europe on a field of slaughter, caused by his incapacity. Unable further to conduct the battle, he now sounded a retreat, leaving the *elite* of the French troops to surrender, or cut their way through the victorious enemy(*a*).

Blarsac, their commander, bribed by Marlborough, or paralysed by fear, advised a surrender. The youthful blood of France grew indignant at this base desertion of national honour, and offered to cut their way through the enemy's ranks, or perish in the attempt. Officers become grey in the service, who had weathered forty campaigns, felt their blood chilled by the magnitude of the disaster, and stained the character of the French army by yielding to the dastardly opinion of their general. It was night; the enemy were fatigued, and the greater number would have escaped; military subordination, however, triumphed over the spirit of the young officers, and twenty-seven battalions and twelve squadrons

(*a*) Cox's Life of the Duke of Marlborough.
(*b*) Turenne's Modern War.

of French dragoons surrendered themselves prisoners of war.

I have been thus minute in the account of the defeat sustained by the French at Blenheim, the most fatal they had sustained since that of St. Quentin, because the Irish regiments, though implicated in that disaster, still maintained their character for valour and discipline, were unbroken in the midst of the universal route, cut their way out of the village of Oberklaw, and effected their retreat to the Rhine, with the remains of the finest army that had ever invaded Germany(a).

In Piedmont the campaign of 1704 was consumed in sieges. Vendome captured most of the strongholds. The regiments of Dillon, Galmoy, and Berwick mounted the trenches at Vercilli, Ivrea, and Verrua. At the last of these Colonel Connock, who had distinguished himself at Cremona, was killed by the bursting of a shell.

In 1705 an augmentation of officers took place in all the Irish regiments. A second captain, two second lieutenants, and a sub-lieutenant, were added to the companies of the colonel and lieutenant-colonel. The great bravery of the Irish officers, always courting danger, and heading their men in charges of the bayonet, required this addition to supply the vast mortality that took place among them in every engagement(b).

(a) Quincy, vol. iii. p. 286.
(b) Manuscript Memoir of the Irish Brigade.

In the years 1702, 1703, and 1704, parts of Languedoc and Dauphiné had been disturbed by the insurrections of the Protestants.

The Edict of Nantz had restored religious harmony to a people long torn into the Huguenot and Catholic factions, and France reaped harvests of domestic peace and prosperity for an entire century. Sympathies excited by persecution touch the hearts of persons of the same persuasion, however remote, however separated by geographical boundaries, or forms of government. But the policy of each of the states of Europe had also long been to compass uniformity of religion within its territories, with a view of extinguishing a community of feeling or sentiment between its subjects and those of other countries. Michael Tellier and his son Louvois, the ministers of Louis XIV. were imbued with those maxims of policy, which soon afflicted France with edicts of intolerance, and ripened into practices of cruel persecution. The revocation of the Edict of Nantz(a) was a proceeding even more oppressive than the penal code in Ireland. It suppressed all the privileges granted by Henry IV. and Louis XIII.; inhibited the exercise of the Protestant religion; enjoined the banishment of all its ministers within fifteen days; held out rewards for converts; and prohibited keeping schools, or bringing up children in any but the Catholic religion. Dragoons were sent into Languedoc, Dauphiné, and Pro-

(a) 18th October, 1685.

vence to enforce this decree. 100,000 Protestants, the most industrious and peaceable subjects of the French monarchy, fled from the sword of persecution, and brought with them to Germany, Holland, and England, their arts, arms, manufactures, and resentments. In every field of battle in Europe they displayed the same invincible valour against France that was evinced by the Irish against England. In Ireland they oppressed the Catholics; in France, the Irish exiles oppressed the Protestants(*a*).

Poverty compelled the poorer classes to remain, and the dictates of humanity aimed at their conversion. It was presumed that ignorance would easily yield the tenacity of religious opinions to interest, and that the preaching of missionaries was more consistent with the spirit of the Gospel than the dragooning of military. The impressions of youth in many instances yielded to the allurements of interest, and the Catholic churches were filled with converts who outwardly professed and inwardly detested the doctrines imposed on them. But the mountainous districts of the Cevennes were peopled by an honest and hardy race, whose early impressions would not yield to the eloquence of the apostles of persecution, nor to the corrupting influence

(*a*) The Court of Rome, and many of the French clergy mitigated the persecution. Bossuet's mind was tinged with bigotry, but the mild character of Fenelon shone with effulgence by the contrast of liberality. Pere La Chaise, the King's confessor, is said to have been an advocate for the cause of humanity and the spirit of the Gospel.

of proffered reward. They gave shelter to the ministers in their fastnesses, and they in return inflamed their passions and exasperated their feelings. The history of the Cevennes and of the mountainous regions of Connaught bears a strong resemblance. The Irish priests were sheltered in caves and recesses by the attachment of the Catholics, and were hunted down by blood-hounds, whose scent was even more unerring than that of the dragoons, who were thus let loose against the pastors of the Cevennes(a).

These persecutions excited heartburnings and discontents, which the belligerent powers allied against France, and missionaries from the French refugees, ripened into rebellion. The war lasted three years with various success, but the Irish Brigade and officers distinguished themselves in most of the engagements. The Camisards(b) (who may correctly enough be termed French Rapparees) made an obstinate resistance, and the Irish suffered severely. In April, 1703, seven Irish officers were severely wounded. In an engagement near Lewes the Irish advanced guard was attacked by a large body of Camisard cavalry, but they stood firm until relieved by reinforcements, who repelled the enemy's charge, but with the loss of several of the Irish officers wounded. At Nages, near Montpellier, Cavaliere, a gallant leader of the insurgents, en-

(a) Court Histoire des Cevennes ou de la Guerre des Camisards. This Court was a native of Nismes, and is the leading authority on the infamous *dragonades*.

(b) So called from *camisado*, a night attack.

countered a very superior force, and, after displaying great military talent, was compelled to fly. The Irish were sent in pursuit of him, and nearly destroyed his whole corps in the midst of the mountains. Some of the Irish officers were killed. Cavaliere himself showed bravery and skill; being pressed hard by a dragoon, he faced about, and killed his horse; the dragoon dismounted, levelled his piece, and missed him(*a*). On the 18th of April, 1704, the old Catholics massacred a great number of the converts, without mercy, and all the horrors of civil war burst forth in the butchery of old men, women, and children, in the burning of whole villages, and the waste and destruction of corn, cattle, and other necessaries for human subsistence(*b*).

Marshal Villiars, who succeeded Monstrevel, by activity and firmness checked these disorders, and the Duke of Berwick, in 1705, finally crushed them. An officer and six Irish soldiers were sent to arrest one of the chiefs of the insurgents in Montpellier. He was killed in a scuffle that ensued. Papers found upon him disclosed the hiding places of other chiefs, who were arrested, broken on the wheel, and their bodies burned; severities which terrified the Camisards, thus deprived of their chiefs, into submission(*c*).

(*a*) Cavaliere died a general in the English service. His gallant career enlivens even Brownrigg's stupid "History of the Huguenots."

(*b*) Quincy, vol. iv. p. 437.

(*c*) Manuscript Memoir of the Irish Brigade.

Most of the Irish regiments served in Lombardy during the campaign of 1705. Dillon's, Berwick's, Burke's, Galmoy's, and Fitzgerald's, formerly Albermarle's, were engaged in all the affairs of posts and battles, which marked the valour and skill of the two great commanders, Eugene and Vendôme, who headed the contending armies.

Eugene descended from the mountains of the Tyrol by both banks of the lake of Garda, threatening the French quarters on the Po and the Mincio, when suddenly he invaded the Bresciano and Bergamasco, and made three several attempts to pass the Adda, either to enter the Milanese, or to divide the French forces, and attack them in detail. Vendôme being induced to divide his forces to guard the passages, left the Grand Prior, his brother, with 20,000 men, at Cassano, whilst he himself, with fifteen battalions and twenty squadrons, guarded the left bank of the river, moving in a direction parallel with the movements of the Prince on the opposite bank, and thwarting all his efforts to pass it. The Prince made a feint to pass, near Iveza, in the Brianza, opposite the palace and villa of the Jesuits of Milan, appropriately called Paradise, from its delicious situation, and being the luxurious residence of the monks of Loyola. Eugene's batteries commanded the opposite bank, and under their tre-

(a) Umicaglia, p. 311 ; Quincy, vol. iv. 605 ; Histoire du Prince Eugene.

mendous fire a bridge of boats was constructed. But Eugene's object was to surprise the army at Cassano. He affected an effort to pass. Vendôme, on the opposite bank, ranged his battalions; the Prince, after a feeble effort, withdrew, burned his pontoons, and marched towards the Oglio, as if to invade the territory of Mantua. Vendôme sent orders to the Grand Prior to march his army to Rivalto to intercept him. He himself, captivated with the delights of "Paradise," to enjoy the repose in which he usually revelled, continued to partake of the hospitality of the rich and luxurious fathers of the Brera.

The Grand Prior, as drowsy when the action ceased, and as courageous when the thunder roared, as Vendôme, was fortunately slow in executing these orders, and when some of his battalions were on the march, a French officer from the roof of an house, espied, by a telescope, the Imperial army, in order of battle, marching for Cassano. The troops were instantly recalled, estafettes sent off for Vendôme, the baggage ordered to cross the Adda, and the troops ranged as well as time and the ground could allow.

The French had been surprised by Eugene at Cremona, Luzara, and Hochstadt. His eyes never winked, his wing never tired, he watched his prey with the piercing eye, and darted upon it with the rapidity of the eagle. The negligence of the French was quite incurable. Waggons, baggage, horses, suttlers, valets, and women, cooped up in an island with one narrow bridge over the Adda, created indescribable confusion, choked up the bridge, and obstructed the passage of Vendôme coming in full speed, at the head of 1500 cavalry. His peremptory orders at once cleared the passage, and waggons and baggage were precipitated into the stream. His presence raised the drooping spirits of men taken by surprise. Shouts of joy announced his arrival, and the Prince hesitated between attack and retreat; if victorious, the French army, from their position, must be annihilated; if beaten, the ground and canals afforded admirable facilities of drawing off without disaster; he resolved upon battle.

The Adda pours down a mighty stream from the lake of Como, narrow, deep, and rapid, no where fordable. On its right bank stands Cassano, with a bridge, having a *tête du pont*, and a redoubt, to defend it. A little higher up, the indefatigable industry of the Lombard peasants has constructed canals to carry off the waters of the Adda in flood time, and to irrigate their fields when the burning suns of their summer parch and destroy vegetation. One of these, called the Retorto, runs nearly parallel with the Adda, forming with a transverse canal, called "the little Retorto," an island inter-

(*a*) Quincy, vol. iv. p. 605. (*b*) Umicaglia, p. 311.

sected longitudinally by a third, called the Pendeno. Opposite to the *tête du pont* was a stone bridge on the Retorto, having a casino in face of it. Vendôme threw eight companies of his grenadiers into the casino, placed another chosen body on the bridge of the Retorto, and ranged his left, centre, and right along this canal. His left was formed of Grancey's, La Perche's, and the Marine brigade, to which Dillon's was attached. Burke's brigade, composed of Galmoy's, Berwick's, Burke's, and Fitzgerald's, commanded by Brigadier-General Ulick Burke, in the centre, touched the right wing, and the rest of the French infantry, forming part of the centre and left, extended along the Retorto(*a*).

Eugene led on his right, which touched the Adda, at the head of the Retorto, and carried the casino with irresistible fury, killing, or driving into the canal the eight companies of grenadiers stationed there. He then planted a battery on the spot, swept the bridge of the Retorto, got possession of the twelve flood-gates, closed them, lowered the waters three feet, and ordered his right to carry the bridge and plunge into the Retorto, to attack the enemy's left. Under a terrible fire the Germans gained the opposite bank of the bridge, broke Grancey's, La Perche's, and the Marine brigades, and nearly separated the French left from their centre. Versac, Heron, and Dillon's regiments maintained their

(*a*) Feuquiere's Memoirs. vol. xi. p. 178.

ground against the most desperate charges. The Imperialists had penetrated between Grancey's and La Perche's, but Burke's and Grancey's, uniting their right and left, cut to pieces those who had broken through. Colonel O'Carroll of Galmoy's most highly distinguished himself on the occasion. Vendôme who rushed into the fight, and animated his men by his desperate resolution, had here a horse shot under him; and now fought on foot at the head of the grenadiers and the brigades of Grancey and Burke; his guards and troops forming a phalanx around him. The Irish and Grancey's brigades, charging with fixed bayonets, next pushed back the assailants to the edge of the Retorto. One of the enemy levelled his piece at the breast of Vendôme, and Colevan, a captain of his guard, rushed in, received the ball, and fell dead at his general's feet: a memorable instance of attachment, which relieves this sad picture of human carnage, and has transmitted a name, not otherwise illustrious, to the admiration of posterity.

The French battalions in face of the bridge, animated by the example of Burke's brigade, redoubled their efforts, rushed on the bridge with fixed bayonets, and drove the Imperialists, with immense slaughter, across it. Eugene now orders Lieutenant-General the Count De Lenange to recover the bridge, and again the Germans plunge into the Retorto; a column presses through; Lenange,

(a) Quincy, vol. iv. p. 608. (b) Umicaglia, p. 311.

performing the duties of a soldier and a commander, falls, struck by a ball in the forehead; his men, disheartened, and attacked with irresistible fury, yield the bridge to the French grenadiers, and the Imperial right is thrown into disorder. During this time their left, and parts of their centre, were separated by the Retorto from their foe. At the distance of some yards they assailed each other with murderous volleys of infantry; both were equally firm, and the fate of the battle depended on the possession of the bridge on the Retorto(*a*).

On the death of Lenange, Eugene hastened to the bridge, pointed out to his officers the importance of gaining it, headed a column, and animating it by his own example, carried the ground in dispute, broke the French left, and pursued the runaways to the *tête du pont* on the Adda. Here the French made the most obstinate resistance, Vendôme and Eugene alike encouraged their men, both equally beloved, equally brave, equally conspicuous, both on foot, exhorting, reproaching, and animating. The French, forming a rampart of baggage-waggons, and branches of trees, kept up from behind it a murderous fire. The Imperialists, on the other hand, struggled to break through it, but were assailed in flank by Verac's, Heron's, Dillon's, and part of Burke's brigade, which, uniting its right flank with the next corps, and facing part of their line to

(*a*) Feuquiere's Memoirs, vol. xi. p. 178.

the Imperial right, maintained their ground against the Imperial centre on the other side of the Retorto, and galled the right wing engaged in front of the redoubt. By the most heroic efforts the Imperialists forced this rampart, and reached the parapet of the *tete du pont*. If this post were carried, another Blenheim would have ensued. 24,000 men, cooped up in the island, with the rapid stream of the Adda in the rere, and the Retorto in front, into which the Prince might have let in six feet of water from the sluices, must have surrendered at discretion. Here commenced one of the most furious engagements recorded in modern history. It is impossible, without horror, to contemplate the picture presented to us by those who have described the fury of the combatants, black with smoke, besmeared with gore, grappling with each other in the struggles of death, and plunging their blood-stained weapons into each other's bodies. In a narrow spot, not more than half a mile in length, and a furlong in breadth, the nations of Europe, from North Cape to Gibraltar, from "l'Ultima Irlanda" to the banks of the Boristhenes, seemed to have sent forth their choicest bands, to try their strength on the banks of the Adda. Norwegians, Swedes, Danes, Irish, Germans, Sclavonians, Poles, Hungarians, Italians, French, and Spaniards, were mixed up in this frightful affray. Thousands of voices roaring in different languages and dialects; 30,000 tubes pouring forth fire and death; and 10,000 bayonets crossing and clanking against each other in the work of butchery, exhibited a scene more horrible and destructive than the conflict of the elements, or the bursting of a volcano from the bowels of the earth.

At the foot of the intrenchment the battle raged with the greatest fury. The Imperial standard at last floated on the parapet. Three regiments of Spanish dismounted dragoons, having plunged into the waters of the Adda to escape the steel of the furious Hungarians, were all drowned. Vendôme brought up some infantry to replace them. His presence, his voice and gestures, reanimated their drooping spirits; and so furious was their onset, that they drove the Imperialists back to the parapet, and precipitated them headlong into the fosse. Eugene, having a superiority of forces, brought up fresh battalions and directed the Prince of Anhalt, who commanded his centre, to cross the Retorto, and attack the French centre(*a*). Anhalt, the most intrepid of soldiers, and the Prussians, the *elite* of the *elite*, the giants of the North, plunged into the stream, were above the middle in water, received a discharge that dyed the Retorto with blood, but reached the opposite bank, when the exhausted brigades of Burke and Grancey were forced to yield to the giant arms and mighty strength of the renowned guards of William, the first of the Prussian monarchs. They crossed the Pendino, rallied behind underwood and bushes on its banks, took a

(*a*) Histoire du Prince Eugene, vol. iii.

sure and deadly aim at these Goliahs, laid hundreds of them prostrate on the ground; and remained secure, from the inability of their opponents to return their fire, their cartouche boxes having been all wet by the water, in passing the Retorto. The Prussians, however, protected Eugene's flank, who again planted the Imperial standard, after a desperate struggle, on the parapet of the redoubt, and drove a portion of the French into an armed work in the middle of the redoubt. But Vendôme, on foot, surrounded by officers, remained outside, as firm as a rock assailed by the ocean waves. Most of these brave men were killed; as the ground was strewed with their bodies, others succeeded to the almost certain death, that spared none but himself. The body of Patroclus was not more furiously contested for than the person of Vendôme; a firelock was pointed at his breast; Coleron, the captain of his guard, rushed in, received the contents, and rolled dead at the feet of his general, a memorable instance of attachment, scarce ever equalled, seldom imitated, but always applauded by the admiration of mankind. The firmness of the French outside, and the fire of those in the inner work, made the Germans reel and stagger. A battery of three guns did terrible execution; the Germans stormed it, and the French, to a man, perished in defence of their guns. The Prince then headed a charge, to carry the inner work; if carried, the waters of the Adda, or surrender, were the alternatives of the French army. The Prince, at the head of his grenadiers, received a musket shot in the throat; he still continued to fight and give orders; a second struck him in the knee; he was carried off weltering in blood, leaving his men discouraged, and uncertain whether the wound of the hero was mortal or not. Vendôme redoubled his efforts; by desperate efforts he cleared the redoubt, and pushed the Germans towards the bridge on the Retorto.

General Albergalle came up at this decisive moment with the fifteen battalions from the camp of Paradise, entered the redoubt by the bridge over the Adda, drove the Germans with irresistible fury out of the redoubt, reinforced the brigades of Burke and Grancey, crossed the Pendino, and drove the Prussians back into the Retorto, leaving after them 600 men killed, and all their wounded in possession of the French. General Bibra, who succeeded Eugene, summoned the last energies of a man in the last stage of a malignant fever, and, in spite of all the efforts of the French, retained possession of the bridge on the Retorto. Night put an end to the fiercest contest that occurred during the seventeenth century; not so murderous as that of Schellenburg, or Malplaquet; but, considering the numbers engaged on both sides, the valour of the combatants, the skill and intrepidity of the generals, and the vicissitudes of the engagement, the most memorable in modern warfare. Both parties maintained their original ground; neither were beaten back; both sung

Te Deum ; and one is at a loss to admire most the genius of the Prince, who conceived the attack, or the valour of Vendôme in defeating it. In such a position the French never dreamed of an attack, and were guilty of the grossest negligence in not throwing up a breast-work in front of the bridge in the Retorto, and not guarding the sluices with a sufficient force. They in a great measure retrieved their negligenee by bravery unexampled; and although, perhaps, the French writers have not sufficiently testified the heroism of the Irish, yet in their accounts, Dillon's, Galmoy's, Berwick's, and Fitzgerald's, shine conspicuous. Verac's and Horan's shared with them the glory of the battle of Cassano. 50,000 men were engaged, and 14,000, more than a fourth of the number, were killed or wounded(*a*).

Both armies on the morning following quitted this Aceldama, leaving the dead and badly wounded a prey to dogs and vultures, bringing those off only whom the science of surgery might restore to another field of carnage. The putrefied bodies in the Adda and the Retorto, and on their banks, mingling with the exhalations of the stagnant waters around, corrupted the air, and infected the Bergamasco and the Bressan, with fluxes and fevers during the rest of the summer. In other fields of slaughter the peace of death unites the fiercest combatants in the harmony of a common grave. The mad quest of glory, and the

(*a*) Umicaglia, ib.

rage of conquest, feel compunction when the storm ceases on the battle-field, and its ravages instil sympathy into the hearts of the most obdurate. But Eugene and Vendôme, in their intrenched camps at Treviglio and Revello were too much engaged in watching each other to attend to the decencies of interring the dead, and the Lombard peasant would not abandon his agricultural labours for a work of abhorrence and abomination. The island inclosed by the Retorto and the Adda was for years after bleached with bones. The survivors who subsequently visited the scene of this memorable carnage, could, from the mounds of bones, and lines of skeletons, point out all the vicissitudes of this bloody encounter. The giant limbs and arms of the Prussian guards indicated the spot where the murderous fire of the Irish brought 600 of them to the ground; the lane of bones along the Pendino traced the line occupied by Dillon and Verac's, by Galmoy's, Fitzgerald's, and Berwick's. There many a gallant Irishman met the stroke of death in his early bloom; no mother to mourn him, no maid with her tears of love, no friend to close his dying eyes, not even a stranger to consign him to a decent grave. In thirty years after, Umicaglia, the historian of these wars, visited this spot, and sat in sorrow over these monuments of human misery, erected by the ambition of kings; he might add, the *persecution of intolerant governments*. Persecution drove these unfortunate Irish from the banks of the Shannon to those of the Adda.

Some of the ancestors of the writer of these pages fell there, *victims of their adherence to their religion, king, and country.* The *inheritor of their wrongs,* he visited this spot after a lapse of one hundred and thirty years; his heart sickened, and his sympathies were excited to tears, on viewing the *last scene* of their sufferings.

Eugene had his wounds dressed at the small house near the Orteria at the bridge of the Retorto, and on the morning following fixed his head quarters in the impregnable camp of Treviglio. Bibra died two days after of fever, and the Prince of Anhalt was removed to Brescia, where he remained oppressed by sickness for several months. Vendôme fixed his quarters at Revello, indignant at the somnolency of the Grand Prior, who during the engagement remained with six battalions at Revello, two leagues' distance, yet dreamt not of the conflict, and in the heaviness of his sleep heard not either the roar of the combatants or the thunders of the artillery.

Lee's, Dorrington's, and Clare's regiments served in Germany, under Marshal Villars, in 1705. The campaign was spent in marches and counter-marches Marlborough sought, in vain, to bring the Marshal to an engagement. Prince Lewis of Baden, envious of Marlborough's fame, and jealous of his command, withheld reinforcements, which disabled the English general from besieging Thionville or Luxemburg; and he was ultimately forced to abandon the Moselle, and return to Flanders, where the incapacity of Villeroy, at the head of the French army, elevated still more his fame, in the capture of the lines of Brabant. Villars, relieved from the pressure of the English army on the Moselle, joined Marsen's army on the Upper Rhine, where he frustrated the efforts of the Prince of Baden to penetrate into Alsace and Lorrain, as he had defeated Marlborough's admirable plan of invading the three bishoprics, Metz, Toul, and Verdun. Lieutenant-General Dorrington, and Major-General Lord Clare, had distinguished commands under him; but the Brigade had no opportunity of signalizing its valour; it shared in all the toils of a most harassing campaign, in which the generals reaped all the glory, and the soldiers suffered all the hardships, and bore great fatigues, in increasing marches, and in passing defiles, rivers, and mountains.

Great desertion prevailed in Marlborough's army whilst on the Moselle, and it is presumed the Irish Brigade was recruited by this desertion. The Marshal, with an inferior army, sought to distract and confound the Prince of Baden, by passing and repassing the Rhine, more than once threatening the lines of Stolhoven, which the dotage of old age cherished with as much fondness as the playfulness of infancy cherishes a baby-house. Feigning a demonstration to attack them, the Marshal fixed his camp on the Ranchin, near the spot where Turenne was killed, and where Hamilton's foot covered the retreat of his army. Some of the officers of that corps, then serving in the Brigade, could have pointed out the precise spot where the Irish legion stood firm against the reiterated attacks of the Hungarian battalions, and might exult in the valour of the soldiers under their command, who had not degenerated from the virtues of their countrymen, and had shed lustre on the land of their birth during thirteen campaigns.

Baden marched out of the lines of Behel to give battle; but the irresolution and caution of old age paralyzed his movements. Villars had time to retrograde across the Rhine to the lines of Moutier. Baden passed the Rhine at Phillipsburgh, approached the Moutier, hesitated to storm the lines, lost an admirable opportunity of storming them, and retired behind the River Stolhoven(a).

Spanish Flanders was lost, by the presumption and incapacity of Villeroy, at Ramillies(b). The French army stationed at Louvain was inferior to that of the allies by some thousands, and instead of evading a battle, and standing on the defensive, marched towards the Meuse, to meet that of the Allies assembled at Meerdorp. The Duke of Marlborough, on the 22nd of May, moved towards Namur by the right bank of the Mehaigne river, and on the 23rd saw, with surprise and delight,

(a) Quincy, vol. iv., Campaign of 1705 in Germany.
(b) 23rd May, 1706.

the French army moving from Judoigne, towards the Mehaigne, with intent to give him battle. The Little and Great Geete have their sources close to the right bank of the Mehaigne, and between these the French drew up in order of battle, having their right leaning on the Mehaigne, the village of Ramillies in front of it, their left leaning on the village of Autre Eglise, and protected from attack, as well as impeded from acting by an impassable morass, formed by the Little Geete. The French cavalry was stationed on the right and left, in two lines. The Irish regiments of Clare, Dorrington, and Lee, and some newly raised French battalions, were thrown into Ramillies, too far from the French line to be supported; and the French order of battle was a *fac simile* of their order at Hochstadt. Marlborough surveyed this defective order with the eye of a great general, and adopted the same tactics as those that gained the victory of Blenheim. He withdrew the greater part of his cavalry, and several battalions of infantry, from his right to his left; drew up his cavalry more in four lines, without intervals, directed the battalions to carry the village of Frauqueuieso. His vast superiority of numbers enabled him to form a reserve, behind his centre and left, of near 20,000 men. These movements could not be concealed in an open plain without underwood, as was the case at Hochstadt. The French inferior officers observed them with dismay; they had no reserves; their cavalry was drawn up in two lines, with intervals; they dreaded the masses of the allied cavalry coming down on them; they expostulated with Villeroy, begged of him to strengthen his right and centre, by drafts from his left, but the presumption and ignorance of this favourite were inaccessible to the suggestions of skill and experience.

During these movements both armies cannonaded each other with little effect; heads flying off, mangled limbs, or shattered bodies, damp not the courage of veterans before the heat of action commences; the thunders and ravages of artillery paralyze new levies and recruits. The troops on both sides were the best in the world, and were long practised in fields of slaughter. Marlborough commenced the action by a feigned attack on the French left at Autre Eglise with the view of inducing Villeroy to make drafts from his right to that quarter. As he made no impression, the French line remained unaltered. The left and centre of the English next pushed on, and were met with the usual gallantry of the French nation. Twenty-four pieces of heavy artillery were in advance of the English line, and twelve battalions of infantry to attack the village of Ramillies. The French cavalry, particularly the household troops, bore down three lines of the English, but whole squadrons of the latter entered into the intervals between the bodies of French cavalry, took them in flank, threw them into disorder, and nearly destroyed them.

During the conflict his twelve battalions, supported by their line of infantry, stormed the village of Ramillies. Feuquieres, in his Memoirs, complains that it was stationed too far from the French line to be supported, and that the infantry stationed in it were foreigners and new levies(*a*). So far as regarded the foreigners, no complaint was ever more unfounded. No portion of the French army fought so bravely as these foreign mercenaries. The attack and defence continued two hours. The Dutch troops, repeatedly repulsed, as often returned to the charge. So long as the Irish were supported by the right wing of the French, they never yielded a single inch of ground, but when the cavalry of that wing was broken, and the infantry taken in flank, they were forced to retreat. Lord Clare, who commanded the Irish, and who, on this occasion, performed prodigies, did not, like the French General in the village of Blenheim, under similar circumstances, surrender his fine corps prisoners of war, but cut his way through the enemy's battalions, bearing down their infantry with matchless intrepidity. In the heroic effort to save his corps he was mortally wounded(*b*), and many of his best officers were killed. His Lieutenant-Colonel, Murrough O'Brien,

(*a*) Memoirs de Feuquieres, vol. ii. p. 188.
(*b*) He died in Brussels.

on this occasion evinced heroism worthy of the name of O'Brien, assuming the command, and leading on his men with fixed bayonets, he bore down and broke through the enemy's ranks, took two pair of colours from the enemy(*a*), and joined the rere of the French retreat on the heights of St. Andre.

Blenheim and Ramillies elevated the fame of Marlborough to the pinnacle of greatness, both gained by the same system of tactics, suggested by Eugene on the plain of Hochstadt, affording the shelter of underwood to conceal the movements, and followed on the plain of Ramillies, which did not admit of any such stratagem. Ordinary capacity would have avoided a conflict with such superior forces, or have met the movements of the Duke by corresponding changes, and the real praise to which Marlborough is entitled, arises from his promptitude and coolness in changing his order of battle, and the steadiness and resolution with which he carried on the attack. Success, adulation, party spirit, the servile pens of hungry poets, have raised his name above the level of his age and country, but much of his glory is shared with Prince Eugene, the companion of most of his victories, and the greatest of the Generals of

---

(*a*) A celebrated English regiment. These colours were suspended in the church of the Irish Benedictine nuns at Ypres. They formed as romantic a memorial as ever was seen, if we recollect the place and the men, where and by whom they were won, and the sanctuary of the "Exiles" in which they were deposited. Lee Forman's Letter on the Irish Brigade.

the 17th century; much of it is built on the incapacity of the Generals opposed to him—Villeroy, a minion without ordinary sagacity, Tallard, shortsighted, and Marsen raised to command by his sanctity, and canonized for his blockheadism. If Marlborough had had to contend with Turenne, Condè, or Luxemburg, his name might have gone down to posterity with the praise of more than an ordinary master of the art of war. But he was never tried in adversity, he never encountered genius or science. His victories of Blenheim and Ramillies will never, in the impartial judgment of posterity, equal the fame and merit of the combat of Vittoria, the defence of Torres Vedras, and the triumph on Mont St. Jean.

In 1706 Philip the Fifth raised two regiments of Irish Dragoons, officered by the reduced officers of the Irish Brigade, one of them was commanded by Mahony, and the other by Colonel Grafton(a); these, with the second battalion of Berwick and Burke's regiment, performed very important services. On the 8th of August Admiral Leake took Alicant by assault, Mahony, the Governor, retired to the citadel. He received three dangerous wounds in the breach, and not having a surgeon, sent for one to General Georges, who commanded the English land

(a) Quincy, vol. v. p. 251; Umicaglia, p. 411.

"Grafton distinguished himself highly at the head of his Irish regiment of Dragoons, at the battle of Guadonna, gained by the Spaniards against the Allies." Bellevan, p. 217.

forces. An English surgeon was sent to him. Leake caused trenches to be opened before the citadal, and threatened Mahony with the last extremities, if he persisted in defending a post considered hopeless. An incessant shower of bombs from the English ships of war destroyed all the buildings of the interior, and in the course of twenty-seven days, reduced the garrison to 134 men. The batteries, mounted with cannon of the largest calibre, played on the bastions and ravelins with such tremendous effect that the whole appeared one mass of ruin ; still Mahony held out, until his provisions and water totally failed, and until a convoy of 50 horses, bringing wine and water, had been intercepted by the peasants. Necessity compelled a capitulation, the bravery of the defence was entitled to an honorable one ; English generosity which had allowed a surgeon to the wounded Governor, allowed it to as brave a garrison as ever defended a fortified town. Sixty-eight Neapolitans, thirty-six French, and thirty-six Irish Dragoons, marched out with four pieces of cannon, two mortars, matches lighted, and colours flying; the English, who admire bravery, were struck with admiration. Such an exhibition of valour had not appeared since the decline and fall of the Roman Empire(a).

The remainder of the campaign of 1706 in Flanders was a continued triumph for the English. All the fortified towns of Flanders, Antwerp, Louvain,

(a) Quincy, vol. v. pp. 4 and 5; Umicaglia, p. 373.

Brussels, Ghent, Ostend, Menin, Ath, and Dendermond, after a feeble resistance, opened their gates. So great was the desertion from the French army, and so depressed were the spirits of the troops, that if Marlborough possessed the genius of Wellington he could have penetrated the iron frontier, and marched to the French capital. Vendôme's arrival from Italy restored confidence to the army, and an impregnable camp between Condè and Lille stopped the career of the English.

The disasters at Ramillies induced the French Council to recall Vendôme from Italy to protect the northern frontier of France, and to substitute the Duke of Orleans in his place. With the bravest troops in the world, the French were every where defeated, through the incapacity of their generals. In Piedmont they besieged Turin, and would have balanced their losses in Flanders if any man of talent headed their armies in Italy. Turin was reduced to the last extremity, and could be relieved only by Eugene's army, distant 300 miles in the Ferrarese, having to cross the Po and the Adige, the two greatest rivers of Italy, and above fifty canals and rivers, at any one of which a small force might have stopped his career. On the 10th of July, under a burning sun, the Imperial General commenced this great enterprize. Several of the men and horses died of heat, and the march was afterwards confined to the night time. After six weeks of suffering and hardships, of incredible perseverance and skill, the Imperialists reached the plain of Piedmont, stormed the French intrenchments at Turin, and gained one of the greatest victories recorded in modern times. During these proceedings, the French and Austrian armies, commanded by the Count of Medavi and the Prince of Hesse Cassel, were actively engaged in the Bresciano. The four regiments of Galmoy, Dillon, Fitzgerald, and Berwick, served there, and had a very principal share in the victory of Castiglione.

Dillon commanded the right wing of the French, having the Irish regiments under his direction, and Saint Pater the left. The Hessian guards, led on by the Prince, on the first onset broke the French right, and three Spanish regiments were utterly and irretrievably broken. The Irish and French stood firm; the opening, made by the flight of the Spaniards, was filled up by the second line. The Hessian guards still advanced with a fury characteristic of their nation, carried the French batteries, killed the cannoniers, and were nearly victorious, but they were taken in flank by the left wing of the French, which totally routed the Imperial right, and drove their cavalry off the field. Medavi, at the same time, came up with his reserves, recovered his artillery, kept up a tremendous fire, and the left of the Imperialists, after the most heroic resistance, was able only to cover a very disastrous retreat. The bravery of the Hessians was equalled by that of the Irish. Dillon was made a Knight of the Order of the Holy Ghost, and raised to the rank of a Lieutenant-General. But this victory, gained the day after the battle at Turin, could not relieve that fatal disaster. Italy was soon after evacuated. The theatre of Irish glory was removed to Flanders and Spain, where we will find the Brigade in future distinguished by the same valour, but not crowned with the same success, because no longer guided by skill, but led on to slaughter by the incapacity of the French Marshals(*a*).

The armies remained encamped near each other during the rest of the summer, watching each other's movements, and both retired to winter quarters late in the season. The Generals returned to their respective courts. Prince Eugene left his army under the command of Reventlau, and Vendôme his under Medavi. The main body of the Imperialists was stationed at Calcinato, having Carpondalo on its right, and Montechiaro on its left. Intrenchments, canals, and rising grounds seemed to render this post inaccessible, and made the Germans unsuspicious of any attack during the winter. Vendôme, usually indolent, would at times display unusual activity; his pride was wounded by the surprise at Cassano, and he sought to retrieve his honour by a counter-surprise. Early in April, he arrived at Milan, gave orders to

(*a*) Umicaglia, 362. Quincy, vol. v. 182.

Medavi to collect his forces ; pretended indignation at the conduct of the commissariat in not supplying the troops in their different stations ; affected to blame Medavi with the disposition of the quarters ; under pretence of a change, directed movements which would collect them at once ; took to his bed, sent for doctors, and took medicines ; of a sudden mounted his charger, and rode in full speed to Medavi's army, 23,000 strong, collected for the purpose of attacking Calcinato. During the night of the 19th of April, after passing some fosses and canals, the French army appeared in front of the Imperial quarters. The Imperialists were completely surprised(*a*).

The brigade of Piedmont, to which Fitzgerald's regiment was attached, formed the right of the French, and was commanded by Brigadier-General Fitzgerald. The brigade of Auvergne, of which Dillon's formed part, was stationed in the centre ; Grancey's brigade was on the left, and comprised Galmoy's. The Marines, commanded by General Walter Bourke, were destined to attack the houses in the suburbs of Calcinato.

Prince Eugene, retiring from Vienna, heard in the Trentine of the movements of the French army. His sagacious mind penetrated at once into the plan of Vendôme; and he instantly despatched orders to Re-

(*a*) Umicaglia, 336. Quincy, vol. v. p. 80.

ventlau, a Dane, who commanded, to collect all the troops in the Bresciano, and place them between Montechiaro and Sonata, having the Saviola Fosse in front, a fine position for defence or retreat in case of necessity, and that he himself would proceed in all haste to take the command. Some regiments refused to quit their quarters so early in the season; some officers disapproved of the position behind the Saviola, and the French anticipated them by crossing the canal, over bridges constructed in all haste, and deploying in the same order of battle on the opposite bank. Reventlau had collected 15,000 men, and finding the Saviola passed, his order of battle was formed with a view to retreat. The infantry was placed between Calcinato and the bridge of St. Marc; some battalions were stationed in the intrenchments in front of Calcinato, and the cavalry on the left to defend the flanks of the infantry in their retreat to the mountains. The troops in Montechiaro were also directed to fall back on the hills to the rere. The impetuosity of the French defeated these arrangements. The brigades of Piedmont, Auvergne, and Grancey, reserving their fire, received the fire of the enemy at half pistol shot distance, and then rushed on with fixed bayonets, not giving the Germans time to reload, and burst through their lines. The Imperial cavalry made a bold but ineffectual attempt to sustain their infantry. They made a furious charge, were received on the bayonets of the French, were unable to break their solid array, and galloped off in full speed to the mountains. The Imperial left wing made a stouter resistance, and sustained several discharges. Grancey's and Galmoy's pressed them in front, and Perche's in flank. Visconti, at the head of the Imperial cavalry, broke the French cavalry, and covered the retreat, which, by the pressure of the superior numbers of the French, became a precipitate and disastrous flight. 3000 men killed, and 3000 prisoners, avenged Vendôme's surprise at Cassano. In this victory the Irish had a principal share; their officers, Lord Galmoy, Dillon, Burke, and Fitzgerald, had principal commands. All the grenadiers of the army, including the Irish, were sent under Fitzgerald in pursuit. The army rallied near a castle on the side of a mountain at two leagues' distance, on the road to Salo, having a deep ravine in front; here they made a resolute stand. Fitzgerald, with the first line of grenadiers, made several bold efforts to cross the ravine, and get to the summit of the hills in the rere, but the post, after six hours' continual conflict, was found inaccessible, and Vendome ordered him to withdraw.

Eugene collected his broken forces at Gavardo; found he could no longer maintain his ground in the Bresciano; evacuated Salo; fortified the passes into the Trentine, and by forced marches descended into the Veronese on both sides of the Adige, and occupied nearly the same ground he had occupied during the campaign of 1701(a).

In the early part of this year Dillon's regiment served in Dauphiné, and guarded the passes of the Alps. Lieutenant-General Dillon commanded a large division of the French, destined to raise the siege of Toulon. Under the immediate orders of the Marshal De Tessè he stormed the heights of St. Catharine over Toulon, and carried that important post. The English, Germans, and Piedmontese, vied with each other in pushing on the works. Fort St. Louis, at the entrance of the harbour, was defended by a Captain Dillon, and was battered from the fleet and the shore. A practicable breach was made. De Tessè sent orders to Dillon to withdraw his garrison; he held out three days longer, and obtained the praise not only of a protracted and gallant defence, but of admirable address, in carrying off his men by water into the town. When the Allies mounted to the assault they found not a man within the precincts of the fort. The season was advancing; the defence of Toulon obstinate; the English were for persevering. Prince Eugene, always against this foolish enterprize, in council yielding to it, merely to extract money and supplies from the English, represented the impossibility of carrying Toulon, made the most skilful arrangements for retiring behind the Var, and effected an admirable retreat. Lieutenant-General

(a) Quincy, vol. v. p. 92.

Dillon was dispatched with thirteen battalions to guard the valley of Barcelonette; he accomplished that object with his usual activity(a).

Lee's and Galmoy's were attached to Villars' army on the Rhine. Lieutenant-General Lee had a principal command, and led on the left wing of the French in storming the lines of Stolhoven. These marvellous intrenchments, the pride and boast of Prince Louis of Baden, the pedestal of his fame in his declining years, yielded to the impetuous assault of the French. Villars, in the stately palace of Rastadt, filled with the trophies of Turkish victories, rioted in the luxuries and riches of the house of Baden; from the terraces of the Castle of Heidelberg he surveyed the whole Palatinate under him, a prey to his arms; and from the magnificent residence of Manheim, he viewed the deep and rapid stream of the Rhine, wafting the fame of his achievements to the camp of Marlborough, and to the capital of the United Provinces. Prince Louis, tortured by gout and envy, broken by age, his fame clouded, and his laurels withered, escaped, by a timely death, the mortification of seeing this monument of his vanity, that exhausted his revenues, and exercised his genius for seven years, crumbled in an hour. His family have raised to their hero a costly sepulchre, a pompous statue, and a storied urn in the church of

(a) Umicaglia, p. 421. Quincy, vol. v. pp. 370–376.

Baden-Baden. The impartial judgment of posterity rejects epitaphs defiled by unmerited praise, and with unerring accuracy traces the outlines of those who have figured in the world(*a*).

Though in the printed accounts of the battle of Almanza, the name of the Irish does not appear, yet Mahony's dragoons, and the second battalion of Berwick(*b*), had a very distinguished share in that important victory. Ruvigni, Lord Galway, inferior in cavalry to the French, interlined his horse and foot, placing on his right five battalions of infantry, and next to them five squadrons of cavalry, and continuing the same disposition along his whole first and second line. In order to outflank the Gallo-Spanish army a portion of the allied cavalry was taken from the second line to extend the first, an irreparable fault, as it weakened the centre.

The Duke of Berwick adopted the usual practice of placing the cavalry on the wings and the infantry between them, all in two lines. Mahony's horse were on the right, composed of four squadrons, Mayne's brigade, Berwick's second battalion forming part of it, stationed in the second line, being the extreme

(*a*) Manuscript Memoir of the Irish Brigade. Quincy, vol. v. pp. 411, 424, 448.

(*b*) Berwick, in the Duke of Orleans' absence, commanded King Philip's army. The Marquis das Minas had the first rank in King Charles's, but Lord Galway seems to have acted for himself. The battle was fought on the 14th April, 1707.

right of the infantry. Mahony commanded thirteen squadrons of cavalry, in the second line of the extreme left. The engagement began on the left of the English, whose cavalry was soon broken by the charge of the Spanish horse, but the English infantry poured such tremendous volleys, that the Spanish cavalry were broken in their turn, which allowed the allied cavalry to rally, and enabled the five English battalions to take in flank the infantry of the French right, deserted by their cavalry. Marshal Berwick, seeing the disorder, directed Mayne's brigade, of which Berwick's battalion formed part, to wheel to the left, in order to front the English. Whereupon this brigade, with their muskets nearly touching the breasts of the English, poured in their fire, attacked them with fixed bayonets, and so totally routed them, that they never were able to rally. Berwick himself, having rallied his cavalry on the right, led them on to the charge, utterly broke the mixed line of the Allies, so as that the fate of the battle remained no longer doubtful. The left wing made a most obstinate resistance, broke and drove off the field the brigades of the Crown and Orleans, withstood and repulsed repeated charges of the Gallo-Spanish cavalry on their left, commanded by Mahony, but being taken in flank by four squadrons and nine battalions detached from the right, retired like lions, and covered the retreat of their shattered army. Mayne's brigade pursued them to the mountains, and did more damage in the pursuit than in the field of battle, as whole battalions and squadrons surrendered the day after, prisoners of war(*a*).

In this engagement the Allies lost near 15,000 killed and prisoners; it was decisive of the fate of the Spanish monarchy: the firmness and presence of mind of the Duke of Berwick were admirable. As cool and as calm as he would be at a review, he provided for every emergency. Wherever his line yielded, he brought up troops from other parts to sustain it. Wherever the Allies yielded, he was at hand to press them with fresh troops taken from his own second line, where his first line was firm, and not in danger of being penetrated. He was every where leading on, encouraging, and exhorting the Spaniards in their tongue, and the French and Irish in the respective languages of their countries.

Three Irish battalions were formed out of the prisoners made at Almanza. They were Irish Catholics, whom poverty enlisted, and persecution induced to join the Brigade, wherein they could enjoy the free exercise of their religion, which in the ranks of the English was denied.

Lord Galway escaped with his cavalry to Catalonia, leaving garrisons in Alcira and Xativa. Mahony sat down before Alcira, which, after five days of open trenches, capitulated. With equal vigour he pressed the citadel of Xativa, which surrendered

(*a*) Quincy, vol. v. pp. 398–403.

soon after. He next blockaded Valentia, having under his orders eleven battalions of infantry, a regiment of cavalry, and his own regiment of Irish dragoons. With part of these forces he besieged Denia, but found the garrison too numerous and well provided, and having himself an insufficient force, he raised the siege. Altea was of vast consequence to the Allies; it protected the country to Denia on one side, and to Alicant on the other. It was attacked with so much skill and vigour, that the garrison parleyed, offering to surrender unless relieved in four days. In a council of war at Alicant it was resolved to relieve it, and Sir Charles Hotham was detached for that purpose, with part of the garrison of Alicant. Mahony had intercepted 30,000 Miguelets endeavouring to throw supplies into Altea, and possessed himself of a great quantity of ammunition and provisions, but on the approach of Hotham's detachment, joined by these Miguelets, he raised the siege.

The Duke of Orleans, who had the command in chief, was chagrined that he had not been present at Almanza to share the glory of the victory, and was jealous of the fame of Berwick. He pursued the allied army to Catalonia, sat down before Lerida, one of the strongest fortresses in Europe, garrisoned by five battalions, two English, two Dutch, and one Portuguese, commanded by the Prince of Hesse Darmstadt. The eyes of all Europe were fixed upon this siege; the utmost anxiety prevailed with respect to its fate; the garrison and the assailants were among the best troops in Europe, commanded by the bravest and most experienced officers. The regiments of Burke, Dillon, and Berwick were not inferior to any of the troops who took an active part in that memorable siege.

Lerida, the ancient Ilerda, is situated in a plain watered by the River Segre, the ancient Sicoris, the scene of Cæsar's triumph over Afranius and Petreius, the lieutenants of Pompey. The arts of modern engineering had been exhausted in repairing old, and adding new fortifications. The waters of the Sicoris filled up its broad and deep fosses; Fort Gardan, on the summit of a rock, accessible only on the side of the town, and connected with it by a covered way, strengthened by additional works, rendered it unassailable on one side, as did the rapid Segre on another. Fort Gardan was built on the hill, so accurately described by Cæsar, where his troops were repulsed by Afranius, and where his admirable genius and presence of mind restored the combat, and saved his army from an irreparable defeat(*a*).

(*a*) Quincy, vol. v. 43–440. "'Erat inter oppidum Ilerdam, et proximum collem ubi castra Petreius atque Afranius habebant planitia circiter passuum, atque in hoc feré medio spatio tumulus erat paulló editior quem se occupasset Cæsar, et communisset ab oppido et ponte et commeatu omni, quem in oppidum contulerant, se interclusurum adversarios confidebat.'—Cæsar de Bello Civili, Liber i. s. xliii. Afranius was encamped on an

Lerida did not make the stand all Europe expected. The Prince of Darmstadt evinced his usual bravery, but the English Governor, Wells, controlled his fire and discountenanced sorties. On the 4th of October, the trenches were opened, and Burke's and Dillon's mounted them, and were relieved

eminence, now included within the fortifications, but then 300 paces distant from the walls, and had neglected to occupy the rock, now Fort Gardan, which lay between the camp and the town. Its importance struck Cæsar. His camp was opposite to that of Afranius, and a little farther from the eminence. He calculated by a rapid movement to take possession of it, and ordered the Antisignani, the *élite* of three legions, corresponding with our modern grenadiers, to carry it. Afranius perceived the movement. The guard usually stationed outside the gate of a Roman camp, were ordered to occupy the eminence; the distance being shorter, they reached it first ; a desperate conflict ensues ; fresh cohorts arrived from Afranius's camp; the three legions of Cæsar, mixed in the combat, were attached in flank by bodies who had marched round the hill unobserved, and were utterly broken and routed. In this emergency, Cæsar put himself at the head of the ninth legion, attacked the triumphant soldiers of Pompey with such fury, that he forced them to fly precipitately into the town of Ilerda, and to the eminence disputed. Afranius, in the mean time, drew out his legions, and having a decided advantage of ground, beat Cæsar's men back, whose intrepidity alone saved them from a total defeat. They made one bold and desperate effort: drove their opponents to the top of the eminence, and under the very walls of the town, and then effected a retreat to their own camp." See M. Guiscard's Campaign of Cæsar in Spain, and Antiquites Militaires, vol. i. p. 358.

by other regiments in succession. On the 12th, a practicable breach was made. Darmstadt wished to defend it. Wells ordered the garrison into the citadel, and Orleans on the 13th marched in without opposition, and gave up one of the principal towns to be sacked by a rapacious soldiery, regardless of all laws, human and divine. The sack was equally disgraceful to Wells, who waited for a practicable breach, and would not defend it, and to Orleans, who took the town without an assault.

The citadel made a better defence. The heroism of Darmstadt triumphed for a time over the pusillanimity of Wells. Trenches were opened on the side of the Segre, and within the precints of the town. Dillon's, Burke's, and Berwick's mounted them in rotation. Darmstadt headed two desperate sallies; drove the besiegers from some houses fortified by them, and levelled some of their trenches. But the works and ramparts soon crumbled under the tremendous fire of the French batteries. General Stanhope, who advised the battle of Almanza, ardent and adventurous, without skill or experience, applied to Count Noyelles to abandon the defence of the Ter, and to join him with 5000 men under his command. This gallant and experienced Fleming refused to sanction the temerity of the English General, incurred his reproaches, and requested his own recall, to prevent further discord, so ruinous to the Allies. On the 11th of November, the breach being still impracticable, Wells, in a council of war suggested the necessity of a surrender. Darmstadt protested against it ; Wells beat a parley, and wanted terms without surrendering Fort Gardan, still untouched. The Duke of Orleans insisted on the surrender of it. Darmstadt required a written attestation of his refusal to concur in the capitulation.

Towards the middle of November, the Chevalier Asfeild and Mahony sat down before Carthagena. The place was garrisoned by one English battalion and a regiment of English dismounted cavalry, who made a show of determined resistance. Hedge, the Governor, to a summons of surrender, replied he hoped to merit the esteem of the besiegers by a gallant defence ; he sent the same answer to a second summons of the Duke of Berwick, who assumed the chief command, but after three days' open trenches he surrendered at discretion.

Lee's and Fitzgerald's infantry, and Nugent's horse, served in Flanders this year. Vendôme, by a Fabian system, disconcerted all the projects of the Duke of Marlborough. In his camp at Sombref, near Fleurus, and afterwards in his camp at Gemblours, he thwarted all the views of the Allies. During a campaign without sieges or battles, the Irish had no opportunity of displaying their usual valour. On one occasion only they highly distinguished themselves ; they were attached to the brigade of Piedmont. Marlborough sought to attack the French in their camp at Gemblours. The French General, wishing to avoid an engagement, decamped on the night of the 11th of August. At 12 o'clock the allied army approached in order of battle. Lieutenant-General Albergotti, who, by his superior talents, deserved a Marshal's staff, but was excluded from that rank by his foreign birth, commanded the rere-guard of the French, composed of Piedmont's and Vendôme's brigades, twenty companies of grenadiers, and two regiments of dragoons. They were pressed by 20,000 men, but so admirable was the order of retreat, so firm were the troops, and so deadly their fire, that the pursuers under Lord Albemarle desisted. This rere-guard joined their main body on the plain of Cambron Abbey, where it had traced out an intrenched camp, which the Duke found impregnable. He soon after returned by the Hague to England, mortified that the skill of Vendôme had not only prevented his adding to his laurels, but had withered those he had obtained through the incapacity of Villeroy and Tallard(a).

Mahony was appointed commander-in-chief of the Spanish troops in Sicily, where his arrival in April secured to the King of Spain the possession of that important island, and extinguished various conspiracies in favour of the Austrians. After performing these important services his presence was re-

(a) Quincy, vol. v. p. 284.

quired in Spain, to command the cavalry of the Gallo-Spanish army.

Two battalions of Berwick's, Grafton's Irish dragoons, and Bulkeley's Irish regiment of infantry in the service of Spain, formed part of the besieging army at Tortosa, in 1708. This place, on the banks of the Ebro near the sea, was strongly fortified, and was garrisoned by some of the best troops of the Allies. The Palatine General, Effrom, made a most gallant defence, disputed every inch of ground, and annoyed the besiegers with incessant sorties. The regiment of Berwick suffered severely, having mounted the trenches several nights. The Lieutenant-Colonel, and several officers and men, were killed; after twenty-one days' siege the place surrendered upon honourable terms.

Vendôme commanded in Flanders, and had under him the Irish troops, who had contributed much to his victories in Italy. O'Brien's was attached to the brigade of Bourbonnois, and Fitzgerald's to the Dauphin's. Unfortunately for the French, the Duke of Burgundy, having the nominal command in chief, being youthful, surrounded by flatterers, and officers disheartened by defeats, was led astray by timid councils, arrogated the privilege of superior command, and rejected the councils of Vendôme. He had penetrated into West Flanders, captured Ghent and Bruges, and was about besieging Oudenarde, when the allied army, superior in numbers, and commanded by Eugene and Marlborough, approached the French camp, between Alost and Ghent, having the Dender in front, and Scheldt in its rere. Vendôme wished to dispute the passage of the Dender; the Duke of Burgundy to retire under the cannon of Ghent, to avoid an engagement, and ordered a retreat behind the Scheldt at Gavern, half way between Oudenarde and Ghent. Vendôme expostulated, he said he knew Prince Eugene too well, who would force an engagement in spite of all their efforts.

Lord Cadogan passed 10,000 over the bridge of Oudenarde, and built a bridge below it for the passage of the rest of the army. Vendôme advised an attack when part only of the Allies should pass the river; some secret impulse pointed to Ghent, but, doubtful and irresolute, the Duke ordered a halt on the heights of Gaverin, as if he wished to dispute the passage of the Scheldt. "The opportunity is passed," cried the Duke of Vendôme, "you should have fought, and not halted." "You are to blame," replied the Duke of Burgundy, "I halted in deference to your wishes." "If you had formed in front of the Scheldt," answered Vendôme, "as I had wished, you would have had room to act. The ground you are now driven to is confined, full of hedges and ditches, and inconvenient to range the troops." To avoid an engagement was no longer possible. At five in the evening the allied cavalry was drawn up in order of battle, and at six the infantry occupied their ground, the right leaning on the Scheldt, opposite to the left of the French, whose army was disorganized, and not sufficiently arranged, in consequence of contradictory orders given by the two Dukes. Vendôme seeing the allied cavalry drawn up, before the arrival of their infantry, ordered the left of the French to charge; the Duke of Burgundy countermanded this order, which, if obeyed, would have led to the rout of the right wing of the Allies. After their infantry was arranged, Vendôme, with his usual impetuosity, led on the French left, and French bravery was never more conspicuous than in this attack. The regiments of Fitzgerald, O'Brien, and Nugent, formed part of this wing. The French right, on account of the difficulty of the ground, was unable to expand, which enabled the Duke of Marlborough to reinforce his right with twenty battalions under the Duke of Argyle. This checked the impetuosity of the French, broke their line, and forced them to a precipitate retreat. Vendôme rallied some fifteen battalions, and carried off the remnant under the cannon of Ghent. The loss of the French in killed was not considerable, but great in their wounded and prisoners. Brigadier General Fitzgerald was among the latter.

The celebrated seige of Lille was the immediate consequence of this victory. The Irish battalion of reduced officers, under the description of the Queen's regiment of Fusiliers, formed part of the garrison. Marshal Bouflers was governor, and Lieutenant-General Lee threw himself into the place. The siege lasted full three months, Eugene commanding the besiegers, and Marlborough the army of observation. The attack, defence, and sorties, carried on with equal skill and resolution, were not less sanguinary than some of the pitched battles we have mentioned. The relation would fatigue the reader; sufficient it is to mention that the Irish reduced officers behaved with their wonted intrepidity. They had been embarked at Dunkirk, on the Chevalier St. George's proposed expedition to Scotland, which failed, and were during the siege of Lille attached to the different regiments in the garrison, and when the siege was over, were again regimented, and in marching out must have excited the sympathy, no less than the admiration of the military of Europe engaged in that siege. Gentlemen by birth, education, and inheritance, victims to conscience and loyalty, famed for valour, reduced from wealth and military station to poverty and to the ranks, they submitted to their cruel destinies, with the same fortitude that marked the heroism of Dundee's officers reduced to the same state, and immortalized in the pages of Dalrymple. Lieutenant-General Lee headed most of the sorties, and evinced equal skill and bravery. He deserved a Marshal's staff, and would have obtained one, if versed in the intrigues of the Court, but being a foreigner, his rewards were confined to the great cross of the order of Saint Louis, and to the fame he acquired. He was severely wounded by the bursting of a shell. Marshal Bouflers nearly monopolized the glory of the defence, being a Frenchman, a Marshal, and chief in command. He merited the esteem of the great Prince whose perseverance and skill carried the masterpiece of the great Vauban. He invited the Prince to dine with him in the citadel, who assented, on condition that the viands should be the same as if the place had not surrendered. The first dish served up was a piece of roast horse flesh; the Prince found it excellent. On the day following Eugene gave the Marshal an exquisite entertainment at his quarters, in the Abbey of St. Loo. History delights to dwell on these trivialities, because they relieve the sad picture of war, and are characteristic of generous hearts.

Prince Eugene and Marlborough finding the French army under the command of Villars, substituted for Vendôme to satisfy the Duke of Burgundy, in an impregnable camp between Lille and Arras, sat down before Tournay, whereon the Irish reduced officers were attached to the different regiments in garrison, as at Lille. They inspired their own courage, and animated by their example, but the defence was not maintained with science. The Marquis de Sourville, the governor, had distinguished himself at Lille under the directions of Bouflers. Placed in the chief command he shewed himself unequal to it, and that the capacity to carry on is distinct from the genius requisite to direct, the operations of war. After the surrender, Prince Eugene threatened Mons: the capture of so many places would open the iron frontier, and lay open the heart of France. Villars's fame was on the decline; he had an army of 110,000 men; he was as vainglorious as he was brave, and his own character, his impetuosity, and the reproaches of his nation, impelled him to hazard an engagement.

Villars, the victor at Friedlingen, at the first battle of Hochstadt, and at the lines of Bihel, though conscious of his own talents, dreaded the responsibility of a battle against Eugene and Marlborough, and requested the aid of another general: Bouflers, his senior, was sent to him. But Bouflers united the pliability of a courtier with the pride of a soldier; Villars was his senior in science, and a favourite with Madame de Maintenon, and his policy or his patriotism submitted to the orders of Villars.

On the plain between Mons and Maubeuge Villars advanced his army, with a view to accept, not to give battle, and at the same time to intercept the operations of the Allies on that side of Mons, and to cut off their supplies. The covering army of Marlborough was encamped at Quevy, between Mons and the wood of Sart. The high road from Bavay to Mons runs through a plain, a full mile in breadth, skirted by the wood of Sart on the left, and the narrow wood of Jansart on the right, between which, and the extensive wood of Lagniere, was another aperture, about half a mile in breadth. The situation was admirable for defence; the Allies, not suspecting an attempt to raise the siege of Mons, neglected it: on the night of the 8th of September Villars occupied it; on the 9th the Allies moved from Quevy, and encamped in front of the above openings; they allowed Villars, during the whole of the 9th, to make his arrangements, and never was made a more admirable disposition. He formed his infantry in a curve, intrenched in and along the wood of Lagniere, his centre extending across the apertures in the plain and little wood of Jansart, and his left forming a curve, in like manner, inside the wood of Sart; his left was protected also in flank by a marsh deemed impracticable. His cavalry was drawn up behind his infantry, in the openings between the woods. The front was protected by abattis of trees, and intrenchments hastily thrown up. His army amounted to 110,000 men; that of the Allies somewhat, but not much, superior. Eugene, surveying their camp on the 9th of September, observed the marsh on the left of the French was practicable, but that without reinforcements an attack was hazardous, and likely to fail. The whole of the 10th was allowed to Villars to complete his intrenchments. The Allies on that day received reinforcements of 30,000 men from Tournay, Ath, and other garrisons(a).

In a council of war the Dutch deputies depre-

(a) Quincy, vol. vi. p. 184.

cated an engagement; some of the allied Generals sided with them. Eugene represented that without a battle the siege of Mons could not be maintained. The French veterans had perished at Ramillies, Blenheim, Turin, Cassano; their new levies would not stand against the troops of the Allies, victors in so many battles.

Lee's and O'Brien's brigades were at the extreme left of the French right, and intrenched opposite the smaller opening between the woods of Jansart and Lagniere; they were formed of the regiments of Lee, O'Brien, Dorrington, O'Donnell, and Galmoy. The French and Swiss Guards were next to them on their right; and the Bavarian and Cologne Guards immediately behind them, in the second line. These were the *élite* of the French army, and upon their firmness Villars placed his chief dependence. Both armies cannonaded each other during the whole of the 10th, the French having 80, and the Allies 120 pieces of cannon; about 400 men were killed on each side(*a*).

A dense mist on the morning of the 11th concealed the movements of the Allies; at 8 o'clock the sun dispelled it, and shone on 240,000 men ranged in battle array; their arms glittering in its beams; their military music rousing to the mortal strife; and their cannons announcing, in repeated peals of thunder, the commencement of a conflict, which was to con-

(*a*) Quincy, vol. vi. p. 184.

sign 30,000 gallant fellows in the prime of life to untimely graves. Marlborough and Eugene rode along the lines, had spirits given to the men to raise their courage, and animated the officers by appeals to courage and glory, and then galloped to their posts, Eugene to the right and Marlborough to the left.

The allied centre commenced the attack, but recoiled on the wood of Sart, annoyed, probably, by the tremendous fire of the horns of the French crescent. Eugene led on the English guards against the wood of Sart. The King's brigade fired, at too great a distance, not a man of the Allies fell. Cheval's brigade reserved its fire till the English were within pistol shot; whole files of the Guards fell, and these *élite* of the Allies retreated a hundred paces, but a portion of the Allies were enabled by fascines to cross the morass, and attack the French in flank: the Duke of Argyle, with part of the allied centre that had recoiled, attacked the left in front. A tremendous struggle took place in the wood of Sart. The French were pressed by superiority of numbers, and by valour the most desperate. Villars sent for reinforcements to the right; Bouflers, who commanded, equally pressed by Marlborough, could spare none. Villars had no resource but to weaken his centre. Lee's and O'Brien's brigades, though in the front line in the centre, were brought to sustain the left wing. Villars had been an eye-witness of their bravery at Hochstadt, and at the lines of Stolhoven; he had more confidence in them than in the French and Swiss guards, in the second line immediately behind them. The Irish, headed by the Count de Villars and the Chevalier Nanges, charged the English, probably with national antipathy, bore down all before them, recovered the ground that was lost, and forced the enemy to the outskirts of the wood. The brigades of Champagne, Charost, Brittany, Tourville, the King's and Queen's, shared in this desperate effort to drive back the Allies.

On the left of the Allies Count Telly led on the Dutch, and their mercenaries, the Scotch and Swiss, against the French right, under Bouflers. The bravery of the troops on both sides rendered the conflict most sanguinary. The Scotch and Swiss carried some of the intrenchments, but were, after two hours, driven out of them with immense slaughter. An opening made in the intrenchments by Bouflers allowed the French horse grenadiers to sally through them, but they were received with such a terrible discharge, that they fled precipitately: but on that side the battle was completely gained by the French, although Marlborough did all that skill, example, and exhortation could perform; 2,000 dead bodies lay piled in front of the French lines(*a*).

On the left also the French were succeeding, when the Duke of Argyle, one of the bravest men of his age, led on twenty battalions against the wood of

(*a*) Quincy, vol. vi. pp. 186–198. Histoire du Prince Eugene, pp. 93–102.

Sart, rallied the troops who had yielded, and by superiority of numbers, as well as signal valour, recovered from Charost's, Champagne's, Lee's, and O'Brien's brigades, the ground they had gained, drove them out of the wood, and reached the plain in rere of it. Villars, at the head of the King's, Queen's, and Perche's brigades, and some dismounted dragoons, charged them with fixed bayonets, and drove them back into the wood. In this desperate encounter he received a wound in the knee, still continued to fight, but from loss of blood was carried off almost senseless(*a*).

Eugene and Marlborough were about to retreat, every effort to break the French line on the plain behind the wood of Sart had failed, and on the right Bouflers was victorious; but Lord Cadogan observing the void left in the French centre by the removal of the brigades of Champagne, Lee, and O'Brien, was not filled up, advised an attack in that quarter. A portion of the troops repulsed by Bouflers marched along the edge of the wood of Lagniere, their cannon, at the same time, pouring incessant and destructive discharges into the French line of cavalry drawn up in the rere. The intrenchments were carried without resistance. Marlborough retained the infantry within the intrenchments, and made openings for his cavalry to attack that of the French in the plain between the two woods. The Prince of Hesse Cas-

(*a*) Feuquiere's Memoirs, 218-232.

sel, afterwards King of Sweden, headed the first squadrons, but was borne down by the French gens-d'armes; being reinforced, the cavalry of both sides, near 40,000 men, were engaged in a conflict, such as had not been witnessed in Europe since the irruption of the Alani and the Huns.

Prince Eugene, from the edge of the wood of Sart, kept up a terrible cannonade on the French cavalry, but their courage was beyond all praise, for two hours they sustained this tempest, and were successful in several charges. The Chevalier St. George headed the French horse guards: if bravery deserved a crown, he shewed himself not unworthy of it. Cowardice was never a failing of the Stuarts. Scotch heroism, sensible at all times of dangers and menaces, and headlong to encounter them, animated nine successive generations of that illustrious family. In reading their sad history sympathy for their misfortunes is relieved by admiration of their bravery.

After a struggle of two hours, in which the Imperial cuirassiers, the English, Prussian, Dutch, French, and Irish (Nugent's), fought with the most obstinate resolution, though exposed to the fire of 200 pieces of cannon, Bouflers, who headed, and claimed success in six several charges, thought it advisable to retreat. His victorious right wing covered it to Bavay, Le Quesnoy, and Valenciennes. The Allies, exhausted by six hours' fighting, by the loss of 30,000 men, and the fearless countenances of the retreating army, thought it advisable not to venture their infantry into the plain, and suffered the French to retire unmolested.

This battle, called by the English of Malplaquet, by the French of Blaregnies(*a*), by the Italians of Mons, was precipitated by the Duke of Marlborough, to balance the triumph of Mrs. Masham over his Duchess in the Queen's affections, and to sustain his declining credit at Court by the popularity of a great victory. Eugene, though sensible of the difficulties of this engagement, sanctioned the views of the English General. He dreaded the defection of the English from the great alliance, and deemed a victory, at any cost, to support the popularity of Marlborough, essential to the interests of his master. The calculations of generals and statesmen are often baffled by circumstances over which they have no control. The number of killed and wounded at Malplaquet, overspread England with mourning and discontent, and paralysed the strength of the allied army. Mons was surrendered to them, but during the three subsequent years of the war, they effected nothing but the capture of four fortresses; the fame of Marlborough declined; the increasing favour of Mrs. Masham dismissed him from the command, and restored to Louis XIV. most of the countries wrested from him by the genius and bravery of the great Eugene.

(*a*) Where Eugene and Marlborough had their head quarters.

Burke's, Dillon's, and Berwick's served in Spain under the Marshal de Berons, in the early part of this year. Count Guy Stharemberg, an officer of great experience, commanded the Allies. Major-General Burke headed the Irish troops. The campaign was not marked by any battles or sieges of note. Dillon's was at the attack of six regiments of the Allies at Montanana, who fled on the first fire, being taken by surprise. Stharemberg, by a rapid movement, surprised Balaguer, captured the garrison, took an impregnable position, and baffled the Gallo-Spaniards till they retired to winter quarters. Dillon's and Burke's had to march from Spain to reinforce the army of Dauphiné, under the Duke of Berwick, who guarded the passes of the Alps so effectually, that the Allies failed of penetrating into France.

Prince Eugene and Marlborough consumed the summer of 1710 in the sieges of Douay, Bethune, Aire, and St. Venant. These places were obstinately defended. The corps of Irish reformed officers were attached to different regiments, and obtained great praise by their conduct. Lee's, O'Brien's, Dorrington's, O'Donnel's, and Galmoy's were under the command of Villars, who confined himself to the defensive, and to intercepting convoys, and beating up the detached corps of the allies(a).

This year vast desertions of the Irish from the

(a) Quincy, vol. vi. 253.

English army in Spain enabled Philip V. to form two regiments, one under the command of Colonel John Cumerford, and the other of Colonel Michael MacAuley(a).

The Archduke Charles of Austria, the competitor for the crown of Spain, brought reinforcements with him to Catalonia, and enabled Stharemberg to quit his intrenched camp, and assume his offensive operations. Mahony surprised Cervera, and captured his magazines; he also took Calaf, besieged the castle, and took it in four days. At Almannara the Spanish cavalry were routed, and at Saragossa Stharemberg forced the Spanish army, under the Marquis of Bey, to a general engagement. Superiority of skill and numbers prevailed. The Spanish army was routed. Lieutenant-General Mahony, who commanded the right wing of the Spaniards, behaved with his usual intrepidity. Stharemberg, contrary to his own opinion, was forced to march upon Madrid, and get possession of the Spanish capital(b).

The General advised a retreat, but the enemy appeared within cannon shot, and a retreat would would be attended with as much loss as a defeat, and Stharemberg resolved to try the chances of war. He had 10,000 foot, and 2,500 horse; the Gallo-Spaniards, 12,000 foot and 5000 horse, but he sup-

(a) Manuscript Memoirs of the Irish Brigade.
(b) Quincy, vol. vi. 416.

plied his deficiency of numbers by the choice of ground and his order of battle, which corresponded with the fame he had acquired in the wars of Hungary and Italy. He was no longer hampered by Stanhope, and in this, the last engagement in which he ever commanded, the boldness of his design, and his consummate skill, raised him to an equality almost with the great men of his age. His front was protected by uneven ground, intersected by ravines and stone walls, which retarded the advance of the enemy. A deep trench protected his right flank; his cavalry was drawn up in his rere, four lines deep, and twenty pieces of artillery on his flanks on a rising ground, swept the whole field of battle. Vendôme observed the veteran infantry of the Germans on their right, and opposed to them the Walloon guards and Flemings, the *élite* of his army; a great portion of his cavalry he placed on the right wing, where he designed to make his greatest effort. Another portion of his cavalry on the left under Mahony, the Murat of his day, called "le Fameux Mahony," was destined to attack the right of the Allies. The engagement commenced with a cannonade, which lasted two hours. Lord Kilmallock's, formerly Grafton's, Irish dragoons were stationed at the extreme. Against these Stharemberg pointed ten pieces of cannon. Lord Killmallock was mortally wounded at the first discharge. A shower of cannon balls raked these immoveable squadrons; immoveable as a stone wall, these intrepid dragoons excited the admiration of the Germans.

On their right, the Gallo-Spaniards came to close quarters under the eyes of Philip, and bore down all before them, 1500 Dutch, Portuguese, and Palatine horse fled in the utmost disorder, and left their right wing exposed ; but the victorious Spanish cavalry fell to plundering the baggage, loaded with the spoils of Castile, and allowed the allied infantry to rally. Vendôme led on the left ; there Mahony and his Irish dragoons, after breaking the allied cavalry, by a rapid evolution came to the rear of their infantry; but, such was the admirable discipline and valour of the Germans, that they continued proof against his most desperate charges(*a*).

The Irish regiments of Mac Donnell, M'Auley, Comerford, and the Walloon guards attacked them in front with the most determined resolution, whilst the dragoons of Kilmallock, with desperate valour, charged them in the rear and flank. Vendôme held the Irish in the highest estimation ; with them he had fought often, gained victories, and was astonished at the terrible charges which these heroes of the army were in the habit of making. On this occasion they fought with matchless intrepidity. The Colonel, Lieutenant-Colonel, Captain Hely, and many other officers of Kilmallock's were killed. Colo-

(*a*) Quincy, vol. vi. p. 447. Bellerue, Camp. De Vendôme, pp. 204, 224.

nel O'Callaghan, of the regiment of Milan, received several sabre wounds. Major-General Grafton headed most of the charges with distinguished valour.

The German infantry, formed in a hollow square, were unconquered; they broke the Walloon guards; filled up every void and gap; recovered their cannon, which had been captured by the dragoons of Kilmallock, and at sunset remained masters of the field of battle.

The decline of the French cause in Spain had induced Louis to send the Duke of Vendôme to command the Spanish armies. His presence restored confidence to the disheartened troops, and reinforcements from France enabled him to take the field.

Stharemberg had anticipated all the disadvantages of penetrating into Castile, an enemy's country, devoted to Philip; remote from his resources, and animated with hatred to the name and heresy of the English(a). Stanhope, and the Whig ministry, conceived that the possession of the capital was the possession of Spain, and forced that famous general into a situation, from which his genius and skill would have extricated him, if the fortunes of war were not paramount to science, and if the negligence of subordinate officers did not frustrate the best concerted schemes. Stharemberg saw the storm approaching, and quitted Madrid, to retire behind the Ebro. Stanhope, with 6000 English, formed

(a) Quincy, vol. vi. 447. Bellerue, p. 76.

his rere-guard. This officer, who possessed bravery without capacity, inflated with his success at Almenara, stopped in the small town of Brihuega, on the road from Guadalaxara to Saragossa, fifteen miles behind the main body of the allied army. Confiding in the bravery of his troops, he had out neither spies nor videttes, nor patroles of cavalry, and lay as secure within the old walls of a Moorish town, as if he were in garrison in one of Vauban's fortifications. Of a sudden he was surrounded by Vendôme's army. In a few hours the old towers were crumbled into ruins, and 6000 English surrendered prisoners of war. The weather was extremely cold; the Spaniards, most probably the Irish principally, wished to strip the English of their clothes. The firmness of Vendôme prevented this inhumanity, and his vigorous orders prevented their being stoned by the populace in the different towns in Castile, where they had committed robberies, plundered the churches, and shocked the religion and superstition of the Spaniards, by gross profanations.

At Cefuentes, twenty miles from Brihuega, Stharemberg was apprised of the approach of the Gallo-Spanish army; of the unaccountable delay of the English at Brihuega; and he estimated their danger by the activity of Vendôme when once in motion, such as he had experienced him in the wars of Italy. He immediately ordered his army to retrace its steps. It marched all day and night, and on the morning of the 10th of November, the ground being covered with snow, he reached the heights of Villa-Viciosa, within five miles of Brihuega, and fired three guns, the signal of his approach. The silence of the English artillery announced the capture of Brihuega. Never did Generals exert themselves more than Vendôme and Stharemberg, they were to be found wherever their troops yielded ; amidst showers of balls ; in danger repeatedly of being killed or taken. Vendôme sustained his former reputation ; Stharemberg added to his fame ; he remained for several hours of the day following in the field of battle, and retired towards Cefuentes. Mahony pressed him with all his cavalry, and summoned him to surrender. He had no cannon, and his charges could have no effect on such steady and firm battalions, who faced about whenever charged, and effected their retreat as victors to Cefuentes(a).

Though Mahony and his dragoons failed in breaking this impenetrable phalanx of Bohemian infantry, they acquired great glory. Bellerue, in his " Campaign of Vendôme," gives the following character of Mahony : " He was not only always brave, but laborious and indefatigable ; his life was a continued chain of dangerous combats, desperate attacks, and honourable retreats. He might have availed

(a) Bellerue, Histoire des Campagnes de Vendôme, pp. 237, 238, 239.

himself of his descent from one of the most ancient families of Ireland, but he preferred advancement by personal merit. If he has risen to the first rank in the army, he has risen gradually, and has passed through all the subordinate military stations to learn their duties. He learned to obey before he commanded, and without sudden elevation to the glorious employments which he has sustained with so much applause during this war. What did not this famous Mahony do on the day of Cremona, on which his conduct, equally bold and fortunate, procured for him the esteem of the Government, and the admiration of the garrison? By his foresight, along with M. Praslin, in cutting down the Po bridge, 10,000 Germans were prevented from joining Prince Eugene. Thus Cremona was saved by the vigilance and valour of the brave Mahony(*a*)... The King made him a Colonel, afterwards a Brigadier. He afterwards entered into the service of His Catholic Majesty, who gave him a commission to raise a regiment of dragoons. Having raised it, he, at the head of these Irish dragoons, performed astonishing feats at the battle of Almanza.

" His Catholic Majesty, convinced of his capacity, valour, experience, and devotion to his glory, sent him, with his regiment, to Sicily, where he served with much distinction, and by his polished and ge-

(*a*) Bellerue, Histoire des Campagnes de Vendôme, pp. 237, 238, 239.

nerous manners acquired the friendship of the Sicilians. The King recalled him soon after to Spain, and made him a Lieutenant-General, and honoured him with the title of Count of Castile. He served in the campaign of Ivaris under Philip V., and made during it many successful military expeditions. He signalized himself as a captain and a soldier at the battle of Saragossa, and, at the head of the Spanish cavalry, charged, with great vigour, the Portuguese horse, whom he broke and drove into the Ebro, in which many of them were drowned; after he had performed this exploit, he got possession of the enemy's artillery, and as he could not carry it off, he cut the sinews of 400 artillery mules, by orders of the Marquis of Bey; if the rest of the cavalry had followed the impetuous movement of the dragoons and the King's guards, we would have gained this battle, although the Allies had 26,000, and the Spaniards 12,000 men only(*a*)."

Mahony also acquired great glory on the day of Villa-Viciosa, at the head of the dragoons. The King was so satisfied, that he gave him a commandery of the order of St. James, worth 15,000 livres annually.

Mahony pursued the retreating army into Arragon, besieged the castle of Dillnerca, in which he made 600 German prisoners. Stharemberg gained

(*a*) Bellerue, Histoire des Campagnes de Vendôme, pp. 237, 238, 239.

Saragossa, remained there some days, and quitted it, leaving some powder behind, with a lighted match attached to it, which, he calculated, would explode about the time the Spanish army would approach it, but a Lieutenant-Colonel of the Irish dragoons having discovered this match, extinguished it.

In 1711, Stharemberg having received reinforcements from England, under the Duke of Argyle, the Irish Brigade served during the whole of the campaign in Catalonia, which was not marked by any actions of note. The Gallo-Spaniards were inferior in numbers, wanted supplies, were obliged to raise the siege of Cardona, after which they retired to winter quarters. The Irish were stationed at Teruel.

In Dauphiné, Burke's, Berwick's, and Dillon's served under the Marshal Duke of Berwick, who, from inferiority of forces, was obliged to abandon Savoy, and to confine himself to guard the passes of the Alps into Dauphiné(*a*). Lieutenant-General Dillon, at the head of the Irish regiments, guarded the passages of the Treve and the Arc. The Duke himself occupied an intrenched camp at Barraux. By his vigilance, activity, and address, he covered the French provinces along the Rhone from invasion, forced the Allies, double his numbers, to repass the Alps by the Little St. Bernard and Mount Cenis, and recovered the whole of Savoy. In all the movements, in climbing precipices, passing ravines

(*a*) Quincy, vol. vi. pp. 240, 242.

and defiles, and in forcing small posts, the Irish had a distinguished part.

Villars commanded in Flanders; Generals Lee, Galmoy, and Nugent served under him, as did also the brigades of Lee and O'Brien, composed of the regiments of Lee, O'Brien, O'Donnell, Galmoy, and Dorrington, and Nugent's horse. The Duke of Marlborough commanded the allied army. Villars had orders not to hazard an engagement, and threw up lines all along the Somme from above Arras to Palluè, having Arras, the Fort de Scarpe, and Arleux, as outposts. Arleux he strongly fortified, turned the waters of the Scarpe into the old canal of Arleux, and prevented the working of the mills of Douay. Marlborough made two several attempts upon Arleux; he carried it in a third attack, but it was retaken by the French. He then made a feint to attack the lines above Arras, and having drawn a portion of the French army to that quarter, he made a rapid march by night, behind Mount Elloy and Arras, having given orders to Cadogan and Hompesch, governor of Douay, to attack the French lines on the Somme, opposite to Arleux. The manœuvre succeeded. Villars was out-generalled. The French lines were carried for want of sufficient numbers. Murrough O'Brien, at the head of the fine regiments of Irish, forming the brigades of Lee and O'Brien, made an admirable manœuvre at Palluè to cover Cambray, and saved that important city until Villars came up with his whole army, and forced

Marlborough to confine his operations to the siege of the small town of Bouchain, which was taken after a siege of a few weeks(*a*), and which terminated the military career of the great Marlborough; female intrigues at Court removed him from the command of the army, displaced the Whig Ministry, effected a peace with France, and a total revolution in the military affairs and political state of Europe.

The Duke of Ormond was substituted for the Duke of Marlborough, in the command of the English army in Flanders, with secret directions not to act offensively against the French, but to maintain appearances of acting in concert with the Allies. At the head of 16,000 men he joined the allied army under Eugene at Tournay. They passed the Scheldt at Neuville and encamped near Cambray, being 110,000 men, including the English, as fine an army as that which fought at Malplaquet(*a*).

Villars commanded the French army, inferior in numbers and in the quality of the troops, and formed an intrenched camp between Arras and Cambray, having there two fortresses in his flanks, and the Somme in front. The Irish regiments of Lee, Galmoy, O'Brien, Dorrington, O'Donnell, and Nugent, formed part of his army, and Lord Galmoy, Lee, Booth, and O'Brien, acted as Generals(*b*). Villars had private information, from the head quarters of Ormond, of the

(*a*) Quincy, vol. vi. pp. 516, 517.
(*b*) Quincy, vol. vii. p. 46.

strength of his opponents, their intended movements, and the strongest assurances of the determination of Ormond to frustrate the plans of Prince Eugene, who held a council of war, in which he proposed to march to the sources of the Somme and the Scheldt, and thus to take the French army in the rere, and compel it to fight or abandon its position, and leave Arras and Cambray open to attack. The Duke of Ormond refused to support this movement, insidiously requested time to consult his Cabinet, and Mr. St. John, afterwards Lord Bolingbrooke, had the meanness to boast that this trick had saved the French from an irretrievable defeat.

Eugene could not, without the aid of the English, venture into Picardy, and sat down before Le Quesnoy, a strong fortress, a few miles to the south of Valenciennes, a hazardous enterprise, because he had to draw his supplies from Marchiennes, on the Scarpe, by Denain, on the Scheldt, close to the French garrison of Valenciennes, and liable also to be intercepted by excursions from Villars's camp, yet he succeeded in capturing this place, although Ormond, to defeat it, proclaimed a cessation of hostilities between the French and English.

Great success, consciousness of great talents, and contempt of the enemy, often betray great men into presumption and temerity, and never was there a more signal instance of it than in the siege of Landrecy by Prince Eugene, immediately after the capture of Le Quesnoy. The French were in possession of the course of the Scheldt, from its confluence with the Scarpe to Cambray, with the exception of Bouchain; Condé and Valenciennes threatened all his communications. Mons, Maubeuge, and Le Quesnoy, in his possession were, to the south of the Scheldt, a secure course of communication. In that great man's military career a material error is not discernible, this single one excepted. Some apology may be made for him. He was conscious of the difficulties and dangers of this siege. The French seemed to be dispirited, and he relied, like Cæsar, on his own fortunes, the chances of war, and the policy of keeping the Allies together by some important enterprize. The Dutch, a nation of shop-keepers and pedlars, incapable of enlarged views, and practising the rigid economy of their domestic expenditure in their military operations, refused to make Mons the depot of the supplies for the allied army. They found great economy in sending up boats, laden with ammunition and provision, by the Scheldt to its confluence with the Scarpe, and from thence by the Scarpe to Marchiennes, where the park of the old Abbey, surrounded by a thick wall, was fossed, palisaded, made a *place d'armes*, and a depot for the supply of the grand army; from thence to Landrecy was more than thirty miles; the Scheldt intervened between them, the passage over which was by Denain, between the two French garrisons of Cambray and Valenciennes, so that it was difficult to protect the convoys and cover the siege of Valenciennes.

After expostulating in vain with the Dutch deputies in his camp, Eugene raised intrenchments on both sides of the road from Denain to Marchiennes, for the security of his convoys, being a distance of eight miles, and placed 8,000 men to guard them, under the Earl of Albemarle, whom he directed to build a second bridge over the Scheldt, near Denain, covered by works, to give Eugene an opportunity of coming to his relief in case of these lines being attacked. Eugene himself, at the head of a large portion of the army, beat up the country in the enemie's possessions, and protected the country between Denain and the camp at Landrecy. Of these movements, of the want of sufficient troops to guard the lines of Denain, Villars was apprised, by the treachery of Ormond, who marched off with his English, and surprised Ghent. Eugene relied on the activity and vigilance of Albemarle in defending these lines, and giving him timely notice of any attack.

Villars made a feint to attack Eugene's convoy army near Landrecy; of a sudden wheeled back to the Scheldt, had four bridges laid over it at Neuville, between Bouet and Denain, a distance of four miles only, passed over his whole army unobserved and without opposition. Albemarle fired signals of distress too late, Eugene, eight miles distant, marched with the utmost expedition to relieve him, but before he could arrive, Villars formed his army into eight columns, one of which was composed of the Irish brigade, stormed the intrenchments(a) on one side, whilst the garrison of Valenciennes attacked them on the other, carried them in an instant, captured or killed the whole of the defenders, broke down the bridges on the Scheldt, and prevented the advance of Prince Eugene. In a few days after, St. Amand and Marchiennes, with their immense stores, fell into the hands of the French. Eugene was forced to raise the siege of Landrecy, and Villars, in the course of the summer, captured Douay, Le Quesnoy, and Bouchain(b).

The preliminary treaty between France and England, consequent on the death of Joseph I., and on the accession of the Tories to office at St. James's, was signed so early as the 8th October, 1711, but it was not till April, 1713, that the Congress of Utrecht terminated. As the Emperor of Germany did not accede to this treaty, the war continued on the Rhine and in Italy. The death of Louis XIV. produced no settlement, nor was it till after repeated pauses and ruptures, that, by the series of treaties made at Vienna, Seville, &c., peace seemed restored to Western Europe. It only seemed so, for in October, 1733, war was renewed, but again rested at the peace of 1738. During this slackened, yet tremendous war, the Irish troops were constantly in action, and the fields and the records of Parma,

(a) 24th July, 1712.   (b) Quincy, vol. vii. p. 69.

Guastalla, and Philipsburg, testified to their fiery and constant valour,

In the great war of the Austrian succession, the deeds and fame of the Irish troops rose higher than ever. The profound and daring Saxe was at the head of Louis's main army, and often, when defeat seemed inevitable, the shout of the Irish Brigade daunted his enemy, and their charge bore back and shattered the exulting columns of the Allies. The plain of Raucoux, the rampart of Lafelt, but, beyond all, the slopes of Fontenoy(*b*), proclaim, to all time, that a better friend, or a more dangerous foe, never swept a battle field, than the disciplined Irishman.

Into the details of these " glorious days"(*c*) we cannot now enter, but they sustained the character which, against the malice of Voltaire, and the ignorance of some nearer home, I have shewn to be the

---

(*a*) 1st September, 1715.   (*b*) 11th May, 1745.

(*c*) The following letter from Lord Clare, who commanded the Brigade at Fontenoy, suggested this phrase, and will, probably, be welcome to the reader.

"*Paris, October*, 1746.

" DEAR M'DONOUGH,—I congratulate you on your marriage, but trust it will not induce you to retire from the Irish Brigade. I hope you do not forget the memorable day they had at Fontenoy, and the other glorious days in which they had a share. Your promotion goes on, and all are wishing for your return. With your assistance and O'Brien's, the ranks are near filled up. I hope to see you soon. How does my old friend and relative,

due of the Irish soldiery; they look worthily beside the memories of Blackwater, Benburb, Limerick, Ramillies, and Almanza, and they justify the motto on the parting flag presented to "The Irish Brigade" by the Bourbons,

" 1692–1792.
" Semper et ubique fideles."

We might lengthen greatly the catalogue of the military services of the Irish. We have been silent on their early career against the British races who "groaned" to the Consul Ætius. Scattered through the English chronicles we find sad proof that the Irish served the aggressions of the Edwards on Wales and Scotland, that their blood rained on the Red and White Roses, and that under the flag of the Tudor kings they distinguished themselves in France(a). At the close of Hugh O'Neill's war, Spain received her first recruits from Ireland, and

---

Captain Dermot O'Brien, get on? Is he in good health, and permitted to live and pray in peace?

" Your's,
" CLARE.

" To Monsieur A. M'Donough,
" Co. Clare, Ireland."

Clare, it may be added, was a great recruiting county for the Brigade. On its stern coast the French used to land smuggled claret, brandy, &c., and take away wool, and, what was more precious, "Wild Geese," for such was the name usually given to the recruits for "The bold Brigade."

(a) Leland's Ireland. Lynch's Feudal Baronies.

ever after sought them eagerly(*a*). During the wars of the Commonwealth, the Irish served the Stuarts in England and Scotland, as well as Ireland. A division of Strafford's Irish army garrisoned Carlisle, and so efficient were the Irish, that the Republicans proclaimed that Irish soldiers taken in England, or at sea, should have no quarter(*b*). The strength of Montrose's army, in 1644-6, consisted of 1500 Antrim Irish, in three regiments, under Alister Mac Domhnall (the Colkitto of Milton), and their steady fire (for they were veterans) won his chief battles(*c*).

We have passingly mentioned the Irish in the Imperial service. In it they served with honour, and some of them attained its highest ranks. Marshal Browne, the conqueror of Frederick, and Marshal Lacy, the organizer of the Russian army, were Irishmen(*d*). The Pennsylvanian line, Washington's surest troops during the war of American independence, were five-sixths Irish; and in a native of Donegal(*e*) the young republic found her second ge-

(*a*) Strafford's Letters, vol. i. pp. 395, 440, 466, 471, and vol. ii. p. 243, &c.

(*b*) See an instance of the enforcement of this annexed to the account of the battle of Benburb, in "Thorpe's Pamphlets," in the Dublin Society Library.

(*c*) Ormond Letters, vol. i. pp. 73-76, &c. Napier's Life of Montrose, *passim*; Dublin Magazine for April, 1843; Introduction to Mac Domhnall's March.

(*d*) Life of Marshal Browne. Manstein's Memoirs.

(*e*) Montgomery.

neral. Nor need England complain of the services of Ireland to her enemies; throughout the last war, from Assaye to Vittoria, and from Vimiera to Waterloo, the Irish battalions maintained their fame and her flag; and high in services and renown, above all the generals who ever drew sword in her name, was the Irishman, Arthur Wellesley.

Let no one asperse the character of the Irish, because they fought so often under foreign colours. Exiled, persecuted, and loyal, they lent their valour to the states which supported their dethroned kings, their outlawed religion, their denationalized country, their vow of vengeance, or their hopes of freedom. Viewed carelessly at a distance, their varied services seem evidence of an unprincipled Prætorian race; examined in detail, with references to the creed, politics, and foreign relations of Ireland at each period, they only prove an amount of patriotism, piety, and valour, which, concentrated at home to national service, would have made Ireland all we could wish her.

APPENDIX.

MEMOIR

CONCERNING

THE IRISH TROOPS,

FROM THEIR ARRIVAL IN FRANCE TILL THE PRESENT TIME.

JAMES THE SECOND having been obliged to leave England, on account of the so well-known revolution which displaced him from the throne, to set thereon the man who had driven him from it—his son in law, the Prince of Orange—repaired to France in the month of December, 1688.

As Ireland had remained faithful to him, he went thither in the month of March, 1689, and found that the nobility of that country had raised, clothed, equipped, and, in a great measure, armed, at their expense, 30,000 men for his service, through the instrumentality of the Duke of Tirconnel, Viceroy of that kingdom.

The late King Louis XIV. sent, at the end of that year, seven French battalions into Ireland, with a great quantity of arms.

King James sent him in exchange six Irish battalions, forming three regiments, which embarked in the fleet commanded by M. De Chateau Renaud, and arrived at Brest the beginning of the month of May, 1690.

These regiments were, Mountcashel's, an old regiment, a long time embodied, composed of two battalions, divided into sixteen companies, consisting of 100 men each; the regiment of Clare, raised by the grandfather(a) of the present Lord Clare, and commanded by his eldest son, which also was composed of two battalions, disposed like the former; Dillon's regiment, raised by the grandfather of the present Lord Dillon, and commanded by his son, M. Dillon, who died Lieutenant-General in France, in 1734, which regiment was also composed of two battalions of 1600 men, and two companies.

The Colonel's company of each of these regiments was not limited, and as many men were taken into it, above the stated number of 100(b), as could be found. There were twenty cadets in the Colonel's company of the regiment of Mountcashel(c), who were retained in it until the year 1714, at the rate of 10 sols per day. In 1703, sixteen cadets were established in Dillon's(d) regiment, who remained in it until the above-named year 1714, with the same pay. Each company was composed of a captain, two lieutenants, a sub-lieutenant, and an ensign(e).

This brigade was called the brigade of Mountcashel, and was commanded by Lord Mountcashel, Lieutenant-General

(a) Who raised, at the same time, a regiment of cavalry, and a regiment of dragoons.

(b) See the Order for the payment of the troops, 4th October, 1692.

(c) Ib. 4th October, 1692, and the others until 1714.

(d) Ib. 1st October, 1703.

(e) Ib. 4th October, 1690, the 25th September, 1694, and of the 21st September, 1696.

of the King's armies, brother of the Earl of Clancarty, head of the ancient and illustrious house of Macarthy, who, on arriving in France, made a stipulation for the corps he led, by which the officers should receive full pay, such as they have at present, the soldiers one sol more than the French soldiers had at that period, and the colonels one sol per livre for all the payments which should be made, as well for the appointments of officers, as for the maintenance of these regiments. Lord Mountcashel had the benefit not only of the sol per livre for the necessaries of his regiment, but likewise of the sol per livre on the pay of the two other regiments of the Brigade, independently of the sol per livre which the colonels received for themselves.

At the end of 1691, after the capitulation and reduction of Limerick, and when the whole of Ireland had submitted to the Prince of Orange (King William), two companies of the body-guards of King James passed into France, together with the

CAVALRY REGIMENTS.
Sheldon,
Galmoy,

of two squadrons each; and of

INFANTRY.

The Guards,	2 battalions.
The Queen's,	2 ,,
The Marines,	2 ,,
Dublin,	2 ,,
Limerick,	2 ,,
Charlemont,	2 ,,
Athlone,	2 ,,
Clancarty,	1 ,,

Each company consisting of a captain, two lieutenants, two sub-lieutenants, an ensign, and 100 men(*a*). There were also several half-pay officers attached to each of these regiments. Besides these there were

> The King's dismounted dragoons, 1 battalion.
> The Queen's, ... 1 ,,
> —
> 17 ,,

Each regiment composed of six companies, consisting each of a captain, two lieutenants, two cornets, and 100 dragoons.

Three more volunteer companies, called Rutherford's, Lee's, and Brown's, consisting of 104 men each, were regimented, having each a captain, a lieutenant, a sub-lieutenant, and an ensign(*b*). These regiments were placed on the same footing as the French regiments, in regard to pay. Some supernumerary men having come from Ireland with these corps, and who could not find vacancies, two new companies were formed, of 100 men each, for each of the regiments of Mountcashel and Clare, which, by this arrangement, formed three battalions of 600 men, divided into six companies of 100 men each, instead of 800 men to each company, as it had been before then(*c*). Dillon's regiment remained, consisting of two battalions of 100 men each. There were thus in France, at the beginning of 1692, twenty-five Irish battalions, namely, two dragoon regiments, two companies of body-guards, two regiments of cavalry of two squadrons, and three volunteer companies.

(*a*) See the Regulations for the payment of the troops, from 24th October, 1692, to 1697.
(*b*) See the Order for the payment of troops, 4th October, 1692.
(*c*) See the Regulation for the payment of troops, the 4th October, 1692.

APPENDIX. 375

The peace of Riswick was declared in the month of September, 1697. In 1698, the regiments of Lee (formerly Mountcashel), Clare, and Dillon, were reduced each to one battalion of fourteen companies of fifty men, having each a captain, a lieutenant, and an ensign, without the colonel's or lieutenant-colonel's companies. In the month of February of the same year, the body-guards of the King of England, and the cavalry regiment of Galmoy underwent a total reduction. The regiments of the Queen's Guards, of the Marines, of Dublin, of Limerick, of Charlemont, of Athlone, of Clancarty; the dragoons *en pied*, comprising seventeen battalions, and the volunteer companies, were at the same time reduced to five regiments, a battalion to each, consisting of fourteen companies of fifty men, under the names of

Dorrington's (which had been the foot guards,
and which at present is Rothe's), . . . 1 battalion.
Burke's, ... 1 ,,
Albemarle's, ... 1 ,,
Berwick's, ... 1 ,,
Galmoy's, ... 1 ,,

Total, ... 5 ,,

When the two companies of the body-guards were reformed, as has just been stated, there remained but 105, who were placed in Dorrington's regiment to serve, and replace so many soldiers, being paid at the rate of eleven sols per day(*a*). In 1701, these guards passed into the regiment of Broderick, to serve in it, and to have the same pay as that of Dorrington, where they remained until 1710, when

(*a*) See the Regulation on all the reforms for the payment of the troops, of the 10th February, 1699; on the remainder until 1701.

they were disbanded(*a*). Each company of these battalions, as well as those of the three first regiments, had a captain and a lieutenant *en pied*, and an ensign in the colonel's and the lieutenant-colonel's company(*b*).

There were also captains and second lieutenants retained in many of the companies of each of the five battalions who remained embodied, chosen from amongst the most distinguished and the best conducted.

"REGULATION OF THE 5TH AUGUST, 1698.

"*By Order of the King.*

"His Majesty having been informed, that the colonels of the old regiments of Irish infantry in his service, always received a sol per livre on the payments made to the regiments, as well for the appointments of the officers as for the maintenance of the soldiers; and His Majesty being graciously pleased, that the colonels of the regiments of Lee, Clare, and Dillon, who are at present in his service, should continue to enjoy this advantage; His Majesty ordains, that this sol per livre levied upon the appointments of the officers shall be placed to the credit of the colonels of these three regiments, and that the rebate, held back from each soldier per day for the general fund, shall be taken, to be remitted to the said colonels, in order to be a substitute for the sol per livre, on the payment of the above-mentioned three first regiments.

"Such is the order of His Majesty, given at Versailles, the 5th August, 1698.

"Signed,   LOUIS.
And underneath,   TELLIER."

(*a*) See the Regulation for the payment of troops of the 15th October, 1701, and the remainder, until 1760.

(*b*) Ib. 10th February, 1799.

APPENDIX. 377

In the month of January, 1699, two companies of each of these Irish regiments were non-commissioned, in order to reduce them from fourteen to twelve companies of fifty men, like the French battalions, having each a captain, and in many, a second captain, and lieutenant *en pied*, besides an ensign, in the colonel's and the lieutenant-colonel's companies; and in 1701, there was added to each company, a sub, or non-commissioned lieutenant(*a*).

From 1705 until 1711, there were attached to each company, composed of fifty men, a *capitaine en pied*, *capitaine en second*, a lieutenant, two second lieutenants, a sub-lieutenant, and one ensign, in the colonel's or lieutenant-colonel's companies(*b*), and several non-commissioned officers attached to each regiment.

The same year, 1705, all these non-commissioned and disbanded officers were marched to Les Cevennes; where they were brigaded; they served very usefully under Marshal de Monnedel, De Villars, and De Berwick; were sent to Flanders in 1708; formed a part of the embarkation which took place at Dunkirk, in favour of the King of England, the Chevalier de St. George; and after the unfortunate failure of this expedition, were reassembled in Lille, where they served, attached to different regiments, during this siege, and those of Tournay, Douai, Bethune, and Aire.

In 1712, each company was placed, in respect of officers, on the same footing as in 1701; that is to say, that there was but one captain, some second captains in some of the companies, lieutenant *en pied*, and lieutenant *en second*, and an ensign, in the colonel's or lieutenant-colonel's companies.

(*a*) See the Regulation for the payment of troops of the 5th October, 1701.
(*b*) Ib. 1st October, 1705, and the remaining ones till 1711.

Burke's and Dillon's regiments being at Cremona at the time that city was surprised on the 4th of February, 1702, and having achieved wonders, and principally contributed to drive out the enemy, the King, to mark his satisfaction at their services, augmented(a), by 25 sols per day, the pay of the *capitaine en pied*, not only of Burke's regiment, but likewise of the four others which were on the same footing as the French, and that of the lieutenant *en pied* to 12 sols, 6 farthings per day. The allowances of captains and of second lieutenants were increased in proportion. The soldiers had also an increase of a sol per day(b). Dillon's regiment, which had also signally distinguished itself, obtained but a simple gratuity, and no increase of pay.

Sheldon's regiment of cavalry, since Nugent's, and at present Fitz-James's, marching, at the close of the campaign of 1701, to take possession of the fortifications which had been assigned to it, between Cremona and Mantua, encountered four regiments of French cavalry, headed by M. de Clermont, who running away, pursued by the Baron de Merci, who commanded a body of hostile troops, Sheldon's not only stopped, but charged them, unassisted; threw them into confusion; and took General Merci prisoner. The King, to signify to the regiment the satisfaction he received by

(a) Captains had at that time but 50 sols, and lieutenants but 20 per day. Soldiers had but 4 sols 6 farthings, when the pay of the French officers and soldiers was increased in 1716. The Irish regiments, of which mention is here made, were left as they were, which caused the captains and the lieutenants to receive, as they do at present, the first, 8 sols 4 farthings more, and the second 10 sols a day more than the French. The soldiers, in regard to treatment, were on a par with the French soldiers.

(b) See the Regulation for the payment of troops, of the 1st October, 1704.

the distinguished manner in which it had conducted itself on this occasion, granted to the non-commissioned officers, who were attached to this corps, the same allowances as to those who were embodied on full pay.

Berwick's regiment formed a second battalion in 1703 at Arras. It was sent into Spain in 1711. The first served at that time in Italy, and these two battalions did not rejoin each other in Spain until 1807. The King of Spain, Philip V., began, in 1708, to raise two dragoon regiments, and three Irish battalions, composed of English prisoners, taken at the battle of Almanza, the 25th of April 1707. The non-commissioned officers, who were attached to the Irish regiments in France, composed this body(a).

Peace with France having been signed at Radstat, the 6th of March, 1714, by the Emperor, and concluded at Baden, the 7th of September of the same year, between France and the Empire; the 15th February, 1715, three companies were added to the regiments of Lee, Clare, Dillon, Rothe, and the first of Berwick's battalions, to make them from twelve to fifteen companies, containing each forty men. These companies were taken from the regiments of O'Donnell (formerly Albemarle and Fitzgerald), of Galmoy, and from the second battalion of Berwick's, which were reduced and incorporated; namely, O'Donnell, one half into Lee's (which is at present Bulkeley's), and the other half into Clare's. Galmoy passed virtually into Dillon's; the one half of Berwick's battalion passed into its own first battalion, the other half into that of Roche.

(a) *Vide* order of King Louis XIV., to furnish the forage to the non-commissioned officers attached to the Irish regiments of infantry of Dorrington, Galmoy, O'Donnel, Burke, and Berwick, the same as to the commissioned officers, during the winter quarters of 1710 to 1711.

As to Burke's regiment, as it had almost always served in Spain, it requested permission, in order to avoid the reduction, to offer its services to the King of Spain; which having been granted by the late King, and accepted of, with joy, by the Spanish monarch, it sent over its arms and baggage to that country, where it served afterwards, with distinction, and in Sicily, in Africa, and in Italy, in the war of 1733, under the King of the two Sicilies, on whom the King, his father, had bestowed it. It is at present at Naples, bearing the name of the King's regiment, and augmented by the addition of two battalions.

On the reduction of the Irish regiments in France, which has been just mentioned, the King of Spain was enabled to form six battalions from supernumerary officers who had been in France. They served at Oran, in Sicily; and in Italy, in 1733 and 1734, with the greatest distinction. Four of those battalions had the good fortune, in 1743, with the Walloon Guards, to repulse the enemy at Veletri, and to save Don Phillippe, who was on the point of being taken. At the reduction of 1715, there was but one captain, and a lieutenant *en pied* in each company, as likewise an ensign, in the colonel's and lieutenant-colonel's company(*b*). All the others were non-commissioned officers(*c*).

(*a*) These officers had been sent into Douay, Bethune, and Aire, the defence of which towns has been so famous.

(*b*) See the Regulation for the payment of troops of the 10th April, 1715.

(*c*) " His Majesty, wishing to treat with favour the non-commissioned officers who served, attached to the Irish infantry regiments of Dorrington, O'Donnell, Burke, and Berwick, in consideration for the services which they had rendered him the last campaign, and to facilitate the means of making the next, he sends to, and commands the prefects of the departments, in which their regiments were then in winter quar-

In 1716, a captain and a second lieutenant were attached to each company, besides those *en pied*, so that the Irish regiments had four companies, besides having an ensign in the colonel's and lieutenant-colonel's companies(a). Brigades were formed of those for whom there were no vacancies, the officers of which had the same pay as the regiments which they had left.

It is to be noticed, that the captains and the lieutenants of the regiments of O'Donnell and Galmoy, and of the second battalion of Berwick's, who went, with their companies, into those of Lee, Clare, and Dillon, had the allowances of these regiments, but took rank after all the captains and lieutenants of the latter regiments, without any regard to the dates of their commissions.

The Chevalier de St. George, King of England, now at Rome, having gone, at the close of 1715, to Scotland, a great part of which had revolted for him, and formed an army, commanded by the Duke [Earl] of Mar, and having marched into England, the Duke of Orleans, the new Regent, notwithstanding the anxiety he felt to follow him, deemed that he could not properly do so at that moment, just as peace had been concluded, but ordered that the Irish battalions should be reduced by 150 men each, that is to say, taking ten men from each company, to whom means should be afforded to pass into Scotland. This trans-

ters, that the same quantity of forage should be given to them per day, as to the officers *en pied*, during the present winter quarters only. Such is the command of His Majesty, given at Versailles, the 18th March, 1711. Signed, Louis, and underneath, Voisin."

The same treatment was adopted towards them during the winter quarters of 1711 to 1712, and from 1712 to 1713. These regulations were not printed, but the minutes of them are at the War Office.

(a) See the Regulation for the payment of troops, the 30th October, 1716.

action took place at the end of December, 1715; so that the Irish battalions thenceforth consisted but of fifteen companies (one of which was of grenadiers), containing thirty men each, making in all 450 men(a).

In 1718, the king having made a new regulation for the whole body of his troops, in order to give the army a permanent and solid form, an order was issued, that the colonels of the three first Irish regiments should no longer receive the four farthings per day on the pay of the soldiers, which had been assigned to them by the order of the 5th of August, 1698, and in lieu of it a pension was assigned them, in form of an annual gratuity, of 2700 francs.

In 1725 the Irish regiments were increased, by adding ten men to each company, which made the battalions consist of 600 men, comprising fifteen companies, with forty men to each. 100 francs was granted for the enlistment of each man; and fifteen francs for his equipment; the King furnishing the coat, vest, trowsers, hat, firelock, and bayonet.

In 1727, Nugent's regiment of cavalry, formerly Sheldon's, and at present Fitz-James's, composed of eight companies, was increased by one. The King gave 22,000 francs for the raising of this new company, by which means the captain raised men, bought horses, equipped both, and provided himself with arms at his expense.

In 1733 this regiment acquired three additional companies. Each of the three captains had fifteen men mounted and equipped, taken from the three old companies. The King secured to them 11,000 francs more, whereby they were required to raise, equip, arm, and horse each fifteen other men.

(a) See the Regulation for the payment of troops, the 30th October, 1716.

APPENDIX. 383

The regiments of Bulkeley, Roche, and De Berwick, had remained in Flanders during the campaign of 1735; those of Clare and of Dillon were the only Irish regiments who went through that of Germany. As they were not comprised in the order for the gratuity made to the French battalions, during the preceding winter, Lord Clare and Lord Dillon made representations, which gave occasion to the following favourable letter addressed to Lord Clare, in order, in some measure, to make amends to them.

" COPY OF A LETTER FROM M. DANGERVILLIERS, WRITTEN TO LORD CLARE, FROM VERSAILLES, THE 17TH SEPTEMBER, 1735.

" SIR,—Upon the information which I gave the King, on the subject of the letter which you did me the honour of writing, the 18th of last month, by which you state, that the regiment you command, having found itself entirely re-established, at the review in the month of April, is in the position to enjoy the benefit of the gratuity granted to the French regiments for their last winter quarter, His Majesty has been pleased, by especial favour, to grant an extra gratuity of 3,000 francs, for which you will find the order annexed, to be a substitute for this pay, although it does not, in any manner, concern the Irish regiments. His Majesty has desired me to recommend you expressly to consider this a special favour, and to cause the entire amount of it, together with the other advantages attendant on winter quarters, to be applied to the filling up of the different companies.

" I am, &c.
" Signed, DANGERVILLIERS."

Lord Dillon received a similar letter.

In 1736, peace having been concluded, five men were reduced in each of the Irish companies, as well as in the French regiments. Lord Clare having requested, that of the five men who were to be reduced in the commencement of 1737, there should be formed two new companies in each of the Irish battalions, to raise them from fifteen to seventeen companies, like the French battalions, this was granted, and consequently, the 8th January, 1737, these two new companies were set on foot, and the companies reduced to thirty men, in order to form battalions of 110 men in seventeen companies, one of which were grenadiers, like the French battalions. It was laid down in this order of the 8th January, 1737, which regulates this arrangement, that the captains and second lieutenants who would be appointed to the new companies, should not be replaced in those from which they were taken, and that the new companies were not to have either second captains or second lieutenants. As it did not appear very clearly, by this ordonnance of the 8th of January, 1737, whether the under officers of the Irish regiments were to be replaced; Lord Clare having represented to M. Dangervilliers the necessity of explaining himself on this subject, and the importance of their being replaced, received from him a letter, dated the 28th June, 1737, of which the following is a copy:

"SIR,—I received the letter which you did me the honour of writing the 10th of this month, and I informed the King of it. His Majesty has willingly entered into the views it contains, of engaging in his service young Irish Catholic gentlemen(a), who are capable of conducting recruits, for

(a) This reasoning, it appears, should have still more force at this period, 1749, than in 1737, since, during this last war, more rigorous laws than ever were made against Catholics. It appears that the King's piety and greatness of soul were concerned, to open asylums for the regiments of this nation, and he is willing that the officers and non-commissioned officers who may be wanting hereafter for each of the companies of the regiment which you command, or who may at present be wanting, should be replaced; but this arrangement will not affect the places of half-pay captains and lieutenants, who have been chosen to form the two new companies and which are not to be filled up. So His Majesty has ordered, by the second article of his Ordonnance of the 8th of the month of January last, reducing the companies and regiments of the Irish infantry; with regard to the two new companies, they are to remain the same as they are, viz., one captain and one lieutenant only, according to the Ordonnance.

"I am, &c.

"Signed, DANGERVILLIERS."

Fitz-James's regiment of cavalry remained composed, after this reduction of 1737, of three squadrons, and it was only affected by the number of men and of horses, constituting the companies.

The 15th May, 1741, it was ordered, that all the Fusilier companies of the Irish regiments should be increased by ten men each, in order to raise them from thirty to forty men each, and those of the grenadiers by fifteen men, in order to raise them from thirty to forty-five grenadiers. Fifty francs were granted for the raising of each man, and the King supplied his coat, hat, and musket and bayonet. With fifteen francs gratuity, which was given to each man,

persecuted Catholicity, according as its enemies make the greatest efforts to oppress it; besides, can a noble people be sufficiently allured into this country, whom His Majesty has seen, under his own eyes, serve and expose themselves so bravely and so usefully?

the captain was obliged to furnish the sword, the belt, the cartouch box, and the accoutrements, and to take upon himself the making of the coat.

The Irish colonels having requested permission to nominate (for the Royal assent) subalterns for the four companies of their regiments who had not any, accordingly the following Ordonnance was proclaimed:

" ORDONNANCE OF THE 5TH OF AUGUST, 1741.

" *By Command of the King.*

" His Majesty having examined into the representations made to him by the colonels of the regiments of the Irish infantry which are in his service, of the necessity they are in to employ on the sea coasts several detached officers of their regiments, in order to assemble and bring together the recruits of their nation, His Majesty has ordained, and ordains, that after the 1st of next September, there shall be maintained, besides the officers *en pied* who are actually in each of the seventeen companies of each battalion, a captain and a lieutenant *reformé*, allowing, for the future, the colonel to propose persons to fill the places of those who shall be raised to the companies, as also the lieutenants *en pied*, according as they shall become vacant, in the abovementioned regiments ; and, for that purpose, doing away with that which had been commanded by his Ordonnance of the 8th January, 1737, and others of later date, which latter shall be put into execution only so far as they shall not be inconsistent with these presents.

"His Majesty commands the Governors and Lieutenant-Generals in his provinces and armies, the Directors and General Inspectors, the Prefects of said provinces and the

Commissaries of War appointed for the discipline of his troops, to put in force the execution of this ordonnance.

"Given at Versailles, the 5th August, 1741.
"Signed, Louis.
And underneath, DE BRETEUIL."

In 1743, the cavalry regiment of Fitz-James (formerly Sheldon's and Nugent's), consisting of three squadrons, made a fourth, composed of four new companies. The King furnished the horses, and the captains raised, clothed, armed, and equipped men and horses at their own expense.

In 1744, the English having sent into Flanders, where the Irish regiments were, a great body of troops, it was thought that many of the enemy would desert, and that this would be the means of raising new battalions. The proposal was made to the Court, which, before taking further measures to adopt it, addressed a letter through the Count D'Argenson of the 29th February, 1744, to M. De Ceteret, the copy of which is annexed.

"*Versailles, the 29th of February*, 1744.

"SIR,—The King having been informed that several Irishmen present themselves on the frontier, with the intention of serving in the regiments of their nation actually in his service, and that most of these regiments being complete, the supernumeraries could only find their means of subsistence at the expense of the captains, if it were not otherwise provided for; His Majesty, in consideration of the useful services which he has received in the preceding wars, and of those which his Irish troops continue to render him daily, commands me to acquaint you, that the Commissioners of War appointed to the direction of the five Irish regiments which are in his service, are to comprise, in their returns, all the supernumeraries capable of serving, who may present themselves, taking care to hold a separate register of those who shall exceed the full number of each regiment, in whatever number they may come, and shall see that their pay be remitted to them, at the rate of six sols six decimes per day each, until His Majesty shall come to a determination of raising the regiments of this nation which he maintains by one or more battalions. I request you to make known this resolution to M. Deseichelles, Prefect of Flanders, in order that he may act conformably, and, on his part, look to its exact performance.

"I have the honour, &c.,
"Signed,   D'ARGENSON."

By the order of the 1st October, 1744, the payment of the sergeants, corporals, grenadiers, fusiliers, and drummers, was augmented by two sols a day.

In order that the King might not be put to greater expense than that at which he was before the increased pay, four companies were retrenched from each of the Irish battalions, so as to reduce them from twelve companies of fifty men, to sixteen companies of fusiliers, of forty men, the grenadier companies remaining composed of forty-five men.

After this modification, the Irish battalions consisted of 645 men, instead of 685, which they were before. Sixteen cadets were given to each Irish regiment, each paid at the rate of thirteen sols per day.

Of the supernumerary officers of the five Irish battalions, after this arrangement, as well as of the forty men who were retrenched, the formation was set on foot of a new regiment, made up in the same manner as the others, arranged by M. De Lally, on the same footing as the two last regiments.

APPENDIX. 389

Fifty francs were granted for the raising of each of the 445 men, who were required to form this regiment, besides the 200 men whom the Irish regiments had furnished, as also 31 francs, 15 sols, 5 decimes for their equipment, and 15 francs of gratuity for each man. The companies having been complete, at the review of April, 1745, the fusee and the bayonet were given gratuitously from the magazines of the King; who, moreover, granted a gratuity of 4000 francs to each of the companies of this regiment, in order to indemnify them for the expenses they had been at for the raising of it, over and above what the King had granted, and for the repairs and the clothing of the men, which the other regiments had furnished to this regiment. The officers of the five old regiments, who could find no vacancies in this new corps, and who were found to be supernumeraries, after the reduction of the four companies by battalion, of which mention has already been made, remained attached to the regiments, and were not to be replaced; but the battle of Fontenoy, which took place six months after, that is to say, 11th May, 1745, cut them off.

When the pay was augmented, as has been just mentioned, Lord Clare, by the consent of all the colonels and chiefs of the Irish regiments, and in virtue of his office of inspector, made the following rules and regulations here annexed, which have been constantly followed and executed until the present time.

" REGULATIONS.

" The captains of the companies who shall be reduced, will deliver honestly every thing they may have belonging

(a) The colonels of the three first Irish regiments lost 750 francs more a year of their revenue, by this operation, a proof of their disinterestedness, for it was they who had proposed the arrangement, in order to provide for the general good.

to their companies, to the captains who shall remain on duty. If they do not give the whole of the equipment and armament for thirty men which should remain to them after the balloting of M. De Lally, they will be obliged to account for what became of them; the whole certified by the *etat* Major. If any thing may have been lost by negligence or otherwise, they will be obliged to keep an account of it on the terms hereafter named. Whatever shall be given up belonging to the reduced companies, shall be drawn for equally amongst those who shall remain embodied.

"Whatever the King shall please to grant to the captains whose companies shall be reduced, must be applied to the service of the general body, and to liquidate the debt of the company, and shall be placed on the books of the major; what remains, if any, shall be paid to the captains, whose companies shall be reduced, provided seventeen men remain, after M. De Lally shall have withdrawn ten men.

"In case that there be not this number of men, there shall be retained, on what may remain for the necessaries, 40 francs for each man who shall be wanting of the 17.

"40 sols for the belt.
"30 sols for the sword.
"4 francs for the cartouche.
"20 sols for the powder horn.
"12 francs for the firelock and bayonet.

"Making, all the abovenamed sums together, that of sixty livres, ten sols, for an equipped and armed man.

"If in the number of seventeen men, who are to be given, there be anything wanting to their equipment or armament, it shall be stopped from the pay of the non-commissioned captain, or the amount shall be made good by him.

APPENDIX. 391

"If in the reduced companies there be found above the number of 17 men, the men over and above shall be drawn by lot, by all the companies who may remain embodied, and the captains to whom they shall fall will pay them according to the rules above mentioned, &c. &c.

"Drawn up at Bassearme,
2nd October, 1744."

"*By Command of the King.*

"SERVICE REGULATION FOR THE IRISH REGIMENTS, AND SCOTCH ROYALS AND D'OGILVY'S, NAMELY(*a*):

	Francs.	Sols.	Farthings.
"Each of the two sergeants of the companies of grenadiers shall have, every month, bread and meat deducted,	12	16	3
Each of the corporals,	9	1	3
Each of the three under corporals,	8	6	3
Each grenadier and the drummer,	7	11	3
Each of the two sergeants of the twelve companies of fusiliers shall have, every month, bread and meat,	11	6	3
Each of the three corporals,	8	6	3
Each of the three under corporals,	7	11	3
Each of the cadets of the colonel's companies of the six Irish regiments,	12	6	3
Each soldier and drummer,	6	1	3

(*a*) This regulation was read after the drum was beaten at the head of each battalion in battle, at the beginning of each campaign, and from the first day that the troops have received the pay of campaigns, it will be necessary to act hereafter in the same way, at the beginning of each campaign, when the war will recommence.

"The sergeants of the Irish regiments, those of the Royal Scotch, and of D'Ogilvy, shall have their bread, conformably to the regulation: namely, two rations per day, otherwise they must content themselves with the payment that the purveyor shall make, and of which the discount will be made up for them, at the same time as that of the officers. The meat shall be furnished the 31st of each month.

"An account shall be kept for each sergeant, corporal, under corporal, grenadier, fusilier, and drummer, of the Irish regiments, and of those of the Royal Scotch, and D'Ogilvy, of 1 sol, 5 farthings and a half for each Friday of the months that they shall be in campaign, on score of the meat, which sum shall be delivered to them at the end of the campaign, or in course of the first month they shall be in garrison.

"Six farthings shall be retrenched from each corporal, under corporal, grenadier, soldier, and drummer, for his linen, shoes, and stockings, according to the regulations of the King, the discount of which will be made up for them every two months.

"Drawn up at the camp before Tournay, the 6th May, 1745."

"The aides-majors of the six Irish regiments of Bulkeley, Clare, Dillon, Roche, Berwick, and Lally, shall have the same necessaries that they had, when these regiments were composed of seventeen companies each, instead of thirteen, as they are at present. The aide-major of the Royal Scotch regiment shall have the same necessaries as those of the six Irish regiments.

"Drawn up at Bilsen, the 12th May, 1748."

In order to avoid the out-bidding each other in enlisting men, and the risk of an unseemly competition among the officers in endeavouring to engage as recruits the deserters from the English army, who came to the general quarters, it was arranged, with the consent of the chiefs of the Irish corps and of the Scotch, that there should be one officer of the Brigade established at the general quarters, to raise recruits for it in general, and for the Scotch regiments.

Lord Clare, in consequence, in his quality of inspector, made the following regulation, which was approved of by Marshal Saxe, commander of the army, and by the Minister of War, as may be seen annexed. This custom and regulation was in operation during all the campaigns of the war of 1741. It was highly approved of, and it is necessary on this occasion to say, that union has prevailed to so great a degree, in the Irish Brigade, since all the corps were thus made to serve together, that the most trifling dispute or altercation never took place, so that it appeared as if the different battalions formed but one single regiment, well united and unanimous.

It is considered, that this conduct was as creditable to it, as the exactitude and the willingness with which it served, and as the splendid and transcendant actions by which it distinguished itself.

" INSTRUCTION FOR THE OFFICER DEPUTED TO RAISE RECRUITS FOR THE IRISH BRIGADE.

"This officer shall fix a price for the enlisting of each soldier; he shall endeavour, as far as he can, to give it equally, and to make his bargain so that the soldier shall not receive it until he shall be arrived at the regiment which he is to enter; and that the sum agreed upon shall be given to him every two months, or every month, on his entering one winter quarter. So often as there shall be an officer of the Royal Scotch regiment, or of D'Ogilvy, in the same place as himself, he shall yield all the Scotch about to be enlisted to these gentlemen, who shall divide them amongst themselves. If there be no Scotch officers in the same place, he shall engage, if he can, indiscriminately, Irish, English, and Scotch.

" Neither the Scotch officers who may be in the same place with him, nor any other officers deputed to make recruits for the Brigade in general, can enlist, or treat of enlisting, nor make any offer to the English and Irish deserters who may come to be enlisted.

" Scotch officers shall be prohibited from giving higher enlisting money, or making any other conditions, with the soldiers of their nation whom they may wish to enlist, than those agreeable to the Irish officer charged in general with the enlisting of recruits.

" All the English, Irish, or Scotch, that the officers of the Brigade may be able to find, five leagues distant from the environs of the place where the army is, or may be engaged, shall be taken in a body in general, and conducted to the officer deputed to raise the recruits for the Brigade, in order to be drawn by lot, and divided by him.

" It is forbidden to Scotch officers to make any proposals for enlisting, to the Irish and English, in any place where the Irish officer may be recruiting for the Brigade.

" It is also forbidden to all the officers of the Irish Brigade to make any private proposals, in the cities and environs, to the deserters of any of the three nations who may come to the camp, they must send them all to the Irish officer deputed to raised recruits, in order that he may treat with them."

" To LORD CLARE.

"*At Mayence,*
" *28th September,* 1744.

" SIR,—I received the letter which you did me the honour of writing, the 20th of this month, on the subject of the division which Marshal Saxe ordered to be made of the deserters of the English troops who present themselves at the general quarters, according to which the English and Irish shall be placed in the Irish regiments, and the Scotch in the Royal Scotch regiment. This arrangement must be approved of, as every thing that Marshal Saxe may judge proper to regulate on this matter.

"I am, &c.,

" Signed, D'ARGENSON."

In 1748, Marshal Saxe, in consenting, according to his usual custom, that the officer of the Irish Brigade should remain in his quarters to make recruits, made some remarks upon the regulation, as will be seen by the following letter, written to Lord Clare.

" *At the Camp before Maestricht,*
the 27th April, 1748.

" SIR,—I received the letter which you did me the honour of writing, and I willingly consent to your request to place, as in the preceding campaigns, an officer of the Irish Brigade, at the general quarter, in order to raise recruits for this Brigade, as well as for the Scotch regiments.

" I found, however, that it will be necessary to make some changes with regard to the instructions for the officer who should be charged with them, and I return it with the marginal observations which I have made.

"I have the honour to be, &c.,

" Signed, MARSHAL SAXE."

Adjoined are the remarks of Marshal Saxe, and the answer of Lord Clare thereto, which appeared satisfactory, and gave rise to the letter of approval of M. D'Argenson, the copy of which is here annexed.

Copy of the Letter written to Marshal Saxe by Lord Clare, at Bihon, the 28th April, 1748.

"My Lord,—I received the letter which you honoured me with, the 27th of April, with the instruction I drew up for the officer of the Irish Brigade, whom you permit to raise recruits for it at your general quarters, and also the observations which you took the trouble to make.

"*Observation with Regard to the Article where it is laid down:*

"'When there shall be an officer of the regiments of Scotch Royal, D'Ogilvy, and of Albany, in the same place as himself, he shall yield all the Scotchmen to those gentlemen, who shall divide them amongst themselves. When there shall be no Scotch officers in the same place, he will engage, if he can, indiscrimately, Irish, English, and Scotch.'

"Permit me, my Lord, to represent to you, that by the stipulation which the Irish made on coming into France, and by the ordinances then published, it is permitted to the Irish regiments to have English and Scotch enlisted. In the regulations for the establishment of the Scotch regiments, it is laid down that they shall only have Scotchmen. However, the Scotch officers have the power to engage indiscriminately the Irish and English in every place where there are no recruiting officers for the Brigade in general, as they are engaging them at present at Antwerp and elsewhere, and we have no officer for the general, except at your general quarters.

"I am very confident that there are not forty Scotchmen in the six Irish battalions, and there are many Irish and Englishmen in the Scotch regiments, for which reason there would have been a considerable loss on the Scotch side, if they drew lots equally amongst the Irish and Scotch for the men of their nation.

" The law appears impartial, when the Scotch may enlist Irish and English, in every place where there is no officer for the general ; that the Irish may, in the same manner, enlist the Scotch, according to their stipulations and the ordinances, in all places where there is no Scotch officer who acts for the general of the Scotch nation.

" *Observation on the Article:*

" 'It is equally forbidden to all the officers of the Irish Brigade, to make any private proposals to the deserters of the three nations who might come to the camp, into the cities, and to the environs; they should be all sent to the Irish officer deputed to levy recruits, in order that he should treat with them.'

" It is in order to remedy the inconveniences which I experienced last year, that I drew up the Article which you approve of, because many officers (for the purpose of having these men for themselves) used to go to meet the deserters, and make them exorbitant offers, to bring them into their companies; by this means they outbid each other, and made null all the arrangements of the first Article, wherein it is laid down, that there shall be an equal price fixed by the recruiting officer. I was obliged, at the middle of the campaign, to take the steps that I propose in the last Article, with the consent of all the officers of the different corps, who complained of this species of robbery. It appears to me that it succeeded to their satisfaction.

" I have the honour, &c.,
" Signed, CLARE."

" To LORD CLARE.

" *At Versailles, the* 15*th May,* 1748.

" SIR,—I received the letter which you did me the honour of writing, the 30th of the last month, on sending me the instruction which you gave to an officer of the Brigade of the Irish regiments, to whom Marshal Saxe has granted permission to remain at his general quarters, in order to make recruits there, as well for this Brigade as for the Scotch regiments. It must be approved of, and I am very much obliged to you for having communicated it to me.

"I remain, &c.,
"Signed, D'ARGENSON."

The infantry regiments of Royal Walloon, of Buffler's Walloon, raised in 1743 and 1744, and reduced in 1749, having complained that the Irish officers enlisted soldiers of their nation, and refused to give up those who were already in their companies, M. D'Argenson wrote, on that subject, to M. Bulkeley, the following letter:

"30th *January*, 1745.

"SIR,—The officers of the French and Walloon regiments complain of the facility with which the subjects of the Low Countries are received into the Irish and Scotch regiments in the King's service. As the intention of His Majesty is that there be admitted but English, Scotch, or Irish, and as it is only on this condition that so considerable pay is granted to them, I have the honour of informing you, that you cannot be excused from giving up to the officers of the French or Walloon regiments, the soldiers who are in your regiment, born on the land under the dominion of His Majesty, in the part of the Low Countries dependant on his sovereignty; and to the officers of the Walloon regiments in particular, the subjects of that part of the Low Countries dependant on the House of Austria, on receiving for each soldier, who shall be reclaimed, the sum of thirty francs, which His Majesty has fixed as the price for engagement.

"I remain, &c.,
"Signed, D'ARGENSON."

But, upon the representations of the Irish colonels of the losses their regiments had sustained in the preceding campaigns, and of the difficulty which they found, under this circumstance, to raise recruits of their own nation, they were permitted to enter into a compromise with the Walloon officers to retain them(*a*).

At the battle of Fontenoy, fought on the 11th May, 1745, the Irish Brigade distinguished itself in the most remarkable manner, in the presence of the King and of the Dauphin. It was this Brigade that principally contributed to restore the battle, which had commenced in a most unfavourable manner, and to achieve the complete victory that was ultimately gained. The King conferred numerous marks of favour on the Brigade. M. Stapleton, lieutenant-colonel in Berwick's regiment, was made brigadier. MM. De Lee and Cusack, lieutenant-colonels of Bulkeley's and Rothe's, got pensions of 1000 and 600 francs. MM. O'Neille and Mannecy, lieutenant-colonels of Clare's and Dillon's, were killed. Commissions of colonel and lieutenant-colonel were given to some of the officers of the different regiments of the Brigade; gratuities to the majors and aides-majors; the cross of St. Louis to those at the heads of the several corps; gratuities of 600 and of 400 francs to the wounded captains, and of 300 and of 200 to the lieutenants.

The town of Ghent was surprised some time after this battle. A great quantity of clothes, of cloth-stuffs, and of equipments, destined for the clothing of the English troops in the service of the allied army, were found here. The King, M. D'Argenson, and Marshal Saxe decided that these goods should be distributed *gratis* amongst the six Irish regiments.

The cavalry regiment of Fitz-James sustained great loss

(*a*) See the Order of the 23rd April, 1745.

at the battle of Fontenoy, and lost a considerable number of horse by the enemy's cannon; the King granted immediately a remount of 74 horses gratis, to replace a part of the loss.

Towards the end of the year, there being some question of sending the Irish Brigade and the Royal Scotch regiment to Scotland and England to sustain the Prince of Wales, Charles Edward, a new scale of pay was proposed.

These regulations were, however, never carried into effect as proposed, the Brigade never having been able to pass over. The regiment of Scotch Royals, a squadron of the regiment of Fitz-James, and the picquets of the regiments of Dillon, Rothe, and Lally, alone reached their destination; but there being neither Commissioners of War, nor Paymasters of the Forces in Scotland, these troops had to be satisfied with whatever pay they could get. They were all made prisoners of war after the battle of Culloden, the 23rd of April, 1746.

The three first squadrons of the regiment of Fitz-James, and the picquets of Bulkeley, Clare, and Berwick, had been captured on the voyage in the months of October, 1745, and March, 1746. All these prisoners, whilst they were in England, received subsistence money, which the Court of France transmitted to them, and which was paid to their order, without deduction. On the exchange each officer received the amount of his allowances during the time he had been absent, at the rate of the English sol, valued as the French sol, and the soldiers and cavalry the same, which comes to nearly the same regulation, as that of which we have given the detail.

The regiment of Berwick having detached ninety men more, over and above its picquet, who passed into Scotland, and were made prisoners with the others, an account was kept likewise of these 90 men.

On the embarkation of Fitz-James's regiment, the King

APPENDIX. 401

ordered, that for its benefit, the horses of a squadron should be sold; but they were the worst of the whole regiment that were chosen for that purpose. The residue were sent to St. Valery, afterwards into Alençon, and afterwards into Lower Normandy. At first there were militia-men chosen to take care of them, who were paid by the King; after some time they were discharged, and it was ordered, that the officers should employ peasants to look after the horses, to whom the King gave 2 sols per day for each horse. These peasants had been computed at that rate of pay in all the extracts of reviews of the commissaries. The foraging for each horse was paid for in all these places, till the exchange of the regiment, and the return of the men into France, at the rate of from fifteen to sixteen sols for each horse's livery.

At that time the King furnished horses gratuitously for the fourth squadron, in exchange for those which had been sold, as has been already mentioned. The men brought back to Calais, on their return, the muskets which they had left at the arsenal, in the place of the fusils with bayonets, with which they had been armed in embarking; but they were obliged to buy pistols, to replace those taken, with the rest of their equipages, at sea.

By these arrangements, and the contributions of the officers towards replacing the clothing, outfit, boots, saddles, bridles, &c. which had been taken at sea by the English, this regiment returned into active service in the month of April, 1748, in the most excellent order.

During the absence of the picquets of the Irish battalions they had been obliged to replace, in each regiment, the two sergeants who had accompanied these detachments. On their return the King willed and directed that these supernumeraries should be retained as third sergeants in those

2 D

companies in which they had been from the 1st December, 1747, till the 1st May, 1748.

The Irish regiments did not serve in the campaign of 1746; notwithstanding which, forage was distributed, in kind, all the summer, to the regiments of Bulkeley, Clare, Rothe, and Berwick, then in garrison in Flanders; Dillon's and Lally's being in garrison in D'Artois, where there was no distribution of forage, Lord Clare made certain representations on that subject, and he received the following letter:

"*Versailles, the 20th July,* 1746.

"SIR,—The King has consented to continue the allowance of eight sols per day, to be given to the officers of the regiments of Dillon and of Lally, for each ration of forage they should receive if it were furnished in kind, and this allowance will be continued, though they should not join the army till the end of the campaign, in consideration of the particular circumstances in which these officers find themselves; but His Majesty wishes that any advantages that may thereby accrue to the captains, should be employed for the re-establishment of their companies, and he commands me to inform you thereof, in order that you may give it your attention.

"I have the honour to be, &c.,

"Signed,   D'ARGENSON."

At the close of October, 1746, apprehensions being entertained of a landing by the English, all the Irish regiments were sent into Normandy and Brittany. They returned to Flanders in the month of April, 1747, to enter on active service, and though they had not taken part in the preceding campaign, as has been said, and had received the winter pay during the summer of 1746, their entire allowances, recruiting-money and conduct-money, were granted in full to each of these battalions.

The army having entered early on the campaign, in 1747, the forage distribution took place before the country was in a fit state to be foraged. The annexed letter was received by Lord Clare from M. Deseichelles, in reply to the representations made by his Lordship as to the smallness of the allowance made to Irish battalions, by which it will be seen that in fact the proportions had been duly observed between them and the French, and that care had been taken at this time, as upon similar occasions, to give the larger share to the Irish in all the distributions.

"*Bruxelles, the* 2nd *May,* 1747.

"In reply, my Lord, to the letter with which you honoured me on the 1st instant, on the subject of the apportionment of sixty-five rations of forage per day, for each of the Irish regiments, I beg to state that pursuant to the scale of forage allotment, and the degrees of rank of the officers, 140 rations per day are allotted to them on the whole; where, according to the scale of the forages due to the officers of a French colonel's battalion, 130 rations only are payable. It is upon this footing that the Irish regiment is placed; where sixty-five rations have been allotted, per day, to your cavalry, a French colonel's battalion has only sixty rations. I believe that you will find that the proportion has been observed; and I beg of you to be persuaded of my attention to the officers of those Irish regiments.

"I have the honour to be,
"Signed,   DESEICHELLES."

The battle of Lawfeld took place the 2nd July. The Irish Brigade distinguished itself very much, and lost considerably upon this occasion. M. de Lee was made brigadier. Pensions of 1200 francs were given to M. Grant, lieutenant-colonel of Clare ; to Mannecy, lieutenant-colonel of Dillon's ; to Barnwell, lieutenant-colonel of Berwick's: and to Hegarty, lieutenant-colonel of Lally's. M. de Cusack, lieutenant-colonel of Rothe, being already brigadier, and having a pension of 600 francs given him after the battle of Fontenoy, had but 1000 francs. Commissions of lieutenant-colonel were given to MM. Hennesy and Arthur, captains of the grenadiers of Bulkeley and Rothe, and to Carroll, major of Berwick's. A pension of 3000 francs was given to Lord Dunkeld, brigadier, who commanded the Brigade. Numerous crosses of St. Louis and pensions were given to the majors and aides-majors, and pensions of 600 and 400 francs to the wounded captains; and of 300 and 200 francs to the lieutenants.

COPY OF THE ANSWER OF THE COUNT D'ARGENSON TO A LETTER ADDRESSED TO HIM BY M. DE BULKELEY.

"*The 22nd July*, 1747.

" SIR,—I receive with all possible esteem the compliment which you were pleased to pay me on the occasion of the victory, which the King has gained at Lawfeld. It is I rather who am more justly indebted to you, for the distinguished manner in which the Irish Brigade (and your regiment in particular) charged the enemy ; and although the duties confided to you at Ostend did not allow of your being present at this engagement, you do not the less partake of the glory, which your regiment has acquired, by these new proofs of its valour. I am aware that the unanimity which prevails in it, is owing principally to the attention of M. de Lee. When you shall have sent me the list of the officers, whom you consider worthy of the King's favour, I shall with pleasure submit it to His Majesty ; and I shall be always very happy to have any opportunity of testifying

APPENDIX. 405

by my attention to whatever concerns you, the constant attachment, with which I have the honour to be,

"Signed, D'ARGENSON."

Peace having been concluded in 1748, the commanders of the Irish regiments and the regiments themselves deemed it advisable for the better procurement of recruits from their native country, to enter into the following regulations, which were written and arranged by each in English.

" 1st. That when any officer, cadet, or sergeant, deputed by an Irish regiment to go to the country for recruits shall meet there with any soldiers, who may heretofore have deserted from the Brigade, he shall be authorized to promise such deserters their pardon, on condition that they be useful to him in the country, and that the regiments, from which they may have deserted, shall not be at liberty to reject such under any pretext whatsoever. That all those who may have deserted and passed back into the country, before the 1st March, 1749, be admitted to this pardon, without any demand for it, inasmuch as otherwise these same deserters might injure the recruiting agents in the country, instead of which, being secured of their pardon, they may employ themselves efficiently in seconding and assisting them.

" 2nd. That all soldiers of the Irish nation who shall be found to have deserted before the aforesaid day of the 1st March, 1749, shall remain where they are without any further notice being taken of them.

" 3rd. That every soldier of the Irish nation, who shall desert after the 1st March, and who shall be afterwards detected in any of the above-named regiments, shall be immediately put under arrest, and punished according to the rigour of the ordonnance. The majors, commanders of the regiments, and captains of the companies, on the detection of delinquents, are particularly charged to have them arrested in their own particular names, and to give information thereof to the majors of the regiments from which they may have deserted, without delaying under any pretext the execution of this order," &c.

In the year 1750, the Irish and Scotch regiments, in consequence of the desire which they felt to fill up their ranks with their own countrymen, and to get rid of the French, Germans, and others whom they had been obliged to admit during the war, which was just finished, sent a great number of officers, cadets, sergeants, and others on the recruiting service to Calais and Boulogne. The excess of their zeal in outbidding each other, having greatly increased the price for recruits, caused the publicans and smugglers of those cities to carry on a shameful traffic in men, prejudicial to the object which was in view, as well as to exact exorbitant prices for their reward, and for the debts incurred in entertaining the new comers. Indiscretion was even pushed to such lengths, that many Irish and Scotch recruiters passed over to England, where they made engagements in London and Dover, with so little caution, and so much notoriety, that some of them were arrested, and one of the sergeants of Rothe's regiment, besides some others, was hanged.

In order to avoid these inconveniences, Lord Clare, Inspector, proposed to the Irish and Scotch regiments the following Regulation, which, having been approved of, and accepted by them, was carried into effect, after having been communicated to and confirmed by the minister, conformably to his letters here arranged.

"REGULATION

"*In the Matter of the Recruits who may henceforth be engaged for the Irish Brigade, and the Scotch Regiments, at Calais and Boulogne.*

"ARTICLE I.

"There shall be but one officer employed at Calais to levy recruits for the Irish and Scotch regiments. Boulogne also shall be in his district; and he shall have a sergeant of each regiment at his orders. He shall supply himself with a registry, in which he will note down the recruits that he may levy, on the day of their engagement, the length of time it is to last, and the sum which shall be paid to each enlister. He shall attentively endeavour to enlist none but handsome men, not under 5 feet 2 inches in height(*a*), well limbed, and at the most not over 35 years of age. They shall be examined by the surgeon-major of the hospital that they have no concealed defects or infirmities. The recruiting officer shall avoid, as much as possible the enlistment of men who are actually sailors; he shall see, with the most rigorous exactness, that he do not enlist any deserter from our regiments. He shall make no engagements but for six years. He will take notice that he will not be paid the expenses of such as are not fit to be received, or of any whom the inspector may have rejected. If he make many engagements on the same day, he will take care to have lots drawn for the men in his presence, by the sergeants of the regiments for which they are destined. Scotchmen by birth shall have the preference in Scotch regiments, rateably out of the recruits levied at Calais and Boulogne; the Scotch regiments making no exclusive claim to men of that country, except when matters are on an equality, that is to say, that if eight

(*a*) French measure.

recruits be at the same time at Calais or Boulogne, and that there be amongst the number two Scotchmen, they by right should join the Scotch regiments. He shall send every month to the major of each regiment an account of the money expended on his own account, as well as that of the men whom he shall send forward, and whom he shall board during their stay at Calais, out of their pay. He shall endeavour to settle a uniform scale of payment in the arrangements which he shall make, and for remuneration of those inhabitants of Dover, or on the other sea side, of whose services he may have the benefit.

"ARTICLE II.

" Each regiment shall contribute to the Recruiting Captain's Fund, which they shall take care, every three months, to renew, if it be exhausted, and sooner even, if it be necessary, or if a number of recruits should come at the same time.

" ARTICLE III.

" The captain, and the eight sergeants, shall he paid at the cost of all the Irish and Scotch regiments; the captain at the rate of four francs, and the sergeants at the rate of twenty sols, a day, besides their usual pay. The sergeants shall have twenty-five sols a day whilst marching, or in case they be employed to escort the recruits to their regiments.

" ARTICLE IV.

" The regiments of Clare, Rothe, and Lally, being stationed the farthest off, shall have two sergeants at Calais, one of whom shall march with the recruits destined for the regiment, while the other shall remain at Calais, in order to take care of those, who may be engaged for his regiment, during the absence of his comrade.

" ARTICLE V.

" With regard to what may be given for the subsistence of each recruit, during the march, it shall rest with the captain at Calais, to arrange with the conducting sergeants on this subject; regulating the expense according to the dearness or cheapness of the several provinces through which they may have to pass.

" ARTICLE VI.

" So often as men shall arrive for some captains in particular, the officer employed at Calais shall facilitate their joining the regiments for which they shall be destined, provided they produce a written certificate from some one who shall have written to them from France, or from the captain from whom they may come, or that they may have some sufficient evidence that they are the proper persons. He shall act in the same way towards the officers, cadets, or sergeants, conducting the men to the regiments to which they are sent; he will charge each of them for the expenses and the advances that he may have been at for the recruits, of which he shall give due notice.

" ARTICLE VII.

" By virtue of the above regulations, it shall not be lawful for any other officers, cadets, sergeants, corporals, or others of the six Irish regiments, or of the two Scotch, to make recruits at Calais, or at Boulogne; and so long as the officer for the Brigade in general shall be there, no private individual shall employ any person at Dover to engage recruits for him.

" When the regiments, which are at present in Flanders, shall leave it to go into Brittany, and those now there shall take their place, the same arrangement shall continue to be adopted, the officer and sergeants only being subject to be changed from time to time."

"To Lord Clare.

"*Versailles, the* 24*th September,* 1750.

"Sir,—I observe, by the memorial which accompanied the letter you did me the honour of writing to me, the 3rd of last month, the arrangements which you have caused the Irish and Scotch regiments to enter into for the future management of their recruiting service, which they can now effect much more easily, and with less risk and expense than hitherto, by one captain and a lieutenant, who with the necessary number of sergeants for each regiment, shall raise all the recruits at Calais and Boulogne. I accord my warmest approbation to these measures, the more so as it will obviate the inconveniences which have taken place, from the excessive zeal of the officers of your Brigade, about procuring these recruits. I have given the necessary directions at Calais and Boulogne, in order that the officers and recruits who go thither shall be lodged, and you will have the goodness, on your part, to make known to the Irish and Scotch regiments, the intention of His Majesty, which is, that they should conform themselves to the arrangements which you have proposed, and which His Majesty has accepted.

"I have the honour to be, Sir,

"Signed,   D'Argenson."

The Count D'Argenson also gave orders to the Commissary of War, at Calais, to furnish to the Irish captain, commissioner of recruits, twenty equipments for soldiers, to furnish the house where he lodged, and to provide the men with beds.

The 655th section of the Ordonnance of the 23rd June, 2750, relating to the staffs of military stations, and to the service therein, confirms to the Irish regiments the custom and the right which they always have enjoyed, since their arrival in France, to hold their council of war, with their commander at the prison, or at any other place they should think fit. These regiments have a further privilege, that their majors shall conduct all proceedings against the men who have offended in criminal matters, according to the practice of their own nation, irrespective of those of the military stations.

The article which immediately follows in this ordonnance, defines the rights of these regiments, as between them and the commanders of military stations, as well with regard to their having permission to assemble a council of war, as to enable them to put into execution their proper resolutions.

The following copy of a letter, written by M. Dangervilliers, to M. Hennesy, Lieutenant-Colonel of Lee's regiment, at Versailles, the 16th November, 1731, shews, that the ordonnance which has been just quoted has only proved, in an unquestionable manner, that which had been practised for sixty years, and authorized by the decisions of all the ministers.

" SIR,—I received the letter which you took the trouble to write to me, the 11th of this month, and the memorial which came with it, repeating what had been done to come at the discovery of a soldier of the regiment of Lee, who had assassinated one of his comrades. The precautions cannot be too highly approved of which have been taken for the apprension of the criminal. From what you say, there is reason to hope, that he shall not escape the punishment he deserves. It, above all, concerns the justice of the regiment to take notice of it, the affair having taken place between two soldiers of the regiment: I write accordingly to M. De Bartant, in order that he may oppose no obstacle thereto.

"I remain, &c. &c.

"Signed, DANGERVILLIERS."

Copy of a Letter from M. DANGERVILLIERS *to* M. HENNESSY, *Lieutenant-Colonel of Lee's Regiment, from Fontainbleau, the* 29th *of September,* 1732, *which shews, that religious Institutions have no Right to give Refuge to foreign Soldiers when Criminals.*

"SIR,—I received the letter you gave yourself the trouble of writing, the 14th of this month, on the subject of the asylum given in the convent of the Capuchins at St Omer's, to a soldier of M. Lee's regiment, who had killed one of his comrades. I return you thanks for your attention in informing me of what passed on this occasion. I write to M. Barteret, that the intention of the King is, that he should prohibit, in the name of His Majesty, all the superiors of the monasteries of this city to receive or conceal any soldiers. It is requisite to make this prohibition public, in order that criminals may no longer flatter themselves that they can take refuge in these establishments.

"I remain, &c.,

"Signed, DANGERVILLIERS."

By the Ordonnance of the 12th February, 1749, concerning the reduction to be made in the Irish and Scotch regiments, on the subject of the peace concluded a short time before, it was ordered, that the ranks of captain, and of second lieutenant attached to each company of Irish and Scotch infantry, should no more be filled up, according as they should be vacated, except in the company of grenadiers, in which the King continued to maintain a second captain.

But upon the representations which the colonels of the Irish and Scotch regiments made, of the impossibility of keeping up these regiments with recruits of their nation, if the hope of promotion were taken away from the cadets, who were the support of the Brigade by the recruits which they brought with them, and also upon representing the expediency of bringing over the young Irish Catholic nobility, His Majesty determined, upon these considerations, and upon what was known to him, to command the regulations of the 5th February, 1751, by which it is decreed that each company of the Irish and Scotch regiments shall be, in future, composed, according as the places of second captains attached to the companies of fusiliers shall be vacated, of a captain and of a first lieutenant, of a second lieutenant, and of an under-lieutenant; and that there be always a second captain attached to each company of grenadiers; in the composition of which no change shall be made, with the exception of the colonel's, or lieutenant-colonel's companies, which shall be composed of a captain, a first lieutenant, of an ensign, and of a second lieutenant.

"His Excellency, the Duke of Feltre, Minister of War, was so kind to communicate to me the original Memoir, above cited, of which this is a perfect copy, which I attest.

"DE MONTMORENCY MORRES (HERVÈ),
"*Adjutant-Commandant-Colonel.*

"*Paris, 1st September,* 1813."

INDEX.

ALICANT, brave defence of, 318.

ALMANZA, battle of, 328.

ALPS, passes of the, forced by St. Ruth, with the aid of the Irish, 103.

ALTENHEIM, memorable retreat effected by the French at, 92.

AMIENS, surprised by the Spanish forces, 42; account of the siege and recovery of, 43.

ARDRES, siege of, 80.

ATHLONE, siege of, 136.

AUGHRIM, battle of, 149.

BAGNALL, Sir Henry, undertakes the prosecution of the war against O'Neal, 12; is totally defeated, 15, 16.

BARCELONA, siege of, 230.

BERWICK, the Duke of, appointed commander-in-chief by Tyrconnel, 123; his operations unsuccessful, 130; defeats the Allies at Almanza, 328; protects the French frontier, and recovers Savoy, 359.

BLENHEIM, battle of, 290.

BOIS-LE-DUC, gallantry of the Irish troops at, 36; taken by the French, and the Irish regiment who garrisoned it enter the French service, 69.

BOMMEL, lodgment effected in the island of, 60; fort erected on it in the face of a hostile army, 62.

BOYNE, battle of the, not absolutely disastrous to James, 105.

BURROUGH, Lord Deputy, killed at Drunflough, 11.

CALCINATO, battle of, 324.

CAMBRAY, obstinate defence of the citadel of, by an Irish regiment, 95.

CAMISARDS, rising of the, 297.

CASSANO, battle of, 301.

CASTIGLIONE, battle of, 321.

CATINAT, Marshal, commands the French forces in Piedmont, 203; defeats the Allies at Marsiglia, 219; employs the Irish battalions to hunt out the Vaudois, 226; is driven back by Prince Eugene, 234; superseded, 235.

CEVENNES, persecution of the Protestants in the, 296.

CHARLES II. obliged to seek Spanish protection at Cologne, 74; his ingratitude to the Irish, 86.

CLARE, Lord, mortally wounded at Ramillies, 316.

CONDE, siege of, 76.

CREMONA attempted to be taken by surprise, 243; is saved by the Irish troops, 246.

DE GINKLE takes Ballymore, 135; and Athlone, 143; marches on Galway, 155.

DILLON and his regiment cross the mountains on the north side of the Lake of Garda, 278; are quartered in Monforrat, 280; his services at Toulon, 326.

DIVISIONS among the adherents of James II. in Ireland, 114.

DUNKIRK besieged by the English and French, and captured, 83.

DENAIN, lines of, forced by Villars, 365.

EUGENE, Prince, takes the command of the Imperialist forces, 231; drives back the French army from the Adige, 234; his character, 259; attempts to cross the Adda, 299; is betrayed, and his plans frustrated by the Duke of Ormond and the English Government, 362; his lines are forced by the French at Denain, 364.

FRENCH troops exchanged for Irish, 98.

GALWAY, festivities in, amidst the general distress, 133.

GAVERN, battle of, 338.

GLOUCESTER'S regiment obliged to surrender at Mont Cassel, 81.

GRACE, Richard, of Gracefield, his honourable conduct on leaving the Spanish service, 75.

HAMILTON, Sir G., raises an Irish regiment for the French service, 87; acquires great glory at the retreat of Altenheim, 92.

IRISH Brigade, commencement of, 97; arrangement of, after the surrender of Limerick, 197.

IRISH campaign of 1690-1, 105.

IRISH colonels, the, offer their services to Charles II. and the Duke of York, 74.

IRISH regiments in the French service, their arrangements, 99, 197; receive an augmentation of officers, 294.

IRISH troops take their departure for France after the surrender of Limerick, 192; are ordered to the Rhine, 264; their services at Dudenhaven, 206.

JAMES II., flight of, after his defeat at the Boyne, ill advised, 108; his ingratitude to the Irish, 115; his letter to Tyrconnel, 116.

LA HOGUE, battle of, 204.

LAUSUN, the French commander in Ireland, incapacity of, 106; withdraws his troops to Galway, 115; is recalled, 120.

LEE, Lieutenant-General, his services at Stolhoven, 327; and at Lille, 340.

LERIDA, siege of, 332.

LIGNI, siege of, 71.

LILLE, siege of, 339.

LIMERICK, siege and successful defence of, 117; second siege of, 170; treaty of, its military provisions, 178.

LUTTREL, Henry, treachery of, 169.

LUZARA, battle of, 263.

MAHONY, an Irish officer, has a principal share in saving Cremona, 245; his modesty, 254; his services at the battle of Almanza, 329; he takes Alcira and Xativa, 330; is appointed commander-in-chief in Sicily, 336; Bellerue's character of him, 356.

MALPLAQUET, battle of, 344.

MARDYKE, unsuccessful attack upon, 81.

MARLBOROUGH, the Earl of, takes Cork and Kinsale, 130.

MARLBOROUGH, Duke of, carries by assault the Bavarian intrenchments at Schellemberg, 382; foundation of his fame, 317; is displaced by the Duke of Ormond, 361.

MOINON, siege of, 71.

MONTECUCOLI commands the imperial forces against Turenne, 89.

MONTENEGRO, the Marquis de, succeeds Portocarrero in the command of Amiens, 52; surrenders on honorable terms, 57.

MOUNTCASHEL'S brigade, services of, at Guillestre, 211; at Embrun, 214; at the battle of Marsiglia, 220.

MOUNTJOY, Lord, opposes O'Neal with energy and success, 19; besieges the Spanish commander in Kinsale, and compels him to withdraw, 24, 26; subdues O'Neal, 27.

NANTZ, Edict of, disastrous effects of its revocation, 295.

NORRIS, Sir John, commander of the English forces, his ill success against O'Neal, 9, 10.

NIEUPORT, battle of, 64.

OATH, an, of fidelity exacted from the Irish by the Spanish government, 79.

O'DONNELL, Baldearg, treachery of, 159.

O'NEAL, Shane the Proud, 4.

O'NEAL, Hugh, Earl of Tyrone, revolts against the English power, 7; makes a successful stand against Sir John Norris and the English army, 9, 10; opposes Lord Deputy Burrough, who is killed in battle, 11; defeats the English army under Sir Henry Bagnall at the Yellow Ford, 16; is more successfully opposed by the energy of Lord Mountjoy, 18; suffers defeat, but holds out in expectation of succour from Spain, 19; which he receives, 20; but without avail, 25, 26; is pursued by Mountjoy into his fastnesses, and compelled to sue for peace, 27, 28.

ORLEANS, Duke of, appointed to succeed Marshal Vendôme in Italy, 320; takes Lerida, 333.

ORMOND, the Duke of, appointed to the command of the English army in Flanders, 361; his treachery to the Allies, 361.

PALATINATE, cruelties practised by the troops under Turenne in the, 87, 88.

PORTOCARRERO surprises Amiens, 41; his death, 51.

RAMILLIES, battle of, 315.

RHINBERG, siege of, 59.

ROSAS, siege of, 225.

ST. GERLAIN, fortress, betrayed by its Irish garrison, 78.

ST. RUTH, Marquis de, commands the French army in Savoy, 100; forces the passes of the Alps, 103; appointed to command the French forces in Ireland, 130; his sympathy with the Irish, 138; his death, 152.

SARSFIELD, Patrick, Earl of Lucan, his character, 120; his death, 222.

SAVOY, operations of the Irish Brigade in, 100.

SCHELLEMBERG, the Bavarian intrenchments on, attacked by Marlborough, 282.

SHELDON'S cavalry defeat a detachment of the Imperialist forces, 240; cut off a body of Imperial cavalry on the Cristallo, 256; distinguish themselves at the battle of Spire, 269.

SPANISH expedition to Ireland commanded by Don Juan D'Aguila, completely abortive, 24–26.

SPANISH succession, war of the, 231.

SPIRE, battle of, 269.

STANHOPE is surprised at Brihuega, and his whole force made prisoners, 355.

STANLEY, Sir Edward, betrays his trust and enters the service of Spain, with the Irish troops under his command, 32.

STHAREMBERG, general, defeats the Spanish army at Saragossa, 351; displays consummate skill in an engagement with the French and Spanish forces at Madrid, 352; adds to his fame at Villa-Viciosa, 356.

STIRUM, General, is overtaken in his retreat from Gremen, and suffers great loss, 272.

TER, battle of the, 228.

TORTOSA, siege of, 337.

TOURNAY, siege of, 341.

TURENNE'S campaign, 87; his death, 91.

TURIN relieved by Prince Eugene, 321.

TYRCONNELL loses the confidence of the Irish, 122; he goes to France, and returns with supplies, 123; his death, 163; and character, 164.

TYROLESE peasantry, their determined opposition to the French, 275.

TYRONE, Hugh, Earl of, history of his campaign.—*See* O'Neal.

TYRRELL, Richard, his achievement at Tyrrell's Pass, 11.

UTRECHT, peace of, 365.

VAUDOIS, the, invaded by the Irish battalions, 226.

VENDOME, Marshal the Duke de, is appointed to the command of the French army in Italy, 254; his character, 257; marches into the Tyrol, 274; crosses into the Trentine, 279; is recalled from Italy, 320; surprises and defeats the Imperialists at Calcinato, 325; disconcerts Marlborough's projects, 335; is appointed to the command in Spain, 354.

VILLA-VICIOSA, battle of, 356.

VILLEROY, Marshal, succeeds Catinat, 235; attacks the Imperialist force at Chiari, 237; is taken prisoner, 248.

WILLIAM III., errors of, in conducting the Irish campaign, 111.

YORK, the Duke of, retires to Flanders, 74.

THE END.

www.ingramcontent.com/pod-product-compliance
Lightning Source LLC
Chambersburg PA
CBHW031248230426
43670CB00005B/90